THE PHYSICIAN WITHIN:
How to attain the quality of life you were meant to live!

by

THE WELLNESS DOC

Bill Warner, MS
Cosmos Institute of Life's Transitions

www.cosmosilt.org.
www.cosmosbooks.us

For information write Author:

Cosmos Institute of Life's Transitions
3509 Southview Cir.
Gainesville, GA 30506
Email: wellnessdoc@mac.com
Website: www.cosmosbooks.us

Author: Bill Warner, M.S. , Wellness Doc

The opinions and ideas expressed in this book are those of the author and stories related to the author from electronic machines and notes taken during his work experiences. Personal accounts as related in the text are as seen and interpreted by the author. Quotes are taken from public records as reported in those sources. Inquiries may be made to the author listed above. The bibliography and glossary list the written reference works which have impacted the author's philosophy and beliefs. The author does not attempt to diagnose or treat any medical issues. For personal medical issues you are referred to your own healthcare provider.

First names of persons mentioned in the text will be used only to protect those individuals not members of the author's immediate family. While all names refer to actual persons, some may still be alive and some have already passed. In some cases I've included the full names of immediate family members as I'm particularly proud of their spiritual association with the author and their inclusion is as much a memorial as well as a part of family history.

Printed in the United States of America

ISBN: 145287137X
EAN: 9781452871370

DISCLAIMER
(Required reading first)

This book is about your wellness and your personal responsibility in life. This book is intended to be read by intelligent, inquiring minds that are interested in researching information to make their own decisions.

Following is the legally mandated disclaimer for whatever I may imply as I relate my educated, researched opinions and suggestions for a long, happy journey on the path of life. Isn't this the land of freedom of the press or is it only a qualified freedom?

Let me make this perfectly clear. I do not diagnose or perform medical treatments for illness, trauma, or disease. I cannot CURE anything or anyone. Only GOD CAN CURE. Only physicians who think they are God have that attitude. I only advocate that you communicate with the Physician Within, who is always available to perform whatever healing your spirit requires.

With that preface said, let me quote my legal obligation so you will be officially informed that what follows in this book is my personal opinions and conclusions. They are based on my study of the Nature Cures tempered with a long life of experience that the secret to a healthy life is a close relationship with the Physician Within and a lifestyle based on PREVENTION by returning to living with Mother Nature rather than trying to improve on her.

The subject matter contained in this book is for informational and educational purposes only. Any comments made by the author or Cosmos Institute of Life's Transitions should not be construed as an attempt to diagnose or treat your illness. The author's purpose is to advocate your taking control of your life and to suggest possible alternatives for your consideration. You should consult with your personal physician or healthcare provider for specific diagnosis or treatment.

Signed in the presence of Mother Nature

Bill Warner, The Wellness Doc

TABLE OF CONTENTS

ACKNOWLEDGEMENT

This book would not have seen the light of day without the encouragement, advice and editorial assistance of Rev. Laura Perry, ND, naturopath and author. She is a friend, colleague and warm, loving human being whose life is an inspiration to me. She spent many hours reading and correcting my manuscript, for which I will be forever grateful. Thanks, Laura, for your labor of love.

She is an ordained minister, a Naturopathic doctor, and a wife and mother who schools her daughter at home. Having such a talented and knowledgeable colleague to work with has really been a blessing and benefit to me and my readers in this book project.

The idea for this project came from my sister-in-law Karen Warner who suggested I publish Cosmos Institute's monthly e-institute in a book form. It took a few years but the motivation finally came while I was preparing a workshop for a health conference presentation.

Thanks to Laura I found the support I needed. My hope is that my readers will find motivation to change their lifestyles for the better and start on the pathways of a happy, joyous and productive journey as you search for the essence of your God.

DEDICATION
BESS (CAPPY) DOYLE

My maternal grandmother, who as spiritual leader of the family laid the foundation for us all as we made our lives a happy event. At an early age we called her "Happy Cappy," a nickname that stayed with her throughout her life. She made her transition in 1965 after 80 years lived to the fullest. She was a role model and teacher to my brother and myself, as she lived in the family home with us during all our growing up years. Her husband, who made his transition before I was born, was my namesake, a moniker I'm proud to carry.

She was a beautiful lady who never met a person she did not like. She has gone before the rest of us to prepare a place for us in our heavenly home.

Much of my philosophy of life is discussed in this book, which had its genesis in the blessings and memories Cappy taught us. It is for that reason I want to dedicate this book to her, as she was a living example of a life filled with service. I know Bill Doyle welcomed her home with God at his side as he said, "Welcome home from a life lived well, my true and faithful servant." Thank you, Cappy, for being my grandmother.

OTHER TITLES BY THE WELLNESS DOC
Available at www.cosmosbooks.us or Amazon.com
An Odyssey into Past Lives: a Personal Exploration into
Cellular Memories
God Doesn't Make Faulty Equipment
Where Have All The Elders Gone?
Cosmos Institute of Holistic Science E-Institute Lessons
Why Did This Happen To Me?
The Metamorphosis of a Business: Thou Shall Not Mess
with Mother Nature
(a work in progress)
If Two is Good, Four is Better

Chapter I

Preface

"I am responsible for my own wellbeing, my own happiness. The choices and decisions I make regarding my life directly influence the quality of my days."
Wellness Doc

Life is a schoolhouse and the lessons are easy but some humans find it difficult to understand them. This book is about those lessons and how to practice them. If it is your desire to maintain a healthy longevity well into the tenth decade of life, learning and practicing these lessons will help make that goal possible. The ideal is that your last five to ten years of life are spent in joy, happiness and financial independence rather than the alternative of sickness, pain, depression and poverty. The choice is yours; all you need do is commit to a change in lifestyle.

Cosmos Institute for Life's Transitions' purpose is to provide the lessons; all you need is to put them into practice. We believe we have a unique story to tell. Some alternative healthcare practitioners expound a specific technique for only one facet of the Body, Mind or Spirit. Some even feel their specialty in the healthcare continuum is the only one that works.

For instance, some medical doctors feel healing can only be accomplished by diagnosing the signs and symptoms then offering the prescribed conventional treatment. Many mental health practitioners feel that only long exposure to psychological therapies will heal mental illnesses. Our spiritual leaders often feel the only way to have complete healing is through the adoption of their particular brand of religious dogma.

Cosmos Institute takes the approach that true healing and a healthy longevity can only be accomplished by the integration of all three protocols. After all, we are all one in the population of the

Universe and until we recognize that, true healing cannot be accomplished. In each human challenge the utilization of all three - Body and Mind and Spirit - is required in order to fulfill the Divine Plan. Each has their place in the total plan and each is synergistic, with all three parts being synthesized into perfect manifestation. No one protocol can be successful by itself – each has its part to play in the creation script.

Cosmos Institute utilizes the following Nature Cure Techniques in our recommendations and in most of our lessons:

Hypnotherapy
Wellness Assessments
Nutrition
Homeopathy
Herbology
Seminars/Workshops
Integration of a spiritual practice into healing

Each chapter in this book, except the first and last, is divided into four (4) subsections. The theme or lesson is carried through the whole chapter but each subsection will cover a different facet of the main theme. Each set of chapter subsections will follow the same pattern: Lesson, Body, Mind, Spirit. The purpose of the subsections is to describe how the Body/Mind/Spirit trilogy applies to the issue of each chapter. Each chapter is arranged as follows:

LESSON: This subsection discusses the main issues involved in the chapter. Each chapter focuses on a particular natural health subject. For example, Chapter One discusses the Body/ Mind/ Spirit connection, except the last chapter that puts it all together. The following chapters discuss such issues as healing, the immune system and hypnotherapy.

BODY: This subsection expands on the lesson subject and how it applies to the functioning of the Body in the Trilogy of Life as well as how it relates to and interfaces with the Mind and Spirit. This includes some ways to integrate the healing of the body based on the main chapter subject - in other words, a 'how-to' for this part of the Body/Mind/Spirit trilogy. The Cosmos Institute of Life's Transitions emphasizes such drugless, non-invasive methods as herbology, homeopathy, nutrition, magnetic therapy, lifestyle improvement and exercise in order to achieve the goals of healing the body.

MIND: Ditto the description above as it applies to the Mind. Our emphasis is in the area of hypnotherapy, light/sound and meditation therapy.

SPIRIT: Ditto the above as it applies to the Spirit. We believe that no healing is possible without the involvement of the Spirit/Soul. We do not advocate any specific religious belief, denomination, dogma or practice since we believe that all humans must have their own spiritual guidance, by whatever name they call the Spirit, in order to achieve complete healing and health. We believe that all life on the planet came from the same source – we are all related and a part of the whole Universe. What better way to start a new day than in a spiritual practice of meditating on the positive aspects of life? If you hold to that belief then your day will also be filled with positive actions. In line with this truth, we advocate the daily use of meditation and prayer, and when challenges develop we encourage the access to your Physician Within.

You are not an accident. You came to earth for a reason and that reason is known only to you and your spiritual guide or God. There is no graduation in this school of life. It is said that if you don't learn from history you will be forced to repeat it, and so it is with life. If you fail to learn the lessons of life, or "cop out" by giving up, then you, too will be forced to repeat it until you get it right. This is why suicide never solves the problem; it only postpones the inevitable.

As you look back upon the events in your life you will recognize a pattern of ever-increasing difficulty in the decisions you are forced to make, just as in school your education continues to build on the previous lessons until you master a particular subject. I refer you to the article entitled "The Station" in the appendix for a beautiful written explanation of this concept – there is no such thing as the final destination in life; when we reach one goal, further challenges are presented to be conquered. The rainbow is a beautiful symbol of this process: you will never reach the pot of gold that seems to be just out of reach, but traversing the rainbow itself is a beautiful experience. That is proof that life's purpose is not contained in the pot of gold but is within the spiritual essence of who we are.

So, let's begin this odyssey down the path of life as we enjoy the daily blessings along the route. Enjoy the trip; your final station will come soon enough as you make your transition from this life and again reunite with your spiritual family that is waiting for you. This book may be thought of as a follow-up to my first book, *An Odyssey into Past Lives: A Personal Exploration into Cellular Memories,* available through Amazon.com or my website: www.cosmosbooks.us.

So let's begin anew with a happy, joyous, peaceful and thankful prayer when we arise each day to continue our journey.

Chapter II

LET THE JOURNEY BEGIN

LESSON: What type of person are you?
"ALL DISEASE AND ILLNESS IS PHYSICAL,
ALL PROBLEMS AND CHALLENGES ARE PSYCHOLOGICAL BUT
ALL CURES AND HAPPINESS ARE SPIRITUAL."
The Wellness Doc

Imagine you want to fly from Atlanta to San Francisco. Could you do it with only the physical possession of the airplane? Wouldn't you also need the pilot and crew to fly the plane? Then, in order to safely and successfully arrive at your destination the pilot would need a guidance system of some kind in order to know how to control the plane so it goes in the proper direction. If the plane represents the Body, the pilot represents the Mind that controls the plane and the guidance system giving information to the pilot represents the Spirit. It is easy to see how this trip is a metaphor for our life's odyssey during this sojourn in this Earthly incarnation. Even the Griswold family had many problems on their trip to Wally World but their trip ended on a happy note by successfully solving the challenges along the way, just as our lives will end successfully if we learn how to make the trip by integrating our tools of Body, Mind, and Spirit.

Let's take a look at who the participants were in the manifest destiny of the human race. Let's go back in time to when the first human-like creatures inhabited the Earth. They comprised groups of small bands that came together to provide protection and support for their clan. They didn't venture far from their familiar territory until the food source began to dry up.

Then out of necessity, one soul ventured out of the group in search of a better home in a better environment. We will call him the Explorer type. He is willing to face unknown dangers to seek something new. His was the early spirit of men like Leif Erickson, Marco Polo, Columbus, Lewis and Clark, and Neil Armstrong. They set out from the safety of the clan to seek new territory.

Eventually, some would return and shout the praises to those that stayed behind and convince others to follow them to the Promised Land, like Moses, Miles Standish or the leaders of the great migration in the early expansion of the West. Included in this category would be the Great Masters of the ages such as Jesus, Buddha, Gandhi, Krishna, Lao Tzu and others. We could call this type Leaders, as they lead others who are afraid to venture out on their own to a new life or embrace new ideas toward a better way of life.

What is left are the good folks who are afraid of stepping out into strange territory through a lack of knowledge or insight; they couldn't leave the familiar surroundings they felt safe and comfortable in. These people are the Followers of the world. Most will only leave their homes in the company of a Leader but many will never leave the territory in which they were born and hence do not benefit from the many experiences life has to offer. They live in the familiar *now* and won't open their minds to anything they can't or won't try to understand.

Whichever type you are is not important – all three types are needed for humans to evolve into the spiritual state we are all destined and desire to attain. All three types can be described in the Body (Followers), Mind (Leaders), and Spirit (Explorers).

BODY:
"Judge not, that you may not be judged. For with the same judgment that you judge, you will be judged, and with the same measure with which you measure, it will be measured to you."
Matthew 7:1-2

In our mythical journey to San Francisco there are many modes of transportation we could choose that would get us to the final destination. We could choose train, bus, airplane, boat, hot air balloon, wagon train, walking or maybe hitchhiking. Each vehicle has its own advantages and disadvantages. Which one we choose will depend on the goals of the trip. And so it is with the vehicle of our life's journey from birth to transition – The Body. We each have the opportunity to decide on this incarnation's body before the trip is started.

Whichever vehicle you choose for your mythical journey, your ability to arrive safely and according to the plan of your trip will depend on the condition of the vehicle itself. We want a vehicle that has its maintenance current and performed by those who know their jobs, a vehicle that uses the proper fuel and in which all the working parts have been checked and repaired regularly. The same applies to our body vehicle if we wish to have a safe journey in our life's plan.

We want to be sure we use the proper fuels in the form of food to keep the body going. We also want to be sure the working organs are checked and repaired regularly by our healthcare practitioners, and that these practitioners are knowledgeable in their business.

MIND:
"People are disturbed not by things, but by the view they take of them."
Epictetus

In order for our vehicle to move from the hangar or parking space it requires a pilot and crew or driver. And if we expect to arrive at our destination we want a well-trained pilot/driver and crew. The Leaders (Mind) of current and ancient times were well trained and knowledgeable in their areas of expertise. This knowledge built confidence and faith with the Followers in order for them to venture out of the clan's territory.

And so it is with the Mind that directs the body. Whatever we think, good or bad, will be manifested in our body. This is why it is so important to control our thoughts. The decisions we make in this life are no different than the decisions of the Leaders whose example we are all striving to emulate. *"As a man thinketh in his heart, so is he!"*[5]

SPIRIT:

"A man is literally what he thinks. His character is the sum of all his thoughts."

James Allen, Author (1864 – 1912)[5]

All of the successful Leaders maintained constant contact with their personal guidance systems. Many of them had different names for their God but their experiences of the higher power were very similar. Each believed and recognized their guidance system, which they knew was the genesis of their life's work as well as the source of the daily plan each followed. They recognized that the Mind would not work without the authority of the Spirit to guide them at all the junctions in the paths of life.

There is no human alive today who can navigate the boulders in life by the use of their conscious mind alone, no matter how smart they think they are. Spiritual guidance is a requirement for a happy and successful life. The magnitude of the success is directly proportional to the time spent in contact with the spirit guides and the Physician Within[6] you (see glossary).

The phrase "boulders in life" may need a little further explanation. To maintain a healthy lifestyle it is imperative that good stress management be incorporated into one's lifestyle.

70%-90% of all doctor visits are stress related. 70% of all prescription drugs are for stress-related issues.[7] Any change in our life or environment will trigger a stress response.

Stress is any change that you must adapt to, from an extremely negative situation (physical or mental) to very pleasant situations like your wedding or the accomplishment of a long sought-after goal. No matter what happens to us, it is our interpretation of or reaction to any environmental condition that impinges upon our minds and bodies.

So a boulder is anything that signals a change or builds a blockage to the peaceful flow of Spirit. See Chapter III, *A stroll down a mountain path,* for a further discussion of "boulders."

The "how-to" for allowing Spirit to guide your navigation through life is through meditation and prayer. The development of skill in these methods and learning to have faith in intuition will provide great benefits in happiness and success in life. Such is the purpose and goal of this book.

LESSON: What kind of transportation do you need?

"Enthusiasm, and therefore success, is knowledge on fire."
The Wellness Doc

In our mythical trip to San Francisco we choose to go by jet airplane but there are other modes of transportation we could have chosen. We choose airplanes because of time, safety, cost and convenience. As improvements in technology increased, our transportation modes also became more efficient and airplanes became more popular as the best choice. The airplane is a lot faster and safer than the wagon train of old, or even walking. So the evolution of transportation, though the knowledge of science, has compressed time and space to make our lives happier, safer and more fulfilling. Through the march of time and evolution the Body/Mind/Spirit has grown and evolved. We have learned to integrate all three parts into a trilogy that together will lead us to the "promised land." No one part of the trilogy can work by itself. They all need to work in cooperation, by recognizing the strengths of each.

You will never arrive at your destination with just the airplane; you need the pilot to guide the Body. The pilot needs the guidance system so he can direct the plane. And at the base of all these technological systems is knowledge: knowledge of the kind of vehicle to choose, the pilot's knowledge of how to drive or direct the vehicle, and access to the knowledge the guidance system is directed by, that spiritual intelligence which is the source from which all knowledge ultimately comes.

Once you know how to tap into this mother lode of knowledge you can travel anywhere you wish. Time and space are no longer a problem. You can go or be anywhere you desired by just asking. Knowledge is so vital to life that without it we would not grow or evolve – and after all, isn't that the purpose of life? Knowledge gives us enthusiasm for life and the will to enjoy it to the fullest. I have heard enthusiasm defined as "knowledge on fire." What a beautiful descriptive definition. If you want to be enthused about anything, all you need to do is to become more knowledgeable and enthusiasm will follow as a matter of course.

Knowledge, and therefore enthusiasm, are only half of the requirements to safely reach the goals you have set in life. We can have knowledge about a lot of things but if we don't have the desire, if we don't put that knowledge to work for us, we won't go far. I'm very knowledgeable about accounting but I've never had the desire to become an accountant. I consider it a necessary evil in my life's work but I don't enjoy it. I have a cousin who has a passion for accounting and had a very successful career as a CPA. So knowledge without motivation will not lead to the accomplishment of our goals. Motivation is a factor of the Mind – the Leader of our life's plan. If you know how to do something but the circumstances don't fit in with what the Mind wants, regardless of whether it is good or bad in the eyes of the rest of the human race, then all the knowledge in the world will be to no avail. The exception is when the increased knowledge brought on by maturity changes your motivation. There will be more on motivation in later chapters.

BODY:
"Nothing happens to any man that he is not formed by nature to bear."
Marcus Aurelius
Roman emperor, philosopher

If the Divine plan in life is to attain a happy and healthy longevity, and during this life we must also help to improve the lives of our fellow human beings, then we must maintain this Body vehicle in perfect working order. We can't contribute if we are unhealthy and constantly afflicted with illness. To do this we must take responsibility for our bodies and be involved in all the decisions affecting the Body. Don't entrust your Body and life to someone else. We don't need to reinvent the wheel every day; we can rely on someone else's expertise but only if we take final responsibility for the actions and the results.

Hence, we need to be aware that if we don't understand something and someone else can't explain it so we can understand, then we need to find out how to develop the knowledge that will give us the understanding we need. Now, we can't know everything, but knowing everything isn't necessary. In relation to our bodies all we need to know is how to stay healthy. All this requires a basic knowledge of how the Body works. If necessary, get a good book on biology; you don't need a college level text - a high school level biology book is sufficient to give you a working knowledge of your body. It's not necessary to know how the body's immune system works, just that the source of life (God) gave us an immune system to fight off all the toxins we come in contact with during our Earthly sojourn.

Then become aware of the information available through newspapers, magazines and Internet sources. Mostly, pay attention to HEALTHY LIFESTYLE issues. The details of the "how to" can easily be found in many Internet sources. One word of caution- what agendas are being promoted? Does the source promote the need for cooperation of all three human systems of Body/Mind/Spirit? Do they recognize that all three are important for a healthy life? If they insist that theirs is the only solution to your problem, check out some other alternatives. Develop the ability to ask the right questions.

In developing the skill of asking the right questions, consider the problem facing the president or owner of a large company. He is faced every day with the need to make many decisions that have a great impact on the company (or nations). He obviously cannot and is not an expert or knowledgeable on all subjects needed to make intelligent decisions. This is why he has many different vice presidents and experts to advise him. You, too, need to know where to go to get advice in areas in which you can't become knowledgeable in the required time. But in the final analysis you are the ONLY one responsible for the decision, so the good and bad of your decisions are also your successes or failures. This is why I try to remember that if I am not happy with the results of my life, the one I need to see about it is always available 24/7.

The final word is that you are responsible for everything that happens to you. Once you realize that, your condition will improve immediately. We all know what it takes to have a healthy lifestyle and following each of these will result in a healthy body: Don't put anything into your body that the body doesn't need for life (this includes avoiding substance abuse and having good nutritional habits), develop good stress management skills, exercise, and access your spiritual guidance system daily.

MIND:

"The significant problems we face today cannot be solved at the same level of thinking we were at when we created them."
Albert Einstein

Once you truly believe you are the architect of your life and body, you will immediately experience positive changes in your life. Then there is no excuse to look for exterior causes to blame for the conditions of your life. When you understand the root causes of your difficulties, you will be able to grow in wisdom and enlightenment. With enlightenment comes healing. When we take responsibility we can then take control of our minds by reframing all the negatives into positive affirmations that will manifest themselves in a healthier body.

Negative conditions are a false reality. They only exist in our minds and therefore are not real unless we let them become real. If you don't like the conditions you find yourself in, the person you need to speak with is always available. If the nature of God is only "good" then it is our perception with our conscious minds that translates into negative conditions. Hence, all we need to do is to recognize the good in everything; by reframing our thinking and accepting our good through faith, good will be manifested in our lives.

When we do this we must be able to accept change and be prepared to change our minds not to accept what appears as reality to the conscious mind. Most of us find it difficult to accept change but we can do it if we realize that change is a part of the divine plan and is a necessary part of life. The mind is one area we all have definite control over, and if we want good in our lives we must think only positive thoughts about ourselves and all that is around us.

SPIRIT:

"The soul is the only part of you that is real."
Wellness Doc

Our good comes from our Spirit; that is the pipeline to our divine plan. For a practical matter then, we need to develop techniques to access the Spirit that dwells within us. One technique that works for many who practice it is to be still and seek guidance from that Spirit at the beginning of each day and to give thanks for all the blessings at the end of each day. *Ask and it shall be given unto you, seek and ye shall find.* This is from the Christian Master Jesus but is an excellent piece of advice if we wish to know the contents of our divine plan.

Start each day with a quiet time of asking for guidance for your highest good, and then put God at the head of your activities today and everything will work out for good. Albert Einstein was once asked in an interview, "Of all the questions you have ever asked, what was the most important?" The interviewer was surprised when the answer wasn't a deep theoretical mathematical problem. He replied, "Oh that's easy, is the universe a friendly place or not?" I'm not sure it is worthy of such a philosophical effort; what the universe is to you depends on your perception of it, what it means to you. Isn't how you perceive reality the only real question? The world is good, friendly, dangerous or happy if you want it to be. If you want to understand the cosmos you must begin with understanding yourself. And the place to start is that "still small voice" within.

LESSON: What is your motivation?

22

As our analogy of the journey of life as a trip from Atlanta to San Francisco continues we now focus on motivation as an important adjunct to knowledge. So, now let's examine the importance of motivation.

A true story that illustrates this point comes to mind. When I was a teenager I was involved with sailing and racing sailboats on Tampa Bay. In those days there was a popular sailboat race from Tampa Bay to Havana, Cuba that was called "The Havana Race." Often the boat skippers invited one of the Junior Yacht Club skippers to come along as a crewmember to gain valuable experience. Of course, you can imagine this event also developed into a big drinking and gambling party when they reached Havana. When it was my turn to be invited to participate, my Dad felt I was too young (15 years) to have that kind of experience, so I was encouraged to wait a few years. But by the time a few years passed I had found out about girls and lost interest in sailboat racing.

There was one skipper who decided to invite a six-member crew made up entirely of beautiful women. Well, that boat never arrived in Havana and so the U.S. Coast Guard spent four days searching before they finally found them. There was much speculation by the whole community about how an experienced skipper could become lost in the Gulf of Mexico. But my Dad had what he considered proof that they were not lost. He said the skipper was his navigation instructor during flight school when he was in the U.S. Air Corps during WWII. It was impossible for him to become lost but he could 'disappear' if he didn't want to be found. So our party-loving skipper had the knowledge; he just wasn't motivated by circumstances to finish the race. He had to appear at a USCG inquest and I'm sure whatever pleasures he enjoyed were short-lived when his meeting with the Coast Guard was over.

So motivation has to be a part of your life's goals or purpose. Without motivation you will never take that first step. To live an enthusiastic life you have to become passionate about life. If you want to change an entrenched lifestyle you must first find a motivator that will keep you on your desired path. All the willpower in the world will not work unless you are truly motivated to succeed. Just find out what your motivator is, the most important thing in your life, and you can do anything.

BODY:

"All great spiritual teachers want us to change, and the self is the vehicle for that change. Becoming new is an illusion unless the self you inhabit every day and recognize in the mirror starts to lose its old habits and conditioning."
The Third Jesus: The Christ we cannot ignore by Deepak Chopra

Earlier we mentioned that to have a full and healthy life we must be considerate of our Body temple. We need to know about whatever is put into or upon our bodies. The usual excuse people make is that "I was born with this or that condition. I can't do anything about it." If we recognize that we are born with the bodies that God gave us for a reason and that our purpose in life is to overcome and grow from that challenge, then we can spend our lives in positive pursuits without feeling sorry for ourselves. Our purpose is not to walk a mile in someone else's moccasins; to understand, yes, but to pay attention to our own mile in our own moccasins. There is a reason for every Spirit and this is why it is so important to respect ALL life in whatever form we find it. Helen Keller is an example of what can be done when we are born with handicaps.

We are all a product of our mothers and fathers. If we believe we choose our parents in this life for a purpose then spending time feeling sorry for ourselves or blaming our situation on our parents does nothing to promote growth and happiness for ourselves. Some may consider having parents that are abusive or who lived an unhealthy lifestyle before and after we were born unlucky but I believe anyone can rise above such a situation. There are many examples of souls that were born into slums and tragedy and soared above it to a fulfilling life. Since we don't know the mind of God, there is also the possibility that we were born to fulfill the karma of our parents.

A special word to all who hope to become loving parents. Remember, the baby is a product of what the mother feeds it during its development within the womb. This is why most medications have cautions for use during pregnancies. And since she has the responsibility of what she puts inside her body, she is also responsible for the resultant product. You can't blame it on bad DNA. Our genetic code, while a product of our parents, it is not a death sentence. It is not formed in stone. It is a propensity toward a particular condition but any condition can be changed if we access the spiritual guidance system and it is within God's plan.

MIND:

"People have to be responsible for their thoughts, so they have to learn to control them. It may not be easy, but it can be done.
First of all, if we don't want to think certain things we don't say them.
We don't have to eat everything we see, and we don't have to say everything we think. So we begin by watching our words and speaking with good purpose only..."
Rolling Thunder, an American Indian Medicine Man

Once our Minds have accessed the Spirit to determine the goals in life then we can go to work on developing the plan to attain those goals. We need to establish what kind of knowledge and experience is required to reach those goals and then direct the Body vehicle to condition itself to make the journey. What the Mind directs the Body to do will follow; hence it is important to be sure we feed the Mind only positive, productive thoughts. Remember, the Mind is the part we definitely have complete control over. Our moods and actions are controlled by our Minds. And we don't have to do anything special to exercise this control. What the Mind conceives, the Body will manifest. This is why, if we just treat or maintain the Body without the direction of the Mind, the Body vehicle will not go. The Mind is part of the fuel equation. If the plane does not have a properly motivated pilot it will self-destruct in the sea of life. Neither the Body nor the Mind can keep from getting lost in the sea of life if we don't maintain continual contact with the Spirit for the compass readings on the chart of life. You can't become lost in the Gulf of Mexico if you have a compass because any direction you will eventually hit landfall.

How can you keep your Mind on course with all the negatives in the environment? You might begin with the attitudes expressed in the quote above. Then if that doesn't work, silently repeat the following affirmation: "Oh God, may the words of my mouth and the meditation of my heart be acceptable in thy sight." This quickie affirmation generally changes the direction of any thought processes to one that is more productive rather than destructive.

SPIRIT:

> *"The event horizon is the passage into the after life."*
> Wellness Doc

Western scientific thought considers only three states of consciousness: waking, sleeping and dreaming. But there is really a fourth state that fewer people are able to access. It transcends these three states into a realm where the super-conscious can take over – into the area of spirituality where all knowledge exists. We all know we can access the three physical states of waking, sleeping and dreaming by helping our Minds attain the beta, alpha and theta brain waves with the aid of programmed sounds. But this elevated fourth state can only be experienced after the Mind has let go of its normal activity and we have moved into the spiritual state of meditation. Life would be so much easier if we could access this meditative state easily and at will. It is in this meditative state that we can experience the cosmic oneness with all creation. It is here that the answers to our problems will be revealed. Could this be the ultimate goal of self-actualization as outlined by Abraham Maslow?

Self-Actualization…. What is it? According to psychologist Abraham Maslow, it is a goal of life, a continuous desire to fulfill potentials. Self-actualization is a process by which an individual becomes the most complete, the fullest –"all that you can be."

Maslow framed this system of attainment in his HIERARCHY OF NEEDS. Simply stated, the hierarchy outlines a level of needs required for human beings and the order in which these needs must be met. The illustration below shows the pyramidal structure of Maslow's grouping of needs and the order in which they manifest themselves.

```
                   /\
         ┌──────────────────────┐
         │  SELF-ACTUALIZATION  │
         └──────────────────────┘
              /    ESTEEM    \
            /    BELONGING     \
          /       SAFETY         \
        /      PHYSIOLOGICAL       \
```

The <u>physiological needs</u> include oxygen, water, protein, calcium and other minerals and vitamins. In addition, other physiological needs include activity, rest, sleep, the avoidance of pain, sex, etc.

The <u>safety</u> and <u>security</u> <u>needs</u> revolve around finding safe circumstances, stability and protection.

The <u>love and belonging needs</u> include the need for friends, a sweetheart, children, affectionate relationships and even a sense of community.

The <u>esteem needs</u> focus on the respect of others, the needs for status, fame, glory, recognition, attention, reputation, appreciation, and dignity. Other esteem needs include self-respect, confidence, competence, achievement, mastery, independence and freedom.

Maslow felt all of these needs were survival needs – requisites for the maintenance of health. Before you can hope to attain the highest level of self-actualization, you must have these lower needs fulfilled. People who have reached <u>self-actualization</u> are reality-centered, which means they can differentiate what is fake and dishonest from what is genuine and real. They are problem-centered, meaning they treat life's difficulties as problems demanding solutions. They have a need for privacy, they exist independently of culture and environment, they resist enculturation... that is, they are not susceptible to social pressure. Open to ethnic and individual variety, they enjoy intimate personal relationships with a few close friends instead of shallow relationships with many. Furthermore, people who have attained self-actualization have a benign sense of humor, an acceptance of self and others, an enjoyment of spontaneity and simplicity, and ultimately a freshness of appreciation.

For a further discussion of self-actualization see Chapter 6, Lesson 3.

There have been many studies about meditation and all have resulted in the conclusion that regular practice of meditation produces significant positive change in both bodily and mental conditions of the subject. Hence, it is worthy of your study and practice.

While this cannot be considered current by any standard, a brief outline of the research done on meditation will be of interest to all who wish to understand this important spiritual technique. One of the earliest Western scientists to study meditation was Robert Keith Wallace, who in 1967 began his Ph.D. research into the physiological changes that take place during Transcendental Meditation. He measured the subjects' blood pressure, brain waves, heart rate and oxygen consumption to indicate the metabolic rate of cells. He found that practiced meditators reached the alpha wave brainstate and a state of deep bodily relaxation within only a few minutes. Normally when we go to sleep it takes from four to six hours to reach a very deep state of relaxation while meditators were able to reach this level of relaxation in just a few minutes.

What was most significant about these meditators was that they hadn't gone to sleep, were not in one of the three consciousness states, but were still fully awake internally, nor had they gone into a trance. They experienced an increased sense of awareness. Wallace called this state "hypometabolic wakefulness."

After a decade of working with these measurements and phenomenal mind body states, he turned to the study of aging. He set out to find out if the normal stress we have in life from environmental toxins, negative emotions, diet, substance abuses, and the fast-paced lifestyle of modern Westerners were responsible for normal aging; then he wanted to know if meditation could slow the aging process even while a person is exposed to these detrimental factors. He investigated a group of adult meditators for biological aging factors. Wallace discovered that meditators, as a group, were significantly younger biologically than their chronological age would indicate. And the difference in these ages was very large; in the female subjects they averaged at least twenty years younger. There was a correlation between the amount of this age difference and the number of years the subject had been meditating regularly. Wallace concluded that for every year of regular meditation the biological age was reduced by one year. In a later study this was confirmed again. A typical 60-year-old who had meditated five years or more would have the physiology of a 48-year-old. Imagine that, looking twelve years younger with no surgery.

So meditation is well worth the time and effort. By putting in the time now you will extend your effective chronological lifespan.

LESSON: What are the environments in your life?

"Everything that appears in your life and affairs, physically, mentally or otherwise has at some time been sent forth from your thinking faculty. It makes your heaven and it makes your hell!"
Charles Fillmore

The paths on the charts of life are already drawn in. We need to access them continually, just as we would our global coordinates in our mythical trip to the west coast. Before the invention of global positioning systems, travelers still got lost by using just a compass.

When they had a chart to go with the compass fewer travelers were lost. But with global positioning no traveler is ever lost. Hence, if you want to arrive at your life's goal without becoming lost you need to advance your spirituality.

Our ancient explorers found it possible to reach their destinations but it wasn't easy nor was it safe. A lot of them got lost trying to find their way. Now we can invest in the technology that insures our safety but it takes time and effort to open the channels of spirituality. It can't be done for you; you have to invest the time. All three parts of our being are required for a successful life. This is why we can't heal by healing only the Body. All three MUST work synergistically in order to become healed. Until we learn this truth of life we will never be able to become a happy and healthy centenarian. This is important because God created our bodies for a life span of 110-120 years. Anything short of that means we must take responsibility for a failure in a decision somewhere along the journey. We tried to force our Body or Mind into something without consulting the guidance system, our Spirit, for the compass readings.

No one element of life (water, air, light, nourishment and rest) is more important than the others. Each is a requirement of life in its own way. As in nature, it is also true in our health therapies – all three elements, Body/Mind/Spirit, are necessary to sustain life. Emphasis on only one will not be sufficient. This is a truism of life.

If you want just the elimination of symptoms then visit your allopathic physician who will provide you with the appropriate medicines; but if you want to be healed and cured of your illness you need to also visit the Physician Within your Spirit. Only the confluence of Body/Mind/Spirit can initiate a complete cure and ultimate happiness.

BODY:

"Unless we become the change we wish to see in the world no change will ever take place. We are all, unfortunately, waiting for the other person to change first."

In the last chapter we talked about perceived negative conditions of your birth. But what if you are fortunate enough to be born of healthy, loving parents? Then you obviously have no excuses; there is no question who is responsible for your life. You are most likely an advanced soul whose purpose is a bigger responsibility. Then it is important that you demonstrate to others how to maintain this body temple as God intended it. You have a mandate to help your fellow man in their quest for a better life. You are closer to attaining self-actualization so you can spend your life in evolving to a higher level. There is no need to concern yourself with the basic survival needs as outlined in Maslow's Hierarchy of Needs - those needs being food, shelter, clothing, sex, love and socialization. When I found out about Maslow in college it was an epiphany experience for me and may be for you.

So, we were lucky to be born of healthy, loving parents; can we avoid the toxins of our environment? Most of the toxins were man-made so we know who is responsible there. We can control many of the toxins by what we put into our bodies. A cursory list of such toxins might include: chemical-laden food, the wrong kind of synthetic foods, food from animal sources, contaminated water, too much of a good thing like sugar/alcohol/tobacco, chemicals applied to our largest organ (the skin), medications, promiscuous sex and polluted air. I'm sure the list could be much longer with some added thought. Even though this seems like an impossible job, we do have control over each of those toxins without becoming a hermit like Howard Hughes. These natural solutions are all available on the Internet and through your healthcare practitioner.

There is a caution here of which we must be aware. The American people have lost faith in the FDA to insure our non-drug or food substances are safe. We must take control of our own bodies and move the healthy substances out of the "buyer beware" syndrome. With the exploding increased use of non-drug supplements, we need to insure that these natural products are always available to the people who want to take personal control of their health. The real problem is that people do not read the labels and attempt to understand what is on them; they don't discuss their use with their healthcare providers; many healthcare providers frighten their patients into avoiding natural products; and some people misuse supplements and herbals by taking inappropriate dosages. Some of you may remember the Ephedra issue a couple of decades back.

An example of the misuse of anti-oxidants is a case in point. It is well established that free radicals, the result of the body's chemical reactions (oxidation) with various substances, some of which are external toxins, are a source of ill health to everyone. The fact that anti-oxidants are a good way to control the damage of these toxins is well documented. Hence, smokers got the idea that they could defeat the unhealthy effects of tobacco by taking large doses of anti-oxidants and still continue the use of tobacco. Then a study came out that *very high levels of anti-oxidants in smokers actually increase the risk of cancer.* Wouldn't it be better to treat the cause, tobacco use, than try to combat the results of tobacco use by not following manufacturers' recommendations for the anti-oxidant supplements? Seems to me we are putting the cart before the horse.

MIND:
"It is not the dummy drug, the doctor's bedside manner, or the antiseptic smell of a hospital that does harm or good; it is the patient's interpretation of it."
Deepak Chopra, M.D.

What the mind can do to the physical condition of your body was demonstrated by a story Deepak Chopra, M.D. relates in his book *Quantum Healing: Exploring the Frontiers of Mind/Body/Medicine.* He had a patient in her sixties who had suffered from a slow degeneration of the heart muscle from a condition call cardiomyopathy. It expressed itself as shortness of breath whenever she exerted herself, due to an enlargement of her heart. Her cardiologist had suggested she go into the hospital for an angiogram. She apprehensively undertook the test and after it was over the angiographer physician came to her room with the good news: "Your vessels are clean – you don't have coronary artery disease; there should be no need for surgery." However, as he was leaving he said, "If your condition gets much worse the only thing that can be done is have a heart transplant."

You can surmise the rest of the story! No sooner had the woman returned home than her symptoms worsened. Her shortness of breath became so bad even when she lay down, she was unable to sleep and became increasingly more anxious. When she finally got enough strength to return to her cardiologist, he could not find anything which caused the worsening of her symptoms. Finally she told him about the angiographer physician's prognosis. The cardiologist assured her that her condition was not advanced enough to need such a complex and dangerous surgery. He assured her that she had nothing to fear and surgery would not be required. Immediately her symptoms disappeared.

These are just two of an infinite number of cases demonstrating the Mind/Body connection. For another example of the power of the Mind see the story of Michael entitled *You Have a Choice* in the appendix of this book.

SPIRIT:

> *"Pain and suffering are not accidental, but they are the visible manifestation of wrong thinking and acting."*
> Charles Fillmore

Jesus said, "I AM the way and the light." The I AM refers (metaphysically) to the source of all spirit, the oneness, God, or any supreme being by whatever name you wish to use. This means your guidance system is always available. Also, verbalizing or thinking "I AM" followed by any statement, either negative or positive, will bring that thought into manifestation. At age 72 I was testing the fall line on an artificial snow surface with a sled I was personally riding. The fall line was not perfectly straight and the sled crashed through the side rail knocking it over. One of the screws holding the rail penetrated the sled and into my rectum which caused an "ouch" response from me. No one was around so I drove myself to the hospital. Since this was a small town hospital

33

they transported me to Gainesville, Georgia by ambulance. The surgeon was called and said he would have to operate immediately. It wasn't too bad just cleaning out wood chips and closing some torn tissues. However the one thing he couldn't guarantee was whether my splinter muscle would be functional after the surgery. Can't understand why surgeons wait to the last minute to tell you the bad news when there isn't time to change or make up your mind? So just before I lost consciousness I said a quick prayer and affirmation. "I am well, whole, and healthy. My body parts work like a well oiled machine." After surgery I had to stay in the hospital for about five days until they were sure my splinter muscle was functioning. A month later at my last doctor visit when he was to release me he said I was perfect and he had never seen a surgery so clean with no signs of infection. The reason was that I got God on my side from the very start. A non functioning body organ was not an option to me. I repeated that prayer/affirmation at least a half dozen times during the days following the surgery until that final visit. I think the surgeon thought he was wholly responsible for how well it turned out. I knew better – he did a good job with his skills and God and I put the finishing touches together. I'm convinced this was an example of the body/mind/and spirit all working together to accomplish such an excellent outcome.

These are just a couple of an infinite number of cases demonstrating the Mind/Spirit/Body connection. For another wonderful story I refer you to the story of Michael in the appendix, entitled *You Have a Choice.*

CHAPTER III
THE HEALING ART

LESSON: Holistic health history
*"Quantum healing is the ability of one mode of consciousness (the mind)
to spontaneously correct the mistakes in another mode
of consciousness (the body). "*
Deepak Chopra, M.D., Quantum Healing

Health is a condition we are all striving for. The word comes from
prehistoric Germanic times and in modern English its root meaning
is *whole*. A suffix was added later that became the English word
health. The verb *heal* comes from the same source. So *heal* was
derived from the Germanic root meaning *whole*. To be whole is to
be healed. Have you ever looked at the word *health* in this
manner? HEAL – TH.

So to heal would imply to become healthy. Throughout history
humans have searched for external techniques to heal themselves
of the pains, illnesses and trauma that have afflicted them. These
techniques have included many mystical methods: prayer (asking
God to intercede on our behalf), magical medicines (to
mysteriously take away the pain), special foods that will heal our
bodies from the inside, the healing hands of human healers who are
the pipeline for the energies from God to the afflicted human. Why
must we humans have to search for an outside answer when God
has provided the means to remain whole as he intended in the
Divine Plan?

From a holistic viewpoint, whether you are healthy or some degree
less than optimally healthy will depend on the harmony and
balance of the physical, mental, spiritual, environmental, emotional
and social aspects of your individual life. When we are in perfect
harmony and balance with all these forces then the life force in our
bodies is also in a state of free flow, unimpeded by the disharmony
and discord that daily affects each of us. When we were born God
supplied us with the tools to maintain this harmony and balance
and he gave us the choices of when, how and which tools we could

use in any given challenge. The choices we make will determine the extent of our evolution, growth and <u>health.</u>

To realize that inborn healing force is present in all living things, all we need to do is observe nature in the wild and see how animals heal themselves when confronted with injuries. The foundation of the Nature Cures, which through a long evolution of techniques and philosophy became what is known today as integrative medicine, began in the first decade of the nineteenth century. A small boy was tending the cattle on his father's farm on a pasture in the Sudetes Mountains in what is now the Czech Republic. He noticed that a stag which had been wounded by a hunter in the thigh, hobbled into a mountain spring and sat with his injured limb submerged in the cold flowing water. Each day the stag returned to the spring for his daily treatments, guided no doubt by some inner spirit. With the healing power of the cold water that was supplied by the same God who watches over us, the stag improved each day until it finally got well and stopped coming to the healing spring. Shortly after reading about this I noticed a deer just standing in the cold mountain stream near our home in the north Georgia mountains. I think it was also wounded because a wild dog was barking at it and attempting to reach it. The dog finally gave up and I saw the deer near the same spot for two days.

The twelve-year old boy in the story above was Vincent Priessnitz. He never went to medical school yet he became one of the most famous healers of the nineteenth century. Vincent had many opportunities to experiment with cold-water therapy for injuries on the family farm. He once sprained his wrist and realized it felt much better when he held it under cold running water. However, he couldn't keep the wrist under the water and still do his daily farm chores. Not one to be discouraged by a minor problem, he found he could wrap the wrist with a wet bandage and renew the bandage as it dried. This idea was incorporated into modern medicine and today is called the "Priessnitz Compress."[1]

In my 35 years experience in the National Ski Patrol where musculoskeletal injuries are the most common type we see on the ski slope, the use of snow (which is readily available) is the most important treatment tool we carry in our packs. I have 28 years experience in the National Ski Patrol as an instructor with the ski patrol's "Outdoor Emergency Care Course," the required medical course for all patrollers. I often tell my students that if there was ever such a thing as a miracle drug it is <u>snow/ice</u>. We learned that if we could wrap the injury site with ice, then by the time the victim reached definitive medial care they were not in as much pain, the injury was in better condition (reduced edema) and the healing time was shortened. We did this before I was aware of Priessnitz.

BODY:

"Man originally came from the hand of the Creator absolutely healthy and good, without any blemish in body and soul."
Adolf Just (1859-1936)
Early practitioner of Naturism

Hippocrates was a Greek physician who is generally regarded as the father of medicine because he attempted to make sense out of the chaos of the mixture of religious dogma that controlled the medical practice of the day. He traveled widely, practicing and teaching. Some of the writings attributed to him are dated from the tenth century AD. These writings deal with anatomy, clinical subjects, diseases of women and children, prognosis, treatment, surgery and medical ethics. The Hippocratic Oath, while not written by him, forms the code by which modern medicine is supposed to function.

Parts of these surviving documents are divided into two major sections. The first section describes the physician's obligations to his students and his students' responsibilities to him. In the second part the physician pledges to prescribe only beneficial treatments, refrain from causing harm or hurt, and live an exemplary life.

Hippocrates made a special effort in his life to insure that the patient did not come away from him in worse condition than when he arrived. Can we say as much for some of the modern physicians? I'm not making a blanket indictment of all physicians – they are human, too and perhaps the world is becoming so complex that we are expecting the impossible of a human no matter how motivated s/he may be. There is hardly a week that goes by that I don't hear of a physician making a mistake in someone's treatment and causing permanent damage, or delaying proper treatment until the condition became critical.

In fact, it is the lack of faith in the medical community that has driven so many to seek out alternative/complementary medicine. This is why it is so important in today's environment to take responsibility and control of your health. Do everything in your power to keep your body temple operating like a properly tuned engine. Begin today to start making lifestyle changes that you know are healthy; then you will never have to worry about your long term health. Prevention is still the best solution to body maintenance and is cheaper than fixing broken parts. And what about the many physicians whose personal lifestyle isn't what they preach? I personally know a practicing physician who must weight over 400 pounds – obviously, not a good role model to his patients. Take a trip to almost any hospital and you will see many nurses who are overweight. Shouldn't at least these two professions have the knowledge and willpower to keep their bodies healthy?

MIND:
> *"The human body was created to be perfect – to be well at all times, and that within each person was a certain power which regulates his health and strength."*
> Benedict Lust (1872-1945)
> Father of Naturopathy

Efforts to access the mind to perform healings may be traced as far back as the sleep temples of Egypt in 2000 BCE. In sleep we are able to communicate directly with the subconscious mind because the conscious mind is in its resting state and is no longer standing guard at the gateway of the mind. At this point we can program the subconscious with possible healing reinforcements that will manifest in bodily functions. James Braid (1795-1860) coined the word *hypnosis* to describe this phenomenon. Each of us passes through this hypnotic state of mind twice a day, when we go to sleep and when we wake up.

Because the Mind controls everything we are, our memories, images of everything that has ever happened to us, and through its input whatever we will become, then it is important we watch what we expose our minds too. This is why hypnotherapy, visualization, meditation and positive affirmations are so successful. Our lives would become so much better if we learned how to control what we think, hear, see and feel. The nice part about this truth is that our mind is the one thing we have complete control over. It is up to us, through our conscious mind, to control what information our subconscious mind receives. My grandmother understood this by dictating my homework that required memorizing into the recorder and playing it back by a microphone next to my pillow while I slept. We are doing the same thing now by pre-recording healing inductions and playing them back while we sleep, using headphones and more modern equipment.

One of the most common and effective uses for hypnotherapy is to help clients control abusive behavior. Since we are talking directly with the subconscious mind during the hypnotic induction, we are able to reframe the mind with thoughts that become positive manifestations in the body and conscious mind when the client is awake. This is also a drugless application for depression. What a wonderful tool, available to anyone once they can control their mind.

Use of this technique does not mean the therapist can take over control of the client's mind. The client must be willing and want to control the abusive behavior in order for the hypnosis to work. The subconscious mind will not accept a negative statement, nor will the client accept in their mind anything they do not wish to do, or anything that is against their moral code or belief system. Brainwashing is accomplished only over a long period of time involving stressful conditions combined with repetitive suggestions that may be in opposition to your belief system. That time frame is measured in years. So don't worry, no one can take control of your mind unless you want them too. With hypnosis, you will always maintain control.

SPIRIT:

> *"For I will restore health to you,*
> *and I will heal you of your wounds,*
> *says the Lord."*
> Jeremiah 30:17

In order to have a complete cure it is necessary to have access to that Physician Within, that special spirit/soul by whatever name you wish to call it. This is where prayer comes in and is the only way a permanent cure can be accomplished. As far as how to pray is concerned, there are only a couple of things to keep in mind. If it is a serious condition, the more people who are praying with you, the better the results. Remember Jesus said, "Where two or more of you are gathered together there I will be also." This is why church prayer circles or groups are really beneficial. Many church organizations have 24/7 prayer request programs. Every time I've ever used Silent Unity, a positive result happened. I have found and research has proven that intercessional prayer (asking God to intercede by telling him how you want him to help) is not as effective as a prayer of thanksgiving in which you have already acknowledged the positive result you seek.

The point to remember is that I guarantee that without prayer, no true healing will take place. Be thankful and learn from whatever the results turn out to be. In addition to our desires we must realize there is a divine plan and the laws of karma are also working in the events of our lives. Remember the line from Shakespeare, "The fault dear Brutus is not in our stars but in ourselves that we are underlings."

LESSON: A stroll down a mountain path.

> *"Chance is a word void of sense,*
> *nothing can exist without a cause."*
> Voltaire (1694-1778)

The question for our purposes is how to cure the condition, not just heal it temporarily, only to have it come back later. To cure means to get to the root cause of the condition and heal it so the condition

40

will not return. Too often in modern western medicine, temporary symptom relief is the only approach pursued. The objective is to reduce or eliminate the symptoms so the patient feels better; then the medical doctor feels s/he has performed their job properly. Well personally, I'm not interested in the symptoms – they are indications that something is wrong and I need to correct the root cause so the symptoms will disappear permanently.

This symptomatic approach is not always the fault of medical communities. You, as the medical consumer, are responsible for this condition as well. We demand instant gratification in the relief from our illnesses and that can only be done by the use of drugs and techniques that bring about rapid results in how you feel. Mother Nature moves at her own timetable – she will not be rushed. Most medical consumers don't believe they have been healed if the physician doesn't give them a pill to take. This was demonstrated to me when I once went to a dermatologist for a diagnosis of a minor skin problem.

He said the skin problem was caused by a virus and preceded to give me a prescription for an antibiotic, which he surely knew was useless against a viral infection (antibiotics kill bacteria, not viruses). I think he knew that my body would eventually fix itself when the energies were in balance and the virus was eliminated by my immune system. In the meantime I would be taking the antibiotic and would think that was the cause of the healing. I didn't waste my money on the antibiotic, but purchased an herbal product that improved my body's immune system and let it take care of the problem. Of course, had I taken the antibiotic my immune system would have been depressed and the healing would have taken longer. My body did the job in only four days; the doctor gave me a prescription for ten days. I think this scenario is repeated many times each day in the United States. No wonder the population stays ill and the bugs become resistant to the antibiotics. The bugs are probably laughing and celebrating with the fine meal they have come to love. By overuse of antibiotics and other drugs, we have masked the bugs so our own immune systems no longer can identify them.

You need the doctor to determine the diagnosis, but it isn't required that you accept his prognosis. That is your responsibility to determine. And when you think about the treatment, ask yourself the question, does it address all three of the systems, Body/Mind/Spirit? As we have mentioned so often, it is only at the confluence of the three systems that true healing and cure can take place.

Walk with me, if you will, as we take a stroll in the early morning hours down a mountain path. It is early in the morning -- the sun has just cleared the mountaintops and the rays of sunshine are beginning to dispel the morning mist. You are beginning to warm to the sun's rays as you listen to the music of the birds as they are rising from their nests. It is early fall and your feet make a rustling sound as they move through the dried leaves as you slowly meander down the forest path. Suddenly you begin to hear the sounds of water and you know a waterfall is close by so you hurry along the path, which meets the mountain stream just before it starts to cascade over the rocks. When the path turns to follow the flow of the water you see that the water is calm; the stream is wide at this point and obviously very deep. Gravity has control of the water as it slowly flows downstream in a peaceful mood. You pick up a pebble and throw it into the middle of the stream and watch the concentric circles of energy flow from the center until the larger volume of water absorbs them. And you realize the water is so much like our soul/spirit in its natural state.

Life is floating along so nice and peaceful with no stress, worries, pain or illness and then some idiot throws us a pebble and the energy in our bodies is activated, causing waves in our soul/spirit until the God qualities can take over and return us to our natural state. Then as the peaceful and serene stream reaches the drop off, the fall of the water represented by our body is excited again with energy as it tries to resist its environment. But at last it reaches the bottom and the stream widens again and the energy is reduced as it continues its transit through life, secure in the knowledge that every bodily illness event is just as surely followed by the peace and serenity of the resurrection from the illness.

42

As we continue our walk along the bank, we notice the stream starts to bend to the right and as the water flows around the bend we notice an increase in its speed. As you round the bend, you notice the whitewater and the increased noise from the water of life as boulders that are strewn around the stream impede its peaceful flow. When the water is confronted with a boulder it must decide if it can go over it (resulting in some discomfort) or crash into it (resulting in more discomfort, being pushed back and forced to slide around the edges), or change course and make a wide path around it (resulting in the least amount of disruption to the flow of the body functions). If there is time and room, the latter is the healthiest choice. As the water moves through the boulder field and the flow calms, it joins up with the battered parts of the body, which has learned the lessons of how to deal with the boulder (or illness) in our life. The water will continue down the stream and occasionally meet up with the boulders, which represent illness, and as our bodies learn how to deal with them the disruptions become less frequent and the stream eventually meets with the larger body of a river.

As we continue down the river, now meeting fewer boulders or obstructions, we notice another stream coming into the river. Its water is mixed with the river, creating deeper and calmer waters. If we were to travel up the stream we would find that it had pretty much the same type of journey down its path to meet the river, encountering other boulders along the way. Let's call this stream the mind, which has now met up with the larger body of the river. As we continue down the river we realize we meet up with another stream and we notice the situation is just like the previous two streams. We can call this stream the spirit. The spirit stream adds more water to the volume of the river and as a result the trip down the river becomes calmer and hence much healthier. The confluence of the three streams of Body/Mind/Spirit is the only way to reduce the stress, tensions and illness of the healthy person.

BODY:

> *"Ask not what disease the patient has, but why the patient has the disease."*
> Sir William Osler

All illnesses begin at the cellular level of our biology. The cells are the microcosm, in balance with the macrocosm of our living body. If the cells are the source of our illness/disease then it is only prudent to maintain our cellular biology in perfect working order. What are some of the techniques we can use to insure a smooth running body temple?

One of the first principles we must realize is the old computer truism, "garbage in, garbage out." So it is with our body machine. If we feed it good, clean, wholesome food it will be able to keep our body healthy. If we feed it junk, non-nutritious foods the result must be poor health. Nutrition is a big area for investigation, much too large for a full discussion here. There are a few principles we can start with, however. First let's recognize that all cells need food so they can grow, function properly, reproduce and die, leaving their replicated off–spring to carry on. If they are diseased or damaged, that condition also continues in the offspring. Hence, we should feed them only good, healthy foods. These healthy foods include only pure water, proteins, fats, carbohydrates, vitamins, minerals, pure air and sunshine. Anything else is counterproductive and should be avoided.

There are hundreds of thousands of chemical reactions continuously going on within our bodies, which these cells require to live and reproduce. The foods listed above are the required substances that allow these chemical reactions to take place. We should be aware not to allow any toxins to enter our bodies to complicate these chemical reactions. So if we put good food in, we will get health out.

In discussing the toxicity of vaccinations and the fact that a good diet is a better solution to guard against disease than the poisonous vaccines, the World Health Organization said, "The best vaccine against common infectious diseases is an adequate diet."

MIND:

"Pain and suffering are not accidental, but they are the visible manifestation of wrong thinking and acting."
Charles Fillmore
Co-founder of Unity Church and School

Charles Fillmore had this to say about healing and the mind: "If all bodily ills of all the people in the world were healed instantly, they would soon be sick again, unless they were taught the Truth. It is the experience of old practitioners that the disease which they heal, in time reappears, unless the mind of the patient has been renewed through spiritual understanding." A proven technique to bring the mind in tune with the body to bring about healing is the use of affirmations a number of times daily. If the mind concentrates on positive healing thoughts, the body will reflect the desired condition.

If you are experiencing a healing challenge, try one of these two affirmations four times daily. Repeat them sincerely in the morning, afternoon, early evening, and at bedtime. You will be surprised at the results:

(1) *I am a healthy expression of the life of God.*

(2) *The life of God moves in and through me now as healing energy. I am renewed and invigorated.*

SPIRIT:

"From the moment people begin talking about what they need rather than what's wrong with one another the possibility of finding ways to meet everybody's needs is greatly increased."
Marshall B. Rosenberg, Ph.D.

To expect a cure from your illness or disease without invoking the spiritual nature of your being would be as successful as putting all your faith and expectations in a cure of cancer by removal of a portion of your colon. Research has shown that as a group, persons with a daily sincere spiritual practice have a higher rate of healthy members than those without a spiritual foundation.

Modern medicine cannot and will not even attempt to explain spontaneous remissions. Since medicine broke away from the religious philosophy for healing when medicine wanted to divorce itself from the mysticism of religion, anything that smacks of superstition had to be discarded as a pagan practice. But spontaneous remission healing has been seen by medical doctors (who will not talk about it) and aware laypeople (who are afraid to talk about it) for centuries. If a healing happened a century ago without the aid of a medical doctor it was considered witchcraft. I have personally, in today's enlightened society, been called a "witch" because I believe in the power of our spirit to work wonders in our lives.

We know spontaneous healings do happen and are happening more frequently as more people are exposed to its miracles. I choose to let spontaneous healings work for me in my life. We will probably never be able to use the scientific method to prove the value of spiritual healings but it is another tool I carry in my personal health tool chest. I don't feel it is important to understand the how and why of spontaneous remission. I know it comes from my spiritual nature and I am not afraid to call on it when needed. I know my spiritual foundation works in my life and it will in your life if you let it.

LESSON: You are a heat generating machine.

> *"It follows that the maintenance of order requires that some form of work be done on the system. IN THE ABSENCE OF WORK, ORDER DISAPPEARS. Hence, we come to our current sense that an incoherent collapse of order is the natural state of things."*
> Stuart Kauffman,
> *At Home in the Universe*

The body of all animals and plants are really "heat generating machines." This is metabolism at work – it is what keeps us alive. And since we must constantly be generating heat and therefore energy, we come face-to-face with the Second Law of Thermodynamics. This law of physics states that disorder (or entropy) must increase in a closed system until the system runs down. Put another way, this is why there is no such thing as a perpetual motion machine because without increases of energy input all machines will break down eventually. Our bodies will also wear out, because they must obey this basic law of physics.

In the case of our bodies the increase in entropy means that each time our cells reproduce or are attacked by toxic substances, a little destruction of the information system within our DNA is manifested and begins to accumulate until our DNA can no long repair itself and function as it was originally intended. Eventually, aging and cancer is the result and becomes irreversible. This gradual buildup of destruction of our informational system in our DNA causes the loss of our cells' ability to function properly. The genes are no longer able to repair the effects of the environmental toxins. All living systems are open, non-equilibrium thermodynamic systems sustained by a mix of the heat produced by the biochemistry within the system in keeping with the Second Law of Thermodynamics. (see glossary). As your body cools, the cellular activity reduces, causing the energy produced from eating to increase cellular activity. The excretion system will reduce the heat balance but not more than the increase in heat production. If heat drops faster than it is produced, a condition called hypothermia develops and if not corrected, death will result as the body temperature approaches 85 degrees F.

If energy is not imported into the system, entropy (see glossary) will increase and the machine (our bodies) will grind to a halt. This can be demonstrated by someone who has stopped the intake of food – we know he will die, but not before he becomes increasingly weaker. Reducing entropy takes work or in the language of physics, in order to produce work you must input energy. If you don't believe it, try to work without using up energy. Let's assume you have two glasses of water; one is hot and other is at room temperature. If you mix them together the molecules in the cold water will speed up while the molecules in the hot water will slow down until the water eventually reaches the ambient room temperature. This is a condition known as thermo-equilibrium. The entropy is reduced unless more hot water is added to the system. As your body cools, the cellular activity is reduced until there is no more cellular activity and the system dies. The Second Law of Thermodynamics (see glossary) allows energy to flow from hot to cold but not in the reverse. Hence, to stay healthy you must supply your cells with the energy (food) that will keep them healthy.

Medicine has been attempting to make itself more scientific, to evolve out of the mystical world of the shamans and the time when the medical work was done by the clergy. As the twentieth century was closing there was a definite shift to include the spiritual within the arena of body/mind/spirit medicine once again. Today more than half of the American adult population visits what are described as complementary or integrative medical practitioners.

In 1998 Dr. John A. Austin of Stanford University School of Medicine reported in the Journal of American Medical Association, the findings of a national survey. "Users of alternative health care are more likely to report having had a transformational experience that changed the way they saw the world. The finding is an acknowledgement of the importance of treating illness within a larger context of spirituality and life meaning. The use of alternative care is part of the broader value orientation and set of cultural beliefs, one that embraces a holistic, spiritual orientation to life." We no longer wish our medical care to be so scientific and technologically advanced that it becomes separated from our spirituality. We as a nation are beginning to recognize that the river of Spirit is just as important to healing as the other two of Body and Mind. Even physicians are beginning to dare to speak out without fear of condemnation, saying that there is a spiritual component to true healing, that healing is not only a science but an art as well.

The old-time forms of medicine really were not so bad. Maybe our ancestors didn't have the modern-day environmental toxins to deal with. My mother-in-law was healthy until the medical community got hold of her. She had lived a healthy life in the country until she was 93 years young. At this point one of her granddaughters decided she would help her by moving into her house with the objective of taking care of her. The granddaughter was a nurse by training and so felt confident she could handle the job. The problem was, she took charge of everything - cooking, supervision of my mother-in-law's physical activities, rest schedules and healthcare.

Prior to this time my mother-in-law did her own cooking, which was a wholesome diet that included plenty of fruits and vegetables. Now her granddaughter brought the type of diet typical of the modern ages, which were more fast foods and non-farm items. At the first sign of a health challenge my mother-in-law was taken directly to the doctor. Up until then she never went to doctors nor did she take any of the medications usually associated with the elderly. She used to say that if you wait for three days, you would always get better. Obviously she was allowing her natural body the time to do the outside work she was used to and enjoyed. After this change she no longer did the outside work any more, nor was she interested in working on her crafts that she had formerly enjoyed and taken great pleasure in. It took less than two years for her health to take a nosedive. She made her transition while in a nursing home after only a three day stay.

BODY:

"If there were a simple way to increase your life span, virtually eliminate cancer, decrease all forms of chronic disease, and age at half the rate you are currently aging, would you want to know what it is?"
***** See Below *****

Dr. C.M. McKay of Cornell University found the secret to the fountain of youth in 1930 when he made a remarkable discovery. He found that "caloric restriction" is a consistent and reproducible method of prolonging life and vitality in animals. It's been shown to be effective in every species tested, from aquatic organisms to primates. We all know that humans are a member of the primate family. When we refer to caloric restriction we are not referring to dieting, but total reduction of caloric intake. We can still have a balanced diet but keep the total intake of calories down. The goal

49

of caloric restriction is to consume calories just above the starvation level.

To many this idea does not make common sense as it is felt that a well-nourished body is a healthy body, but research has shown that a caloric intake of approximately 950 calories per day will significantly extend a person's healthy life span. However, this goal is not meant for everyone; you should consult with your healthcare practitioner to set your own personal goals. Obviously, the activity level of your lifestyle in relation to the exercise level you obtain will have a lot to do with your caloric needs. The problem lies with the excess caloric input that has a negative impact on health. Remember the energy rule, that energy in must equal energy out. Better to adhere to the wisdom of "live slowly and live longer." The result of caloric restriction is: lower metabolic rates, a longer life span and reduced rates of cancer, heart disease and diabetes.

It is important to remember that healthy goals cannot be attained overnight. It would be counter-productive to attempt to reduce the caloric intake to the 1000 calorie level by starving the body of its needed energy source. However, with planning, the level can be gradually reached over a longer period of time without adverse effects on your health. It's a matter of training the body to reach a healthier condition. Remember, the choice of what and how much of any substance you put into your body is wholly your affair. So you are responsible for your diet and intake of toxins. Be sure you are making the choices now that you will be happy with thirty years from now. So often I see people in the sunset of their lives wishing they had done things differently when they were younger but by then it is too late to fix the mistakes of the past.

MIND:

"*I think, therefore I am.*"
René Descartes

In The Holographic Universe, Michael Talbot had this to say about the power of the mind to manifest either health or illness: "Medical science is at a loss to explain how mental imagery could actually create an illness. As we have seen, ideas that are prominent in our thoughts quickly appear as images in the energy. If the energy field is the blueprint that guides and molds the body, it may be that by imaging an illness, even subconsciously, and repeatedly reinforcing its presence in the field, we are in effect programming the body to manifest the illness. This same dynamic linkage between mental images, the energy field, and the physical body may be one of the reasons imagery and visualization can also heal the body."

The placebo effect is an interesting phenomenon that if understood, can be used to our benefit in helping us heal. The placebo effect occurs when the patient believes in a medication, treatment or the power of the healer. and the healing is credited to the belief rather than the actual treatment. We usually think of the placebo as a "sugar pill" which has no possible ability to heal, but the patient believes the pill is the source of the healing. The effectiveness of placebos provides dramatic support for a holistic view of the human organism, a view that is receiving increasing attention in medical research.

This view holds that the mind and body continually interact and are too closely interwoven to be treated as independent entities. It has been established that an average of 35 percent of all people who receive a given placebo will experience a significant healing effect. Conditions that have proven to be responsive to placebo treatment include angina pectoris, migraine headaches, allergies, fever, the common cold, acne, asthma, warts, various kinds of pain, nausea and seasickness, peptic ulcers, psychiatric syndromes such as depression and anxiety, rheumatoid and degenerative arthritis, diabetes, radiation sickness, Parkinson's, multiple sclerosis and cancer.

A colleague of mine told me that when she was growing up, her pediatrician used to treat warts in his young patients by digging up a handful of change from his pocket. He would give the child the change and tell them that if they spent it all before the end of the day, the wart would dry up and fall off. It rarely failed to work, probably because of the children's deep belief in the authority of the doctor.

When a condition is cured but no relationship can be found as to how the treatment could produce a response then it is often credited as "it is all in his head." I say it doesn't make much difference how it happened; the important point is that whatever works should be fine. It is the objective that is important. When you are up to your waist in alligators it is difficult to remember that the objective was to clear the swamp.

I've often wondered: if the healing rate of 35% is an average for the placebo effect, then how could something like the Tuskegee experiment not have any successes? Then I realized the Tuskegee experiment lacked one very important ingredient for the placebo effect to be successful, that is, the patient and the physician must both believe the treatment will be successful. This is what is meant by the double blind study. It is not always sufficient for just the patient to have faith; all concerned parties need to believe the treatment will be successful. Can you imagine how successful you would be if you didn't believe in the prescription? How successful would Jesus have been in his healings if he didn't believe he could perform the miracles? Or, more accurately, God performed the miracles through Jesus as the channel. What the 35% means is that if your faith is strong enough then you, too can perform miracles. This is probably a reason spontaneous remissions take place. It seems prudent to me that the more healing tools you have in your medicine bag, the more chances you have to be successful. So why not use your mind to heal rather than manifest the illness?

SPIRIT:

"My prayers do not change God,
my prayers change me by adjusting my attitudes
so I can better understand God's divine plan for me."
Author Unknown

Healers, both ancient and modern, have realized that the diseases they heal will in time reappear unless the mind has been renewed through spiritual understanding. They have healed but were not truly cured. Prayer or distant prayer (nonlocal prayer – see glossary) is the usual technique involved with healing the spirit so the body can respond. We will discuss this idea in more detail in the next lesson.

Spiritual healing is the channeling of healing energy from its spiritual source to the patient. How this works is that everyone has a healing spirit that flows through their bodies as an energy force. When in balance this energy force keeps the Body/Mind /Spirit in perfect order. Such conditions as stress, an unhealthy diet or negative thinking can block this energy force from a free flow, resulting in illness. This works the same as plaque build-up in blood vessels that block or reduce the volume of blood flow to the tissues. The channels need to remain open so this energy force can perform its healing activities. In traditional Chinese medicine (TCM) this force is often referred to as Qi or Chi. These energies flow through paths known as meridians and are the sites used in the techniques of acupuncture and acupressure. The discussion of TCM is a fascinating one and quite lengthy so I'll save it for a later chapter.

When a healer lays their hands on you they act as a conduit for the healing energies that go to your pain and free the blockage so the force can flow in balance again. If the healer is a good medium and the healing does not work it is usually because the patient subconsciously "blocks" the healing force because they subconsciously prefer to be ill. This is sometimes referred to as secondary gain. Some people need to be ill for some karmic reason and therefore, healing escapes them.

An interesting study was done in 1990 on 46 healthy volunteers who had incisions made on their arms. Twenty-three of them unknowingly had noncontact spiritual and therapeutic touch and standard wound dressing. Others in a control group were placed daily in an isolated room but were not sent healing treatment to their arm. Both the physician who performed the incisions and the technician who measured the wounds were unaware of the true nature of the study. By day eight the size of the wounds of the treated group was ten times smaller than for those in the control group. After 16 days the wounds had healed in 13 of those who received noncontact healing while none in the control group had healed. (*Wound Healing – double-blind trial: Wirth D.P., Subtle Energies 1990; (1): 1,1-20)*

LESSON: Physics and Healing

> *"When will the doctors stop acting like God?*
> *When you stop kneeling."*
> *Brain Longevity* by Dharma Singh Khalsa, M.D.

No two humans were ever created exactly alike. So why should we expect any standardized protocols for our treatment to work exactly the same? The philosophy of standardization was developed as a result of modern scientific methods and the modern medical community's attempt to control the implementation of medical care. But in health care we are not dealing with the physics of matter but with a biological system of living things. Because they are living they must have a spirit and a mind that directs the vehicle of the body. Since the spirit deals with creation, each living system is a unique creation.

In the realm of quantum physics (see glossary) we know that energy is unpredictable; as we approach that time of singularity the units get smaller and smaller. When I was in high school I was taught that the proton and neutron were the smallest forms of matter in the universe. By the time I left college I was aware of hundreds of particles that were much smaller. We know there are many other invisible particles, which we can only predict, and only in a few cases can we even see the effects of these extremely small particles. In order to see these particles scientists must use a circular accelerator miles in diameter to reach the required high speeds. When the collision occurs we can only witness the resulting product for just a nanosecond.

As I am writing this it was just announced yesterday that the European Organization for Nuclear Research has successfully collided two photon beams traveling in opposite directions to replicate the conditions just after the Big Bang (see glossary). Just before collision the beams reached speeds a nano (billionth)-fraction of a second slower than the speed of light in the 27 mile tunnel 330 feet below ground. The energy released was 7 trillion electron volts. As the data is analyzed over the coming years the scientists expect to find answers to questions like where we came from, how the early universe evolved, how matter was converted to mass after the explosion of the Big Bang and what is the dark or invisible matter that makes up an estimated 25 percent of the universe. This original mass after the big bang is believed to have made possible the emergence of stars, planets and eventually life from the matter that came from the big bang. Scientists said on CERN's official Twitter account, "Experiments are collecting their first physics data – historic moment here!" "Nature does it all the time with cosmic rays (and with higher energy) but this is the first time this is done in the laboratory." What a great day for physics. And also when God said "Let there be light," now science is finding out the 'how' of what happened next.

In the last lesson we discussed the Second Law of Thermodynamics and how it applies to healing. In this lesson we will continue the scientific applications with one of the most significant physics discoveries in the last century – Bell's Theorem (see glossary). If you haven't heard of this theorem don't feel bad because unless you are a theoretical physicist working with quantum mechanics you probably haven't come across this landmark discovery. Surprisingly, it has explained a lot of the mysteries involved with healing and prayer. In fact, it gives the scientific proof for better understanding of healing, prayer and a lot of the psychic phenomena that we know work but that we don't understand.

The Buddhist Nagarjuna understood this theorem hundreds of years ago (200 AD) when he said, "Things derive their being and nature by mutual dependence and are nothing in themselves."

How is this important to us? At the point of singularity of the Big Bang (see glossary), everything in the universe was interconnected, a complete whole, all was one. In the nanosecond that followed, we began to separate into our individual parts. In the latter part of the twentieth century the cosmos was discovered to be a large hologram. The hologram is a beautiful and very difficult concept to understand. In its simplest terms it means that if you take any whole part of matter and break it into smaller pieces, then each of the smaller pieces is a complete projection of the whole. You have seen the application of holograms on driver's licenses and credit cards.

Consider this! Within the last decade we have realized that memory is not confined to our minds but that each cell of our body is a hologram of our life. Every event in our life, as well as previous lives, is stored within each of our cells. There is a fascinating book entitled *The Holographic Universe* by Michael Talbot, if you care to delve more deeply into these mysteries. Many questions have been answered as a result of this discovery. We will discuss some of these in the following sections. I just wanted to introduce you to the concept before we discuss these points in more depth.

As you think about these laws of physics, let's consider some of the following questions. Why does distant healing through prayer work? What is the explanation when a person awakens from a deep sleep with the intuition of an event happening to another family member who is on the other side of the globe? What about the times you go to answer the phone with the sure knowledge of who is on the line and why they are calling? What is the explanation of a déjà vu experience?

The thesis of Michael Newton, PhD's extensive research into the properties of our Spirit/Soul maintains that when we are born into this lifetime only a part of our sprit is incarnated. The remainder of the soul stays in the higher dimensions. In other words, our incarnated soul is really a hologram of our spirit/soul. We are incarnated on this earth with a duplicate of our soul (our soul mate, if you wish) also incarnated somewhere else, who has the same goals and lessons to learn but may make different choices in life than we did. Since we all have free will we are continuing to make choices; some are good and others we probably would do differently if we could. There are so many questions, the ones above and questions such as why are we here? What is our purpose? They can be answered with an understanding of the Second Law of Thermodynamics and Bell's Theorem.

BODY:

> *"To see a world in a grain of sand,*
> *and heaven in a wild flower,*
> *hold infinity in the palm of your hand,*
> *and eternity in an hour."*
> William Blake

Research has shown that through imaging, the brain and each cell in our body can tell the body what to do. This is why visualization has been so successful in correcting the negativity that has manifested in our bodies. By positive imaging or visualizing, the brain and cells can tell the body to recreate the image again, a rebirth. Some medical centers that treat childhood cancer have harnessed this power through the use of video games. The children under treatment are told that the 'bad guys' in the video games are cancer cells. As they play the games, their immune systems manifest an increase in activity against the cancer. The children's powerful imaginations become allies in the fight against the disease through the visualization of the video games.

Images making images, just like two mirrors, reflect each other infinitely. That is the nature of the body/mind connection in a holographic universe. Paramahansa Yogananda taught us that proper visualization by the exercise of concentration and willpower enables us to materialize thoughts, not only as dreams or visions in the mental realm, but also as experiences in the material realm. An excellent resource for learning how to add positive visualization to your daily life is Australian author Liliane Grace's book *The Mastery Club*. The story is engaging and even children can enjoy it, either read out loud to them or reading it themselves if they're older. The earlier you start with good visualization practices, the happier and healthier your life will be. And don't forget, it's never too late to learn these helpful practices. Her book is available in printed or electronic form on her website: www.themasteryclub.com.au.

The lesson to be learned from living in a holographic universe is that we are all part of one big, whole, infinite cosmos. The reality of this is that we cannot hurt another person or another living thing without also hurting ourselves. When I look at a tree, plant, bird or animal I say, "That living thing is part of me." We, all creatures, are connected with all other creatures and if we send love out to those other creatures then we will be safe, happy and successful in living our own creation. So let's remember that every time we think it is OK to cut down that tree or run over that tortoise trying to cross the road, or for that matter cause hurt to another human being. Make the Golden Rule a living symbol of your life. In the name of religion, humanity has committed more crime and violence than from any other motivation. And in modern times there is a close second where humanity, driven by power and greed, commits mass genocide and attempts to control natural resources as well as committing crimes and violence against society. I think it is time for the children of Mother Nature to grow up to respect all living things, don't you?

MIND:

"The power of mind, rooted in experience, only increases as we meet the predictable crises and accidents of life and discover our resilience."
The Developing Person Through the Life Space, 4th Ed.
Kathleen Stassen Berger

In his book *Quantum Healing* Dr. Deepak Chopra tells a story that makes a good point here. It also points up that there is a time and place for modern medicine within the area of complementary medicine. This is why "integrative medicine" is gaining so much popularity. A woman who had been diagnosed with a malignant tumor in her right breast came to see Dr. Chopra . The tumor was large but had not yet spread to the lymph nodes. When doctors had looked at it the fear in their eyes made her scared even though she didn't feel that she was in any immediate danger. Each physician had insisted the tumor needed to be removed surgically, but she insisted on them only monitoring it. She was determined to beat the survival odds and still avoid surgery. She was looking for a sympathetic physician who would help her in her challenge.

Dr. Chopra was successful in controlling his reactions and showed no fear when he examined her. He agreed with her that she was in no danger because she felt that way, but then added in a soft tone, "This tumor is a nuisance. You are denying yourself a more beautiful life by having to look after this. Why not go to a surgeon and have the nuisance removed?" That was a new concept to her. An appointment was made for the surgery, and she said as she left the office, "I don't identify myself with this tumor. I know I am much more than it. It will come and go like the rest of me, but inside, I am not really touched by it." But she left in much happier and positive spirits.

If you take a completely materialistic view, Dr. Chopra said, there seems no difference between the surgeries this woman refused before and the one she agreed to now. Yet now she identifies surgery with healing, whereas before it was violence. It is well documented that in a climate of negativity, the ability to heal is greatly reduced.

SPIRIT:

"All points in space became equal to all other points in space, and it was meaningless to speak of anything as being separate from anything else. Physicists call this property 'nonlocality.'"
The Holographic Universe
Michael Talbot

During December 1997 Harvard University held a conference entitled *"Intercessory Prayer and Distant Healing Intention: Clinical and Laboratory Research."* Over one hundred scientists from around the country gathered to discuss their research in nonlocal (Bell's Theorem) healing, with one common goal: to test whether or not individuals could mentally help heal distant persons who were unaware they were doing so. Most people already know that this works and the proof of it is Bell's Theorem, but these scientists wanted to prove it using the scientific method and take it out of the religious field. There were many experiments discussed in this conference for a multitude of conditions but the real test for Bell's Theorem came while Edgar Mitchell was returning to earth from the Apollo 14 mission after walking on the moon and encountering an epiphany which resulted in his retiring from NASA and starting the Institute of Noetic Sciences.

Back in the space capsule, when the astronauts settled down for the programmed sleep period, each evening Edgar performed his experiment. The only persons who knew of the experiment were four compatriots on Earth. Edgar would write down on a clipboard in a random order the Zener symbols (used in distant viewing experiments): a square, circle, star, cross, and wavy line. At the same time the collaborators on Earth attempted to jot down the symbols in the same random order that Edgar had. The answers were compared when he returned. The results were significantly different than what could be expected by chance, which suggests that information can be shared nonlocally between distant individuals without any sort of sensory exchange.

Hidden within the results of the conference attendees' experiments was the fact that the ability to relax in both the subject and healer was a common thread among all the healings. When you have developed the ability to "let go and let God," any healing is possible and very probable. You, too can learn to go to "your secret place" regardless of the environment around you.

The author has a CD available that provides instruction in how to find your own secret place. It is called *The Serenity Place,* and with a visit to the website www.cosmosbooks.us you to can obtain a copy for yourself. It is an induction to help you move to the secret place of serenity you decide on and while there, attain a state of complete relaxation. With practice you will be able to induce the relaxation response whenever or wherever you feel the need.

CHAPTER IV

HEALING: A Trip Through the Healing Disciplines

LESSON: Pioneers of integrative medicine

has a strong preventive orientation and encourages patients to change their habits before disease appears."
Andrew Weil, M.D.

Many people have had a health challenge or know of someone who has experienced one. Often these health challenges are not handled properly by the modern medical community. As a result the person must search for answers outside the medical arena. They must come face-to-face with the natural way of treatment which has been used since thinking man began to improve his life. This method of healing predates the scientific version by many centuries. We then recognize that the body has what seems like a miraculous ability to heal itself if we but work in cooperation with nature instead of trying to force nature to our will.

When I was very young I learned from my elders that "an ounce of prevention is worth a pound of cure." Hence, by midlife I resolved to look at my lifestyle and make the necessary changes to insure I would be a healthy centenarian. I realized that my lifespan was my decision and I didn't want to be kept alive by the technically advanced medical professions. In other words, I was going to take control of my destiny. And what was the epiphany I had to motivate me toward that decision? I was sitting with my brother at his deathbed just a few hours before he made his transition. The last words he could speak to me were, "Why is my body doing this to me?" I knew the answer but it wouldn't serve any purpose to tell him at that point. It was too late to make any changes. He was dying of cancer at midlife and I wished he had asked that question to himself many years before. He was fortunate, just as I was, to inherit some good genetic material but he was still responsible for his health. I think he knew it, but that knowledge came too late. This is why the message I try to bring to everyone is to make the lifestyle changes in the third and fourth decades of life and then you won't have to say, "Why is my body doing this to me?"

Most everyone knows what it takes to live a healthy life: it is just a matter of motivation to take control. First, you have to recognize that you are really the architect of your destiny. What happens if a medical doctor makes a human error? You die and he goes on with his life, hopefully having learned from his mistakes. The fact that human error can occur is the scary part. The other areas of your life are basically very simple: good, healthy nutrition to feed the body, exercise to keep the body and mind active and functioning, access to a spiritual foundation that provides the guidance needed to maintain a healthy and productive life, commitment not to put anything in or on the body that the body does not require for its maintenance. To keep the toxins out, you must regularly do maintenance on the digestive system (without chemicals) and protect the immune system from depression. And finally, an absence of the word "retired" from the vocabulary. To the mind and spirit of the person using the "R" word, the term is interpreted as "retired from life."

In this chapter we will be discussing the history and purposes of some of the techniques used to aid the healing process.

You know that modern medicine has had successes and failures. In this chapter we will be discussing the "back to nature" health treatments. Since ancient times physicians have been aware of the power of the living organism to utilize its own innate strength to control disease. They even invented a phrase to describe this phenomenon: *vis medicatrix naturae,* " the healing power of nature." This statement refers to the fact that all healing is self-healing. Once we believe that, we are well on our way to becoming a healthy centenarian.

Let's start the trip with the pioneers who started the Integrative Medicine movement; they were called the Nature Doctors. We cannot give a thumbnail sketch of each of them as they span three centuries, but we will try to hit some of the highlights. You may wish to review how nature cures got started with Vincent Priessnitz in the last chapter. Most of these early doctors became involved with nature cures because the medical treatments of the time were not working.

BODY:

"Wherever we are and whatever we do, we cannot avoid being exposed to a multiplicity of physio-chemical and biological agents of disease. We survive only because we are endowed with biological and psychological mechanisms that enable us to respond adaptively to an immense diversity of challenges."
Norman Cousins

I wonder how many of us would submit to the "blood letting" procedures our forefathers underwent only a couple of centuries ago? Our protocols of modern medicine were a learning experience on the path to healing. Hippocrates' dictum to "do no harm" wasn't always followed. How many suffered in the name of medical advancement? Long before there were medical doctors, there were herbalists who kept us healthy and free from disease. The drug or pharmaceutical industries are a relatively new invention in the progress of humankind.

Herbs are medicinal plants with their own life force. These plants offer their leaves, stems, roots and seeds to support our specific healing needs. Ancient healers understood how to mix these whole plants to help people overcome illness and disease. The timeless appeal of herbs rests with the fact that under the care of a knowledgeable herbalist they work, and without the usual, often toxic side effects of current prescription medications. If herbs are so good, why does the drug industry hold such tight controls over the medical profession? I think the answer is GREED! The pharmaceutical industry developed from the herbal industry, not the other way around.

One of my basic philosophies is that whenever I need a medicinal product and a physician writes a prescription, I know that there is always a safer and less toxic alternative among the herbal or homeopathic remedies. I start a search. In other words, I go for the natural and safer treatments first. In their infancy the drug companies realized that within each herb is an active ingredient that accounts for the healing. They extract that ingredient and then try to duplicate it synthetically and make a prescription drug out of it. An example would be aspirin that comes from the willow bark. Why do the drug companies do this? You can't patent a natural formulation. Hence, there is not as much money in the compound as it comes straight from the plant. They must create a synthetic chemical in order to hold a patent and make a proprietary profit.

The problem is that these synthetic chemicals don't represent the whole plant, just a single compound out of many in the original herb. Most plants have dozens of complex ingredients that work synergistically to perform their healing work. They work best when the active ingredients are used whole (the whole plant) and in their natural state. God, not man, performs the final healing. Herbalists prescribe whole herbs in order to heal the whole person. Herbalists prescribe for the whole person, not for the illness. This is in keeping with the philosophy of Holistic Medicine.

Medical herbalism is the use of plants as medicines to restore and maintain health by keeping the body balanced. It uses the curative qualities of the plants to stimulate our own healing systems whenever the body is out of balance. It is this vital force that herbalists and other holistic practitioners use to help their clients heal. All of us possess this vital force that is constantly at work to maintain us in health, physically, mentally and emotionally. It is when this vital force is weakened that we become ill and diseased. Your physical symptoms are an indication that your body is under attack and is trying to fight off the invasion.

MIND:

"The universe was created once, but we re-create ourselves with every thought."
Quantum Healing by Deepak Chopra, M.D.

If the blood letting didn't work, the physician in many past cultures might have prescribed animal dung, powdered mummies, sawdust, lizard's blood, dried viper, frog sperm, crab's eyes, weed roots, sea sponges, unicorn horns and lumpy substances extracted from the intestines of cud-chewing animals. You might wonder how the patient survived and the doctor was not burned at the stake! The people were able to overcome these noxious prescriptions and the malaises they were suffering because they believed in more than the drugs; they believed that what the doctor gave them was good for them and they were going to heal. In most cases the reasons for their healing can hardly be attributed to a scientific explanation. But these prescriptions were considered just as effective in their day as medications are considered today. And the fact is, many patients did survive. We now know the reason - the placebo effect. The word placebo comes from the Latin meaning "I shall please." What the placebo effect proves is the efficiency with which our bodies are able to heal themselves.

These beneficial properties have been demonstrated in hundreds of studies. The placebo effect must be considered when utilizing double blind studies in medical research today. Studies have shown that up to 90% of patients who seek out medical help are suffering from self-limiting disorders - problems that will resolve by themselves in time regardless of any treatment or lack of treatment. Hence, if the medication doesn't kill the patient, the patient is going to survive by allowing the body to heal itself through its own powers.

The power of the placebo can be for good or evil - good if the patient believes the physician when he says it will work, evil if the patient sends the wrong signals to the brain about his possibility to recover. The brain may then send out harmful biochemical compounds that will result in damage to the human body. The placebo effect is proof that there is no separation between the mind and the body, that each will influence the other. Illness and disease are the result of the negative communication between these two forces. Both must work in harmony to effect a permanent healing. So if we know this is true, then all we have to do is to be sure only positive thoughts emanate from our minds and positive images are made for our bodies. Isn't this the real genesis of spontaneous healing? It must begin with us, then the spirit will be able to work through us for our ultimate good.

SPIRIT:

Placebo scholars believe "that the placebo is powerful not because it 'fools' the body but because it translates the will to live into a physical reality."
Anatomy of an Illness by Norman Cousins

The one attitude thread that is common to all healings is the patient's determined will to live. Without the will to survive, the physician's job is an uphill battle which is usually lost. A strong will to live is also very important for the success of spontaneous remissions. The placebo can play an important part in strengthening the will to live by transforming the mental image into positive physical reality. A will to live means a belief in a future and faith in the goodness of that future.

Dr. Albert Schweitzer said to Norman Cousins during a visit to his African Hospital, "The (African) witch doctor succeeds for the same reason all the rest of us succeed. Each patient carries his own doctor inside of him. They come to us not knowing that truth. We are at our best when we give the doctor who resides within each patient a chance to go to work." Norman Cousins says that the placebo is the doctor who resides within. I'm not so sure. The placebo may be getting its power from the spirit that resides within. The *Bhagavad Gita* (Hindu scriptures) say, "The faith of each man is a reflection of that man's character or nature. That, in which each hath faith, is the essence of that man himself. Each man's God – his conception of Deity – is himself at his best, magnified to infinity. By one's Deities shalt thou know the man himself, if thou observest well." To be healed you must start with a spiritual foundation.

LESSON: Nature Cure Physicians

66

"Naturopathy is the mother, all-inclusive, of natural therapy. It is the basic platform for all methods of healing: without it any healing art will be a failure."
Benedict Lust (1875 – 1945)

Naturopathy – The treatment of disease by natural means in order to assist the body to heal itself. Naturopathy evolved out of the philosophies of nature cure, homeopathy, spinal manipulation and other natural therapies which developed in the United States during the 18th and 19th centuries. Those methods and techniques grew out of a long history of natural healing. Hippocrates (460-377 BCE) was probably one of the earliest nature cure physicians since he taught that the body has an innate ability to heal itself. He was credited with saying, "Nature is healer of all diseases."

After Hippocrates there was another early proponent of nature's healing properties, a Jewish philosopher, scholar and physician named Maimonides (1135-1204 CE). He received very little attention as a practitioner of holistic medicine because the medicine of his time (the Middle Ages) was based on superstition and religious dogma. Maimonides prescribed some holistic practices we generally think of as current or modern. He believed:

> "The physician must keep in mind that the heart of every sick person is narrow and that every healthy person has an expanded soul. Therefore, the physician must remove emotional experiences that cause shrinking of the soul. And in order to strengthen the vital powers, one should employ musical instruments and tell patients gay stories which make the heart swell and narratives that will distract the mind and cause them and their friends to laugh. One should select as attendants and caretakers those who can cheer up the patient. This is a must in every illness."

And we thought Norman Cousins was the first to prescribe laughter as a medicine for illness. Cousins did the scientific research to prove the benefits and documented the results as a powerful force in healing. Maimonides also challenged the physicians of the day on the importance of drugs and surgery and argued that diet, exercise and mental outlook were the key elements for attaining health. He understood that the fountain of youth lies within us, in our lifestyles, and does not come from an external source such as the legendary Fountain of Youth Ponce-de-Leon spent a lifetime searching for.

Another important figure in the history of medicine was Paracelsus (1493-1541 CE), who lived at a time when we were evolving out of the medieval dark ages into the period of the Renaissance and the Enlightenment. He burned the medical textbooks of the time in a public display of revolution against the medical practices of the day. He advocated the practice that if you keep wounds clean they will heal. He said, "If you prevent infection, Nature will heal the wound all by herself." In addressing his fellow physicians he said, "Nature is the physician, not you. From her you must learn, not from yourself; she compounds the remedies, not you." Paracelsus also saw that Nature was a two edged sword: "Each natural disease bears its own remedy within itself. Man has received from nature both the destroyer of health and the preserver of health." He was referring to the destructive power of Nature as the healing power.

Many Nature Cure physicians broke with the current medical community because of its' inability to cure the illnesses they were personally experiencing. The person considered the Father of Naturopathy in America was Benedict Lust (1872-1945 CE), who was born in Germany and came to America in 1892. He became ill and developed an acute case of tuberculosis as a result of several surgeries and six vaccinations that were forced on him. After the attempts of many American physicians to cure him, the last physician made out his death certificate in Lust's presence; he decided to return to Germany to die in his homeland.

He managed to travel to see Father Sebastian Kneipp, a student of Priessnitz, who carried on and expanded Priessnitz's techniques, developing what became known as the Kneipp Cure. After listening to Lust's story the Father said, "I don't know whether I can put you back together again or not but I will see what **we** can do." Under Kneipp's care he regained his health within eight months.

Kneipp authorized Lust to take his techniques back to America as his official representative, thus beginning Naturopathy in America. Lust combined Kneippism with other nature cure practices and established a school, a clinic and a magazine. He didn't repudiate the Kneipp Cure but expanded it, making it even more successful. As you can imagine, the growing popularity of Lust's "naturopathy" caused conflicts with the contemporary medical community in America. Lust believed that the naturopath's purpose was "to reach and transform and transfigure everyday lives." He felt that all diseases arose as a result of the violation of nature's laws and that all of nature's creation could be used to heal the disease.

His definition of naturopathy was "a distinct school of healing, employing the beneficent agency of Nature's forces, of water, air, sunlight, earth power, electricity, magnetism, exercise, rest, proper diet, various kinds of mechanical treatments, such as massage, osteopathy, and the chiropractic, mental and moral science."

Lust had many accomplishments for the furtherance of nature cures; not the least was his eventual victory over the power of the medical community. He wrote, "Without free competition in the art of healing, the American people will be deprived of their unalienable rights under the constitution to select the method and the doctor of their choice and to have the best in the prevention and cure of disease." More than forty years after his death we finally began to see the emergence and acceptance of this right. It has been a hard fought fight but Americans are beginning to enjoy the benefits other parts of the world have enjoyed all along.

BODY:
"There is a physician within all of us; that Nature's healing powers are automatic and need only to be encouraged and fostered."
Henry Lindlahr (1862-1924 CE)

A personal experience in my life demonstrated the power of the mind to bring about illness. When I was in my mid-twenties there was a time when I was working sixteen hour days seven days a week for a couple of years. I was obviously tired and was hopelessly behind in my reading. I remember saying to myself, if I could only spend a week in a hospital somewhere I could get rested and caught up. Shortly afterward I began to feel sorry for myself I developed a fistula. I had to carry an air ring around with me for a couple of months before I finally consented to surgery. My hospital stay was only a few days, and that was when I realized that you don't get much rest in a hospital. I also realized it would have been less painful and cheaper to hide out in a motel room somewhere. Since being ill was a new experience to me, I couldn't figure out why the fistula problem came my way, until I remembered my previous wish. That was an early lesson of the truth that you should be careful what you wish for because you will probably get it, though not necessarily the way you want.

If negative conditions result from wrong thinking then you can create positive situations from positive thinking. Your mind is one area you have complete control over, so why not use it to your advantage? This is why hypnotherapy has been such a benefit to those who understand its use. Hypnotherapists believe the subconscious is the source of all human energy systems and as a result determines whom you really are. In healing we can program the subconscious to cure pathological disease. Through hypnosis the causes of illness can be discovered and through positive imaging it can help you release the root cause of the illness. But think how you could use this truth to your advantage by asking for positive results to be manifested in your life.

SPIRIT:

"Only God can cure. First a person has to become healthy inside, then outside. Everyone who wants health must return to Nature. God is so close and so is a handful of earth, the water, the air and the sun."
Adolf Just (1859-1936 CE)

We live in a three-dimensional physical world. The spiritual world operates within a three or twelve-dimensional universe, depending on whose explanation you are using. These dimensions are energy vibration levels. With the human mind we cannot conceive of more than three dimensions, so to those of us who define reality as only

70

that which can be seen and manifested in a physical way, we only experience these three dimensions. But in order to understand any spiritual dimension beyond the physical we must have a spiritual foundation on which to build that awareness. The Body/Mind/Spirit represents the three dimensions of our health. All three dimensions are required for us to live within our three-dimensional world. To prove all three dimensions are required, try describing a three-dimensional object in only two dimensions. Nor can our mathematics describe a cube using the formula for a square. It can't be done, just as healing cannot be described with just the body and mind. The spirit is a required part of our dimensionality.

A spiritual foundation means that your belief system recognizes some supreme power beyond yourself, which provides a meaning and map for your life. Without such a solid foundation you are at the mercy of the winds, without a rudder to guide you through the challenges of life. You must have an answer to questions like: Who am I? Why am I here? What is my purpose in life? These are age-old questions that have plagued man since the beginning of time. The details of your spiritual foundation are not important to anyone except you − but it is vitally important to you. The mechanics of how you access this spirit may vary depending on your belief system. What is important is that you have a belief system that makes sense to you, that you have a personal connection to your spiritual guide. Without it you cannot heal the afflictions of this world. Who or what is your spirit? Can you access this spirit every day and do you sincerely discuss your challenges with your guide? If you haven't done so lately, maybe you should investigate the techniques of meditation and start a personal practice. It will change your life.

As a starting point you might want to visit an interesting website I found: www.beliefnet.com It is a fun site and there are two short tests you should take. The first link is a test called "What's your spiritual type?" You will learn about how your faith affects you and how you compare to others, how the dogma of your religion fits into your belief system. The second link is called "Belief-O-Matic." This test will help you define the "labels" you place on your faith - how much of your beliefs fit into the different sects/denominations of the world. It will then rate your concepts of God, the afterlife, human nature and more according to twenty-seven different faiths. Then by clicking on the names of the faiths you will get a detailed description of what that faith believes. That information alone is worth the few minutes it takes to answer the questions. You might be surprised at the answers. Most people's beliefs do no neatly fit into only one dogma but are parts of a number of different systems. If you want to study your beliefs in a serious manner, the questions will cause you to seriously think about what your belief system really is. It is interesting information but more important, it provides a starting point for your own search for a solid spiritual foundation.

LESSON: Allopathic vs. Nature Cure

"The highest art of the true physician is to preserve and restore, not to mutilate or destroy."
Henry Lindlahr, M.D. (1862-1924 CE)

The area of conflict between western medicine and naturopathy involves three basic principles. First is the action of the vital force, which is the inherent force the body utilizes to heal itself naturally. This vital force is what enables the body to return to a state of health and harmony. It moves the body toward perfect health. Naturopathy's job is to restore the vital force and protect it. The objective is not the absence of disease but a condition in which the person feels physically, mentally and emotionally healthy.

The next principle in which the disciplines disagree is how they understand disease. Disease in all living things is an indication that something in the organism is not working perfectly. Poor diets, ineffective elimination of waste, trauma, genetic factors, destructive mental and emotional conditions, toxic drugs, prescription drugs, a lack of exercise, environmental factors that penetrate the body's defenses, all affect the health of the body's cells and cause the body to be out of balance. Thus the naturopath tries to identify the cause of the imbalance and help the vital force to restore the balance by eliminating the cause.

The third principle of disagreement is in how the different systems view symptoms of the disease. To the naturopath, symptoms are signs that the body is attempting to heal itself and we should not interfere with that natural process. Allowing the symptoms to run their course is considered normal and the body's attempts should not be suppressed by toxic interventions. Rather than vaccinate against disease, we should ensure the strengthening of the body's immune system to fight off the disease naturally. Conditions such as colds, flu, diarrhea, skin lesions, vomiting, etc. are seen as the results of the body's attempts to dispose of accumulated toxins .

All natural treatments are seen as utilizing nature to restore the immune system, to improve its effectiveness in fighting off the invading disease. These natural treatments use water, air, pure wholesome foods, sunlight, relaxation, rest, exercise and a healthy lifestyle.

Modern western medicine is referred to as allopathic medicine. Allopathic treatment options usually involve drugs, surgery, vaccinations, unwavering faith in the germ theory, or the injection of other toxins which depress the immune system, resulting in the suppression of the symptoms. More commonly, however, the symptoms resurface later and have to be suppressed all over again. This sort of treatment may make us feel better for a time but we will have to pay the piper eventually, usually with more pain and more serious symptoms.

Whenever you have a condition that seems to return time and time again, you must suspect that the body is trying to deal with the disease. Healing hasn't taken place —medication has simply suppressed the symptoms but the underlying cause is still there. After awhile the acute disease turns into a chronic disease, which later results in the patient's untimely demise. If, however, you are unlucky enough to be involved in a trauma event, the skill of the allopathic physician and the ability to utilize life-saving techniques is of utmost importance. Sometimes these heroic measures may not be a blessing. While you might technically be alive, the quality of life is so poor you might wish you were dead. But then again, some of these efforts are able to extend a healthy life for many years. The decision as to what happens must come from another source. These problems have resulted in the popularity of the Do Not Resuscitate Orders. If you don't currently have one, it could be well worth filing one. It may save you and your family a lot of pain and heartache.

In case of illness, however, the tools of the allopathic physician produce additional stress to the body's systems. Here is where the naturopathic physician can best be used, as his tools will tend to be less toxic, safer, and in most cases will result in a complete cure. If illness is the problem why not seek out the Physician Within to affect the healing? You don't have anything to lose except a shopping cart full of toxic side effects. Listen carefully to cautions and warnings next time you watch TV commercials for a prescription drug. Then compare those side effects to the appropriate herbal or homeopathic medication. The allopathic physician diagnoses by testing for the signs and symptoms and thereby rendering a name to the medical problem. Each diagnosis has its own set of treatment protocols which the physician administers. The problem with this procedure is it assumes all people are the same. We each have unique features that belong to us alone. Why can't we be treated as individuals? The naturopathic physician uses a detailed history, then through a variety of diagnostic systems determines the cause of the illness and treats the cause. This is called holistic medicine because it seeks to treat the whole person, not just the symptom. 'Holistic' is derived from the word *holy,* meaning *whole* in its original sense.

In the eyes of the naturopath, the secret to a long, healthy lifespan lies in prevention of illness, keeping the body's vital forces in balance. If you live a healthy lifestyle you will be healthy.

BODY:

"Prevention and cure of all these ailments (acute & chronic diseases) lie not in local symptomatic treatment and suppression by drugs or knife, but in the rational and natural treatment of the body as a whole."
Henry Lindlahr M.D.

A safe, natural alternative to toxic drug therapy is the herbalist's medicine chest. The basic premise I've used for years is, when a physician prescribes a prescription drug for me, and assuming I trust his diagnosis, rather than get the prescription filled I look for the appropriate herb to affect that particular body system. While the allopathic drug will suppress the symptom, the herb will assist the affected body part in order to help it return to a state of balance or homeostasis.

Herbalism is a very ancient practice, going back at least 5,000 years and probably longer. Modern research has begun to prove what herbalists have known for centuries, that the living herb or plant is made up of mutually dependent complex compounds just as our bodies are. They work effectively when the whole plant is compounded while in its natural state. The whole herb is then able to help the out-of-balance body system to return to balance and thereby affect a complete healing. You still have to know what you are doing because some herbs may be toxic and sometimes deadly to the human system. But the proper herb under the correct conditions, taking into consideration the whole patient, will be safe, effective, nontoxic and will affect a complete cure. Plants are the pharmacy provided by God to be freely utilized by all other living systems.

With the recent advent of modern pharmacology there was no profit motive for the pharmaceutical companies to support herbal remedies; the plants were readily available and the ingredients could not be protected by patents so these companies attempted to synthesize what they considered to be the active ingredients in the herbs. By formulating their recipes around these synthetic compounds they manufactured our patented prescription drugs. The problem with this idea is that the whole plant works better than the individual parts. You cannot create synthetically what God has created as a living entity.

The proper whole herb is used not only to treat disease but to prevent the disease from recurring, detoxify the body of the poisons that daily invade the system, and support the immune system to accomplish its healing work and maintain the body in balance.

There are many natural therapies that are used to protect and heal the body but the ones we at Cosmos Institute specialize in are herbalism and homeopathy. We do not claim these are the only effective therapies; depending on the situation we might advocate other appropriate therapies. In the next section we will discuss homeopathy.

MIND:

"All that we are arises with our thoughts. With our thoughts we make the world."
Buddha

To be as old as it is (originating around 2,000 BCE), hypnotherapy is one of the most misunderstood and misrepresented of all the alternative therapies. The sleep temples of Egypt in 1,000 BCE where positive suggestions were repeated to heal disease while the patient slept, were no different from the technique used today. My grandmother helped me with my studies in early school by recording things I needed to memorize and playing them back on an old tape recorder while I slept. This experience, and many other times throughout my life when I have used positive mental suggestions and visualization to solve problems, have convinced me that I can use my mind to accomplish anything I want. Many people think of hypnotherapy as an act they witness on the stage as entertainment. While it can be entertaining, it can also be used as a powerful force in healing. We have long since proved that there is a connection between the body and the mind and your mind is something you have complete control over. Hence, you have complete control over your body.

Why is this so? We have known for a long time that the mind has two distinct parts, the conscious and subconscious mind. I also stand with the many who consider a third part called the super-conscious mind. This third mind is where the spirit/soul resides. We talk about this mind during each chapter as we point out how the body/mind/spirit are all interwoven. There are also four wave frequencies of our brains, which are continually working. They are the Beta brain waves (13+ Hertz or cycles per second). This is the fully awake or alert state where you can concentrate on your environment. The next slower brainstate is the Alpha brain wave (8-12 cps). This is where you are daydreaming and learning recall. It is in this state that most of the hypnosis activity takes place. The next slower is the Theta brain wave (5-7 cps). This is the dream state and lucid visualization. Deep hypnosis may be done in this state. The slowest brain wave is the Delta brain wave (0.5-4 cps), the deep sleep state. This is really the slowed down state and we frequently reach this state in our sleep. But as you can see, we each hypnotize ourselves at least twice each day – as we go to sleep and as we wake up. So it is nothing new to any of us.

The conscious mind is thought of as the gatekeeper. It decides what we do and what is allowed to pass to the subconscious. The subconscious is really the active part; it runs all the automatic systems of our body. We breathe and our hearts beat without us having to think about it. The super-conscious often tries to influence the subconscious mind but in our awake state this is hard to do because the conscious mind is always on guard, censoring every word, thought or deed we have. Hypnotherapy works so well because we put the conscious mind to sleep while we talk directly to the subconscious mind. We can then implant good, positive suggestions that will improve our lives. This is how we can say that you can do anything you put your mind to. If you want to change bad habits or make a change in you life, all you need to do is give the proper commands to the subconscious mind and it will manifest in your body or life. If you want to improve your health, the person you need to see about it is always available (your subconscious mind).

Because the Wellness Doc has used this vital technique so successfully throughout his life, he became certified as a clinical hypnotherapist. We realize that substance abuse, overweight conditions and stress are the three biggest factors that have a profound influence on our health. If we want to live to be a healthy centenarian then control of these factors is a must. Hypnotherapy is the easiest, safest and most efficient way to accomplish that. No special equipment is needed and results come rapidly. It is a natural healing technique that anybody can use, provided they realize the enormous power of the mind.

In the next lesson we will see how hypnotherapy can access the superconscious mind and how the information can be used to promote healing and determine goals.

SPIRIT:

"Fast food isn't exactly healthy for our bodies; drugs, in a sense, are an unhealthy fast food for the SPIRIT."
Wellness Doc

In the last chapter I suggested visiting a website: www.beliefnet.com. I hope you took the opportunity to peruse that site, as it will provide an important starting point for your odyssey into your spiritual foundation. The results of the test "What's your spiritual type?" will indicate to you the strength of your personal belief system. When you compare it to the results of the Belief-O-Matic test I'm sure you will have some interesting revelations. If you have a religious denomination in which you are an active member, was that denomination in the top three of your list? If so, you probably had a high percentage (over 70) in the first test and you feel comfortable in your belief practices – congratulations. I'll bet you also would consider yourself an above average healthy person. But if you scored with a low percentage on the first test and found the second one difficult to answer or you didn't like the results – do not worry, it just means you have some work to do with your spiritual self.

Healing is impossible without a sincere spiritual belief system. It doesn't matter what your denomination or sect may be, just that you have a belief system. Where does the responsibility lie? Remember what happened following the 9/11 tragedies. Church attendance skyrocketed. It would be interesting to do a current study to see if the attendance continued and is high this many years later. My guess is that most of the people slipped back into their old lifestyles when the emergency passed. Does church attendance guarantee a place in heaven? Is that what people think? The attendance is not what is important. It is what you believe and how you live your life that matters. If you don't progress up the ladder of spirituality each day of your life then surely there can be no health and happiness in your life. With no firm beliefs you are like the ship without a rudder – at the mercy of the winds. You have no control over your life. To attend church when danger appears, as if your attendance is a shield, demonstrates your lack of understanding of what is meant by a solid spiritual foundation. So attend a church of your choice if you want – but be sure you demonstrate a strong spiritual belief in the affairs of your daily life.

In order to participate, you need to access the spiritual being at the center of your belief on a daily basis. Don't look to someone else or any organization to protect you. Only your deeds are noted in the heavenly records. So to stay healthy start a meditation habit today. We will leave the techniques of meditation to a later chapter so we can devote the proper amount of time to such an important area of our lives.

Since we recognize the importance of the spiritual foundation, how can Cosmos Institute help in an area reserved for the clergy? I was brought up in a very religious family and most of my life was spent within the doctrine of the Unity School of Christianity. In my journey of spiritual growth I have taken what has proved beneficial from many different sects and denominations and discarded what didn't make sense or was dogma obviously expounded by man rather than God. I believe God is the creator and is omnipresent, omnipotent, and the universal intelligence, that God is accessible within each of us if we will but ask. It is through this inner spirit that we can access the healing power. We recognize that we humans and other life forms are a global community, and we need to support each other and live together in peace and harmony. To do this, we must understand the religions and cultures of the other people on Earth. That doesn't mean we have to agree with them but they have a right to their beliefs just as I have in mine. And remember, everyone has a story to tell; we all ought to listen. Freedom of religion is a right we are blessed to possess in the United States, but do we honestly give that right to those who happen to have a different belief system from ours?

In your search for meaning in the spiritual issues of the planet, consider what your answers might be to the following, published shortly after the 9/11 tragedy.

"The attacks on September 11, 2001 stimulated all of us to ask, "Why?" "Why did it happen?" "What are the lessons we need to learn from this?" The urge to make sense of an event that seems so horrible, painful, and evil is the urge within us to know the mind of God. If we can understand how all of this aligns with Universal Law and what our soul needs to learn, then we can take steps to build understanding. With understanding comes peace."

LESSON: Naturopathic Therapies

"We are not punished for our sins but by our sins.
The great all-wise and all- loving Father-Mother principle
does not impose or enforce suffering on its children.
We create it in ourselves through ignorant or willful
violation of the laws of our being.
There is no accident, no ill luck nor misfortune –
there is nothing but cause and effect."
Henry Lindlahr, M.D.

The previous chapters have used the terms nature cure, natural therapeutics, naturopathy, vital force, allopathic physician, etc. Many times they are used interchangeably but there are differences between them. In this section we will bring you up-to-date on how these terms apply currently in the United States. It was Dr. Benedict Lust who emigrated from Germany to the US who developed and named Naturopathy. He took the nature cure techniques he learned in Europe and expanded them in the US by the addition of other natural therapies. He believed that Naturopathy should include all natural therapies and this helped him to separate himself from the allopathic medical community. Dr. Henry Lindlahr wanted natural therapies to be incorporated into the practice of allopathic medicine with a tendency toward more nature cures.

Today the practice of traditional naturopathy involves advocating and educating clients in improving and maintaining their health through lifestyle changes and the practice of all natural therapies that are appropriate. Stewart Mitchell, a British Naturopathic practitioner, defines Naturopathy as "a philosophy which provides a heath-care approach but offers much more than merely an alternative medical system. It encompasses a view of life, a purpose in human health and suffering and a model for living a full life." Within the area of traditional naturopathy this approach is toward nature health and personal responsibility for the lifestyles that result in a good healthy life.

In the first half of the twentieth century there was a split among the practitioners of naturopathy. One faction wanted to maintain the pure nature therapies as practiced by the nature cure doctors, with the addition of the natural alternative therapies. These were becoming increasingly popular, usually as a result of failures of the allopathic physicians' ability to effect real cures. These pure naturalists wanted to divorce themselves from the medical community entirely because they felt that drugs and surgery were contraindicated by Mother Nature. In addition, they believed that symptomatic treatment did not result in cures but only repression of symptoms that later resurfaced.

The other faction wanted to incorporate the naturopathic techniques of nature cure into the practice of allopathic medicine. They felt it was better to join them than to fight them. However, the pure philosophy of the naturopath who believes in the power of the vital force to heal is not compatible with the symptomatic repressions of the allopathic physician.

Some states have instituted licensure laws for the practice of Naturopathic Medicine that includes the ability to diagnose disease, prescribe medications, perform minor surgery and other invasive procedures, and use other modalities that are opposed to the Naturopathic philosophy. They want to bring the naturopathic practitioner closer to the allopathic medicine philosophy. They practitioners are called "Naturopathic Physicians."

In the last couple of decades the term Alternative Medicine has come into play to try to separate the Allopathic Physician from the non-conventional, natural techniques. Anyone who was not an allopathic medical physician was considered an alternative practitioner. As alternative medicine gained in popularity, some allopathic physicians took up the banners of some of the alternative therapies and began referring to themselves as practicing complementary therapies. The term complementary was more acceptable than alternative to the traditional medical practitioner.

To cut to the chase: A naturopathy practitioner practices the natural therapies including the recognition of the vital force in healing the whole person. The naturopathic physician also practices naturopathy but in addition will utilize the skills of the allopathic physician when he feels they are indicated. However, he can't truly be a naturopath if he doesn't believe in the vital force to heal the diseases and uses the drug therapy of the allopathic physician. As Dr. Lindlahr says, "If true healing is to occur, the vital force must never be suppressed." To suppress symptoms will effectively suppress the vital force. The belief in the necessity for the Body/Mind/Spirit to be an integral part of the healing process is fundamental to the naturopathic practitioner.

BODY:

> *"Miracles happen, not in opposition to Nature,*
> *but in opposition to what we know of Nature."*
> St. Augustine

Millions of people depend on a safe, reliable, natural form of medicine called homeopathy. Homeopathy is not a drug or invasive procedure like surgery. Its genesis dates from 500 BCE in Greece with the father of medicine, Hippocrates, who first introduced homeopathic remedies to his patients. Homeopathy did not find much use after Hippocrates until the 18th century when Samuel Hahnemann reinvented it. Hahnemann was concerned with the violence and the invasive procedures used in his day. The increasing spread of disease from poor hygiene and medical practices that used powerful, often toxic, medicines produced terrible side effects. While working as a translator in *A Treatise on Materia Medica* he made the discovery that led to the founding of Homeopathy. Homeopathy is a form of holistic medicine using animal, vegetable and mineral preparations to cure a person's illness.

Homeopathy is a medical system which treats the whole body and aids the body to heal itself. Its philosophy evolved from the simple observation that "like cures like." This means that substances that cause symptoms in a well person can also cure those similar symptoms in an ill person. This view is in opposition to that held by the conventional medical community. An allopathic physician would treat the symptom with a substance that is the opposite of the symptom. If you had a rapid heart rate he would give you a medication to slow the heart rate. This would heal the symptom but not correct the cause of the problem.

In contrast, the homeopath would prescribe a substance that fixes the cause of the problem. He does this by using very small doses of the substance, which if given in the large doses of the allopathic physician would cause the rapid heart rate. Allopathic physicians treat the symptoms of the disease because they view the symptoms as the manifestation of the disease. They prescribe large doses of medications to suppress the symptoms. The Homeopath views the symptoms as evidence that the body is trying to heal itself so he prescribes small non-toxic doses to help the body do its job. The homeopath wants to support the body, not suppress it, so true healing can take place. In fact, under the homeopathic philosophy the patient sometimes gets worse before he gets better and naturopaths call this a healing crisis.

As an example of how the homeopathic remedies are made, take a single unit of the substance and dilute it in 100 units of water or alcohol. Shake well then take one unit of the resulting mixture and dilute it again in 100 units of water and alcohol. Do this 30 times and you will have a solution referred to as a 30C potency. As you can imagine, there are hardly any molecules of the original substance remaining. This is why allopathic physicians cannot understand how it could work. But the homeopath knows it works because of the vital force, which it can influence and cause the body to heal by itself. These homeopathic remedies are so diluted that they are safe for infants, pregnant women and the elderly.

The scientific proof of how the homeopathic remedy can still work even though none of the chemistry of the original substance remains in the final dilution is another application of the reality of Bell's Theorem. See the fourth lesson in Chapter III where we introduced this theorem of physics. A more complete explanation is found in Chapter VII, first lesson and the glossary.

If you visit a homeopathic practitioner be sure to be truthful in answering all their questions. Some may not seem relevant but they are important because in order for the homeopath to choose the proper remedy he must have all your symptoms, since he does not treat the disease but the whole person. The more information the homeopath has, the more accurate his suggested remedy will be. In the event you try the wrong remedy for your body, you will know it right away, not because it will produce ill side effects but because you won't see any change in the symptoms. Because the dosage is so low there are no toxic effects, so you simply try another remedy. The Materia Medica gives first, second and third choices for most symptoms. The homeopath only needs to find which of the remedies covers the complete list of symptoms you present with.

What I have found in my personal experience, and the reason I don't use any prescription medication, is that there is a homeopathic or herbal remedy for any condition you can think of and without the harsh side effects of pharmaceutical drugs. In addition, you are completely cured of the illness rather than just suppressing the symptoms only to have them reappear at a later time.

MIND:
"Another way to access the healing force within us is to bypass the thick armor of doubt and skepticism that exists in our conscious minds. Like a surgeon reaching in and altering the condition of an internal organ a skilled hypnotherapist can reach into our psyche and help us change the most important type of belief of all, our unconscious beliefs."
The Holographic Universe by Michael Talbot

Hypnotherapy is useful to do so much more than just provide relaxation and help with addictive behavior. Remember, the way the subconscious mind works is in conjunction with the super-conscious mind, which is really the spiritual or vital force of the body. The spirit, or our spiritual guides if you wish, communicates with us through the subconscious mind. It knows it would have too much flak from the conscious mind. By bringing the spiritual into our lives there is so much more that we can accomplish. The super-conscious also contains all the images and records of everything we think, experience and say in these current and previous lives. Of course, in order to appreciate and access this realm you need to believe in past lives. A discussion of this concept may be found in my book *An Odyssey into Past Lives* found at www.cosmosbooks.us as well as a tremendous volume of other books and studies on the subject of past lives. Over seventy percent of the world's population believes in past and eternal lives, so if you agree with the majority it will open up a world of opportunities for you.

Through the hypnotic state you can participate in understanding your past lives that will shed light on questions you have during this life. If you experience a situation in this life where you seem to have a particular condition continue to come up or never seem to be able to get out of a rut, like continuing to develop close or intimate friends that have the same bad habits, then you have probably hit upon a lesson you have failed to learn yet and the lesson will probably be revealed in the memory of a previous life.

Time line therapy is a technique of finding the root causes of phobias, releasing negative emotions, or determining limiting decisions that may have their roots in previous lives. Psychotherapy does this by having you relive these traumatic events and then releasing them. You have to do that with each event and work backwards from the most current one. In many cases this takes fifteen years and a lot of pain, and often a complete healing never happens. That is because you never reached the original event that set up the trauma in the first place. Time line therapy is a procedure that can go straight to the original event and clear all the events at one time. So what could take fifteen years with psychotherapy could be accomplished in thirty minutes with time line therapy. This is a learned technique and with practice you can do it for any problem whenever you wish to. In addition, you can project yourself into the future time line. This is how psychics like Nostradamus, Edgar Cayce and the modern Sylvia Browne can be so successful. With training and practice you, too can access your own Akashic Record (your Book of Life). See glossary for more information about the Akashic Record. If you are interested in these concepts or do not have a personal hypnotherapist to visit, Cosmos Institute can help.

Other areas where hypnotherapy can help include pain control, during medical procedures (in consultation with your physician), altered states (without LSD), distant viewing, problem solving by ideomoter response, stress management, goal setting, control over health issues, developing your own psychic healing powers, mental telepathy and astral projection, success manifestation, plus many more where hypnosis has been successful. Try hypnosis; it can be an exciting adventure.

SPIRIT:

"We are addictive to our beliefs and we do act like addicts when someone tries to wrest from us the powerful opium of our dogmas."
The Holographic Universe by Michael Talbot

The last half of my life and to date I've been troubled with the institutionalized church. It seems to me that most organized churches by necessity must be run by human beings, who let their personal egos take control of their hearts. Most churches teach a dogma of some sort which is dictated by the denomination of the particular faith. When conflicts surface and power struggles provide negative undercurrents, it seems the members forget the principles taught; particularly they seem to forget the golden rule which is the basis of every sect or denomination of which I'm aware. Then fractures develop and the membership is split, resulting in major upheaval and divisions within the church.

I'm not saying that institutionalized churches are bad; for many they provide a very effective spiritual foundation. If they work for you, please give them all your support and energy.

But in my case I've found that I have developed a personal relationship with my God and spirit that has been guidance to me. A guiding philosophy in my life has been that any spiritual relationship is a personal thing and I leave others to enjoy their God the way they see fit. I always promote freedom of religion because there is good in all sects and denominations. As the global community gets smaller it is more important than ever to understand that tolerance and peace are possible. By studying other religions you will increase the strength of your own beliefs or you may alter some of your beliefs. Either way you will grow in spiritual awareness. There is no doubt that we live in a global community; as the affirmation states, "Let there be peace on earth and let it begin with me TODAY."

A solid spiritual foundation is so important to your health and longevity. What can Cosmos Institute do to help those who have lost contact with their church through the situations listed above, or are confined to their homes through disability or lack of their faith where they reside? Is there a need for a completely interdenominational and non-sectarian spiritual program to help those who are lost and searching? I've seen many examples of people who are unable to go to a church for a multitude of reasons and are forced to spend time wandering in a spiritual void. We at Cosmos Institute are considering increasing our program to include tapes that can be ordered for shut-ins or anyone who wants to take a non-sectarian and non-denominational approach to their spiritual quest. What do you think? Maybe an e-chapel called Cosmos Sacred Circle: The Back to Nature Chapel. It has been said that a sacred circle is formed when two or more gather in prayer, with affirmative thoughts of life and healing, peace and understanding for all peoples.

CHAPTER V
STAFFING YOUR DEPARTMENT OF DEFENSE

LESSON: Psychoneuroimmunology explained
"Mind-body medicine is a metaphor for an approach to health that
focuses not just on the physical body and the conscious mind, but also
incorporate unconscious emotional life and an individual's spiritual
dimension."
Mind-Body Medicine: A Clinician's Guide to Psychoneuroimmunology
Dr. Alan Watkins

PSYCHONEUROIMMUNOLOGY: That tongue twister word refers to the rapidly advancing field of research that investigates the mind/body connection. Broken into its subparts it means mind (psychology), brain (neurology) and the body's natural defense mechanism (immunology). If we are to learn to stay well and healthy we will have to come in contact with this field of study. As a follow-up to the previous lessons on healing techniques we want to expand on immunology as this science describes it. The mind and brain aspects have been discussed before and will be referred to during this section as well. Without a healthy and well-functioning immune system, good health and a long lifespan are impossible. Research has also shown that a dysfunction in any of the three systems will result in a dysfunction or failure in the others. We continue to promulgate the proposition that the natural healing methods are the only methods to successfully work in conjunction with Mother Nature.

There is a large body of scientific research that has developed irrefutable evidence that all of our defense mechanisms are directed by the central nervous system. This research has proven that our thoughts and beliefs result in a neurochemical and hormonal reaction that trigger the immune system into action - action that protects and maintains our bodies in a healthy condition.

Hence, the protection of our immune system reaches high priority if we wish to avoid the devastation of ill health as we age. The well-woven belief that for every offense there is an appropriate defense is absolutely true for our human lives. In our daily lives the poisons, toxins, microorganisms and our polluted spirits dictate we must be on the defensive. The choice is up to us as to how we wish to organize our personal department of defense. It would not be unrealistic to describe life as a personal war to defeat the terrorists of the world and the devil from robbing us of health and happiness.

It is not my intention to make this series a technical discourse on biology but there are a few points we need to establish at the start in order to understand the natural principles involved. We must realize that we humans are an advanced creation of biology but we are functionally pretty much the same as all other members of the animal kingdom. Hence, we are spiritually entwined with all "lower" forms of animals. We can't kill off any animal without the act having repercussions to us. This is a divine truth that we must all become aware of and practice in our lives.

All animals have pretty much the same biological body functions and vary only slightly in complexity. An animal is composed of the following biological systems: digestive, respiratory, circulatory, immune, urinary, nervous, skeletal, integumentary, muscular, endocrine and reproductive. As the laws of physics dictate, the subsystems of biology are composed of subatomic particles, atoms and molecules that form the cells of all the above systems. All of these components are held together and allowed to function through an energy/electrical system many nature practitioners refer to as the vital force. I believe this vital force has its origin in the spirit that is unique to each animal. It is important to understand that each of these systems has an interdependence with all the others and any dysfunction anywhere is felt in some way by each of the other systems. Thus we see the fallacy of treating only the symptoms which manifest in any one system.

The complexities of each of these systems have led to the proliferation of medical specialties because a full understanding of the wonderful workings of God requires a lifetime of learning and practice. I don't mean to diminish the importance of specialties in any way but sometimes I think they become myopic in their viewpoints. The process of interaction between these systems that keeps the body stable and healthy is referred to as *homeostasis*. It is this aspect of homeostasis that each naturopathic practitioner strives to maintain.

While each of these systems is important to our health and well being I want to concentrate in this lesson on the immune system. It is a system that, without its vital function, we would be as defenseless as a castle without cannons and shot. There is an aspect of the immune system that is so complex and important that we will save it for a deeper discourse in a later lesson. That is the situation with stress. We may make reference to it during this lesson but keep in mind that the effects of stress are vitally important to our overall health and survival and will be treated more fully later.

BODY:

"Few things are more exciting about the human body than the wide array of forces within it that are poised to do battle with invaders or abnormalities. The body possesses an immune system designed to meet the challenge of illness."
Head First by Norman Cousins

In an investigation of the efforts of our bodies to defend against invading microorganisms we must confront the issue of antibiotics. Let's be perfectly clear when discussing the role of antibiotics: they are only effective against bacterial infections. When antibiotics were developed they represented a great advancement in the battle against bacterial infections and diseases. But with every bright side or advancement there is always the corresponding negative consideration. Bacteria also have a life so when their world was threatened with extinction they fought back and adapted to the antibiotics. In order to counter this bacterial defense mechanism, pharmacies had to develop stronger and stronger antibiotics. With each new development the detrimental effects on our bodies became more severe. Just as on the world's battle fields when one army develops an advanced weapon, the opposite side finds a defensive weapon to use – and the cycle continues ad infinitum until such a destructive weapon is developed that no one can use it – like the H bomb.

This situation is caused by the over-prescribing of antibiotics. Whose fault is this? We, the patients are demanding ever more antibiotics to cure minor assaults and in many cases demanding antibiotics for use against viruses such as the common cold or flu. The physicians realize this will not work but comply because that is what the patient demands; they feel if they don't comply the patient will go somewhere else. The sad case is that in addition to their diminishing effectiveness antibiotics also depress the natural defenses God gave us, the immune system. We are depressing the one and only defense that will always work if we keep it maintained and in good working order. In fact while antibiotics, antifungals, antivirals, anti-anything are specific to a particular species of microbe, our immune system is designed to fight off any and all foreign invaders. If the substance doesn't belong in our bodies the immune system will eliminate it. In fact, this was one of the major problems with organ transplants – to find a way to prevent the immune system from rejecting the foreign organ.

The reason I do not use any antibiotics is because I don't want my body to build up immunity to the foreign substance and at the same time depress one of my most valuable defensive assets. Also, there may come a time in my life that I may need a strong antibiotic if a determined invader overwhelms my immune system. I don't want to waste my bullets unnecessarily.

The unpleasant side effects of antibiotics are also an important consideration. So when I have an infection I begin immediately to find a way to naturally enhance my own immune defenses before the invaders overwhelm me. I've been successful in the use of a good nutritional program, homeopathy and herbalism to defeat any invaders I've encountered. These methods work with the immune system instead of against it with almost minimal side effects. And the infection stays gone.

So when you have a physical problem, begin first to use the God-given tools you have to defend yourself. When you do you will find the harsh chemical solution is not necessary.

MIND:
"Perhaps the only limits to the human mind are those we believe in."
Willis Harman

There is a wealth of scientific evidence that shows that depression is the result of a serious or fatal diagnosis given to the patient by their physician. What we have found is that depression will seriously compromise the effectiveness of our immune cells. At a time when all the weapons at the patient's command need to be brought together to ward off the invaders and take the offensive, this is the time for sincere, positive mental action. In a study conducted by Drs. Sandra Levy and Ronald Herberman to find the link between depression and a diminished immune response after a serious diagnosis of cancer, they showed that depressive behavior (fatigue, listlessness, apathy) was associated with diminished NK cell activity and accelerated tumor spread in breast cancer patients. They demonstrated that NK cell activity was a significant indictor of tumor spread. Since depression is a condition that is completely under our personal mental control then a positive, drug-free mental attitude is a better response than one that will defeat the defender before they are able to face the enemy (cancer).

This is an area where it is important to consult the Physician Within and perhaps see your hypnotherapist to marshal a positive defense strategy, one that will support the "will to live" rather than give in to defeatism.

SPIRIT:
"Limiting decisions are boulders in the path of the life force."
The Wellness Doc

God and the vital force's power are infinite. To place any kind of limit on this power is a self-defeating activity. When we make a limiting decision we are placing a negative cap on our power to realize our good that is God's plan for us. A limiting decision is usually preceded by such statements as "I can't", "I can only", "I was born with a genetic defect", I'm sick", "I will never be able to…", "The doctor said…." or "My immune system must be poor because…". Probably one of the worse case scenarios is when the doctor says, "We can't do anything for you. You probably have about six months to live. I suggest you go home and put your affairs in order." Yet there are hundreds of people who hear similar statements and refuse to accept the diagnosis and then three years later, when they are still alive, the doctor says he can't explain it except that a miracle happened. As long as there is faith and hope there is always the chance that conditions will change. A professional should never leave a patient/client without HOPE. To do so leaves only the strong ones with any hope of healing. If you accept a negative diagnosis and throw away your will to live, whether the doctor was right or wrong is immaterial because the conditions have already begun to manifest themselves. A self-filling prophecy has already been set in motion. I can't think of a crueler indictment that any professional could make. Whatever the condition there is hope – miracles happen every day - there is no reason one shouldn't happen to you.

In such a situation a hypnotherapist would say you made a limiting decision sometime in your past. Such decisions can be reversed with Time Line Therapy by finding out when that limiting decision was made and then unmaking it. Your spirit is willing to undo any limiting decisions so the workings of the divine plan will be possible. There are many documented cases where on Friday afternoon the physician sent the patient home for the weekend with instructions to return on Monday morning to have a tumor removed surgically and when the patient showed up they couldn't find the tumor. What happened? The patient went home and over the weekend the mind and spirit had a conference and they called in the body to have a heart-to-heart. All good coaches will teach that you must never give up no matter what the circumstances. Losers never win and winners never lose! That is just as true in life as in sports. Our purpose in this life is to meet the challenges with faith and hope and the divine plan will manifest in your life. Wouldn't it be better if the physician talked about challenges rather than fatal outcomes? Couldn't he/she have described the challenges facing them and then show how the physician and patient can work on the challenge together?

When my wife was diagnosed with colorectal cancer and the doctor gave her at the most three years to live her reaction to the doctor was: "That diagnosis is unacceptable to me. Here is what we will do, you do the best you can medically and God and I will take care of the rest." It is eight years later and she is cancer free. There was a lady a couple of years ago who asked my wife after her surgery how she did it. This lady refused to leave the house with the words "I can't....." Unfortunately she made her transition within a few months. My wife is a *cancer survivor* because she took back the control of her body by not leaving it up to the doctor to dictate her destiny. The spirit will direct your immune defenses to accomplish miracles if you will let it. After all, that is how this thing called life works. It happens that way every day!

In the USA TODAY of August 19, 2003, the headline read *Most heart attacks caused by unhealthy lifestyle, not bad genes.* The newspaper was reporting on two studies that were just released, which took away all the "cop outs" commonly used by those who don't want to take responsibility for their health. As I've maintained many times, genetics is only a propensity for a condition, not a death sentence. We need to get back to the basics, the traditional risk factors.

The article reported on a large, diverse population study with a 30-year follow up on lifestyle. Basically, the conclusions reaffirmed the fact that roughly 90 percent of the people with severe heart disease have one or more of the classic risk factors like smoking, high cholesterol, high blood pressure, obesity and diabetes. All are factors that can be controlled through diet, exercise and consultation with the Physician Within. When are we going to wake up to the truth as Shakespeare told us four centuries ago: "The fault, dear Brutus, lies not in our stars but in ourselves that we are underlings."

LESSON: The invasions of the microbes.

"In a medical system that viewed itself as infallible and all-powerful, there was no motive to use any but the tried and presumed true methods. However, with the advent of antibiotic-resistant strains of bacteria, vaccine-resistant viruses, drug-resistant parasitic diseases like malaria, and the increasing strength of viral illnesses, the conventional methods are being questioned and the accepted thinking challenged."
Viral Immunity by L.E.Williams, O.M.D

The above quote is a perfect explanation of this lesson and a follow-up to the problem outlined in the previous lesson. The book *Viral Immunity* was written for medical professionals as a resource to integrate natural medicines to enhance their patient's immunity against the exponential growth of infectious diseases facing humanity in the twenty-first century. The theory of infectious microbes as the cause of disease was presented by Robert Koch in 1884 and remained the model for western medicine until the last decade of the twentieth century. We have recently realized that it is the strength of the immune system of the host organism that contributes to their resistance to infection. The current model suggests that disease is the result of the interaction between the host and the infectious microbe and it is not the power of the microbe that is important. The Chinese have taken this model a little further by showing that the strength of the host's immune system is the primary factor in preventing infectious disease.

Every second of your life you are engaged in a life and death struggle with infectious microbes and deadly environmental toxins. It has been shown that your immune system is the only thing standing between a healthy, happy life and extinction. Hence, it is important we understand how such a vital system operates. As most systems that make up our body temple, the immune system is extremely complex. If you wish to delve deeply into its mysteries any good college biology text should give you the technical aspects of the many different cells that make up its physiology. For our purposes the immune system can be compared to any army protecting its host country from terrorist invaders. The rules of war and organization are pretty much the same. So with that in mind, let's take a look at our personal Department of Defense.

Remember, the enemy is any substance that is not natural or normal, a foreigner to our body temple. That may be a microbe who was not born or raised as a local citizen of the body, or an environmental contaminant or microbe brought into the body through holes in the border represented by our first line of defense, the skin and mucus membranes. A small company of soldiers who are commanded by a captain, as represented by your blood and lymphatic vessels, patrols these borders and interior roads constantly. These soldiers (privates and corporals) are called *phagocytes* and are constantly on a search-and-destroy mission. When they encounter an enemy their job is to engage and destroy it by engulfing and ingesting it. They also send messages back to the colonel at regimental headquarters located in the white blood cells giving the intelligence of the size, strength, location and make-up of the invading enemy. The captain sends out reinforcements to increase the strength of the fighting company while the colonel digests the intelligence to take appropriate response. These messengers are hormonal and chemical responses that travel rapidly along the nerve highways. The colonel's response is to immediately send out reinforcements in the form of *macrophages* to the front to increase the committed manpower, along with specialized offensive soldiers. One of these specialized forces is represented by the proteins secreted by the macrophages to request the heat be turned up. The colonel then requests the general at corps headquarter to send in the artillery, air force and naval bombardments. This increases the temperature on the front lines in order to make it more difficult for the enemy to maintain their positions. This is why an increase in temperature is always a sign of a battle going on somewhere and current thinking says we should support and monitor the fever, not suppress it.

The grunt soldiers sacrifice themselves for the first couple of days of the engagement to provide time for the generals to develop the appropriate response forces. Once the intelligence has been evaluated and a battle plan developed then more specialized forces made up of a wide array of specialized T cells, depending on the mission and the make-up of the enemy, are called into the battle. These T cells are designed and manufactured to break apart and destroy the enemy who has been identified by the macrophages.

As the conditions on the battlefield begin to turn in favor of the host army, planning at the Department of Defense takes over to beef up the defenses against that kind of invaders and to start reducing the size of the frontline troops. The defense plan includes the use of specialized B cells that are trained to recognize that particular enemy if it appears again and are charged with patrolling the borders and highways to provide early warning and engage that particular enemy the next time he tries to invade the body (country). These B cells will stand guard for the rest of our lives against that particular enemy.

The Secretary of Defense is charged with long-range defense planning and mobilization of the forces. However, it is the Commander-in-Chief who must set the long-range strategy. The CIC is our MIND. But he also has a boss. He must be re-elected if he plans to stay in power and our SPIRIT represents the electorate. If the objectives of the electorate are not followed, the mind will fail and then the BODY is returned to dust.

BODY:

"In order to reach the objectives of the current model of health, it requires a new paradigm in the way people perceive disease. The new model recognizes that the components of life are related and linked in a functioning Body/Mind/Spirit."
Wellness Doc

A 1983 study and a follow-up study six years later confirmed the fact that a major reason that individuals sought out non-traditional medical treatment was because they suffered chronic illness that developed as a result of doctors failing to cure the underlying cause of the disease but only suppressing symptoms while the illness was in the acute stage. This confirms the thesis of the natural therapies, that suppressing the acute symptoms will only lead to later development of a chronic condition. We have long known that those who practice asceticism (anyone who lives with strict self-discipline and abstinence) in their lifestyles are insuring an immune-enhancing lifestyle that pays off in longevity, health and happiness.

There are many techniques important to a healthy lifestyle and one that is common to every list is that of exercise. The most beneficial aspect of exercise to long-term health is its positive effect on stress management. We will cover stress in a later section but for now suffice it to say, one important anti-stress technique is exercise. We are not talking about the exercise needed for athletic conditioning, but enough aerobic and strength training to maintain cellular oxidation and repair of tissue. If you have not regularly exercised be sure to check with your healthcare professional and take the development of conditioning in small incremental steps. Stretching of underused muscles before a heavy workout is vitally important to avoid the aches and pains of overly enthusiastic programs from the start.

Recent research has confirmed that something as simple as a thirty minute brisk walk three to four times a week is more beneficial to health than a hard workout that stresses underdeveloped muscles and increases the potential for injury. Why not use this time to also listen to educational tapes with a walkman or enjoy the beauty of nature and the therapeutic benefit of fresh air? And if you are fortunate enough to be able to do your exercises in sunlight you will receive the added benefit of generating vitamin D in your skin. Vitamin D is an essential nutrient (actually a hormone) that bolsters the immune system.

In addition to improving the immune system, regular exercise also provides the following benefits: It normalizes blood pressure, increases muscle mass and reduces body fat, lowers total cholesterol and increases high-density lipoprotein cholesterol ('good' cholesterol), improves cardiovascular function, increases energy and improves resistance to fatigue, decreases cravings for sweets and normalizes appetite, improves mood and sense of wellbeing and lengthens life span, among many others.

In recent decades it has been shown that the best exercise program is a complete system of physical and mental health that trains the Body/Mind/Spirit, known as Hatha Yoga (see glossary). Yoga is a safe, gentle exercise system that can be participated in by everyone (old, young or infirm). Yoga benefits the body by relaxing muscles and improving flexibility, fitness and physical conditioning. It helps to control stress, negative emotions and poor lifestyle choices. The practice of Yoga is an ancient exercise program going back to the eighth century and hence has a long history of beneficial use. There are many books and classes for beginners who want to embark on a life-long exercise program that requires no expensive equipment or time investment.

MIND:

"Among the prime assets of the human mind is the ability to cut loose from vengeful or burdensome memories. The easiest way to deepen a grievance is to cling to it. The surest way to intensify an illness is to blame oneself or the Deity."
Head First by Norman Cousins

Remorse, guilt, recrimination, depression, fear, un-forgiveness of an assumed hurt, obsessive ness with the idea of hell or divine punishment are all destructive negative emotions that start in the heart and are fed by the mind. Such emotions have been scientifically shown to be depressive to the health of the immune system. If there is one thing I've learned in my seven decades of life it is that my emotions are 100% under my control. I put those negative emotions in my mind, so I can also take them out. The idea of "let go and let God" is very important. I simply release them and replace them with a more positive or happy emotion. By recognizing the good in every event or situation these negative emotions will not be allowed to fester in the heart and mind. Love, compassion and a faith in apocatastasis (see glossary) have a positive influence on our immune system and healing. When you live by the philosophy that "until tomorrow becomes today men will be blind to the good fortune hidden in unfortunate acts," each day is an adventure and the immune system will not need to expend its energy on negative toxins.

SPIRIT:

"Life is an adventure in forgiveness. Nothing clutters the soul more than remorse, resentment, recrimination. Negative feelings occupy a fearsome amount of space in the mind, blocking our perception, our prospects, our happiness."
Head First by Norman Cousins

When God said to Moses, "I am who I am," he defined the power of spirit when he described his name as I AM. Such a powerful statement speaks to the spiritual foundation we all have within us at all times. It is a God-given potential just waiting for us to manifest it in our lives. Thus whenever we use the words "I AM" followed by any statement, whether positive or negative, that statement becomes manifest in our lives and body. By using positive affirmations when we access the Physician Within we will bring into being the conditions which we choose. Words are what move spirit into reality. Our reality is what we ask for. Therefore, it is obvious that if we keep our minds on only good, healing, prosperity and love, these will become a reality for us. And since we have complete control of our thoughts, emotions and feelings we are able to realize our full potential.

In our discourse with the Physician Within we should affirm our health and well-being and thereby such blessings are immediately manifest in our bodies and mind. The I AM is awakened to health and healing. Can you think of a better blessing to bestow upon yourself at the beginning of every day? The I AM will respond to your healing with the continuous renewal of every cell, tissue and organ in your body and health will surely manifest itself in your life.

LESSON: The germ theory of nature
"The task confronting the natural defense system can be capsulized in six key words: encounter, recognition, activation, deployment, discrimination, and regulation."
Head First by Norman Cousins

Every October I am reminded of the cycles in nature and how important cycles are to our health and life. One of the reasons I moved to the mountains was to experience the *beauty* in the changing seasons that is manifested in the mountains. The autumn can be likened to the autumn of life. Just as the plants let go of their leaves and begin their period of rest until the birth of renewed life in the spring, so birth, life, death and rebirth is a cycle played out in humans. Our immune system continues this divine plan as the *phagocytes* are born at the cellular level then march out to protect their territory. If foreign cells or waste matter are encountered the phagocytes engage the enemy, perform their life's work, then after the threat is gone they die off as the army is reduced to the pre-invasion levels.

Another cycle that is very important to our immune system is the digestive system. In this cycle we take food in to energize the cells, to keep them alive and healthy. The cells utilize this energy source then discard the unusable waste so they can take in fresh energy. The cycle continues unless there is an imbalance or blockage somewhere. When an imbalance or blockage occurs, illness is the result. This will manifest as symptoms of illness when the immune system starts it defensive tactics. At this point allopathic medicine jumps in to destroy the soldiers the Department of Defense sent to combat the invaders. Now these synthetic do-gooders are consumed in the battle, leaving behind a partially destroyed enemy that is due to arise like a future phoenix.

Notice that the unwanted help from the allopathic remedy did not eliminate the waste; maybe some of it was scrubbed away but all that is needed is one wounded enemy cell to be left behind. This is like trying to disinfect with a germ-killing chemical. By definition a disinfectant only has to kill 99.999% of the pathogenic population. This means that in a population of only one million germs (a bare minimum in any infection) there are 10,000 germs left, and this walking wounded will double their population every fifteen minutes. This means you feel better for a time but will be right back where you started before too long. This is why nature's method of healing by getting rid of the source is so practical and effective. If it's true that germs are the only and ultimate cause of disease, why doesn't everyone who inhales cold germs catch a cold? Have you ever wondered why some people seem to get sick all the time while others never seem to catch whatever illness is going around?

Let's investigate this morbid or waste matter a little closer. The fundamental principle of natural healing is that every acute and sub-acute disease is the result of nature's mechanism to rid the body of the infection which allopathic medicine claims is the cause of the disease. This healing that is taking place is the result of the action of nature on the pathogenic conditions that are present. Nature is breaking down this morbid or toxic substance to rid the body of its poisoning forever. Microbes, both so-called good and bad, are always present everywhere in the environment and are constantly searching for their food source (the morbid matter) in order to sustain their lives. When they find this source in the human or animal body they invite themselves to a feast fit for a king. By killing the microbes we have not eliminated the problem. We must eliminate the source. One way to do that is to protect the entrance into our bodies by any of the ingredients that make up this waste feast. This is why lifestyle is the critical issue in our long-term health.

In describing the fundamental principle of the Nature Cure Doctors Dr. Henry Lindlahr said, "We do not endeavor to kill the germs with poisonous drugs, vaccines, serums and antitoxins, but instead we endeavor through natural ways of living and natural methods of treatment to purify the organism of the systemic waste, morbid encumbrances and disease taints which furnish the soil for the development and multiplication of disease germs."

So the germs discovered in Pasteur and Metchnikoff's germ theory are nature's servants to perform her work rather than the cause of the disease. Remember the bell curve; as the food source is destroyed by the germs' voracious appetite or our actions to eliminate the food source, then the symptoms will disappear.

The germ theory of the Nature Cure philosophy, as described in the book *Philosophy of Natural Therapeutics,* is quite different from the allopathic germ theory. 'Bacteria develop from microzymes, the primal units of living organisms, but this occurs only under morbid, pathogenic conditions. These microzymes may be the remains of decomposing bacteria entering the system from without, or the microzymes of normal cells may develop into bacteria under pathogenic conditions within the body. According to this conception the cycle of germ life works out as follows: The microzymes of the normal healthy cells under morbid, pathogenic condition may develop into bacteria. These bacteria feed on and decompose the morbid matter which brought them into being. Thus nature, with the evil, provides the remedy. When the morbid food supply has been exhausted the microzymes devour the protoplasm of their own bacteria until there is nothing left but themselves and they seem to be practically indestructible under ordinary conditions, as is shown by the finding of living microzymes in calcareous rocks of ancient geological formation. It is undoubtedly true that these morbid microzymes may again develop into disease germs if they enter a living body and find morbid soil on which to feed, but otherwise they are not harmful." This is one of the reasons why in every epidemic not everyone dies. A French Scientist, Antoine Bechamp, first described microzymes in the mid-nineteenth century. Allopathic medicine has done such a good job in burying the microzymes germ theory I can't find the word in my medical dictionaries. It means "minute ferment bodies."

BODY:

> *"Disease is not an accident, nor an arbitrary infliction,*
> *but the inevitable result of the violation of nature's laws."*
> *Philosophy of Natural Therapeutics* by Henry Lindlahr M.D.

If you would like to test the Nature Cure philosophy for yourself, why not use this treatment protocol the next time you have a small wound on your skin? I often observe the speed of healing and therefore the efficiency of my immune system by watching the healing time of the numerous skin wounds I receive in my daily activities. If I am slow to heal I realize there is some blockage in my immune system that needs relief. The first step to the protocol is when I suspect I need to boost my immune system because of something that may cause a infection. I immediately take a dosage of 400 mg of a standardized extract(4% *echinacosides*) of an herb called Echinacea. This herb will boost your immune system to counter the potential invaders. Then I clean the wound with distilled or filtered water. I don't use soap or antiseptics because of the residues they leave behind. If you feel you must use some type of "healing" cream, use a homeopathic arnica cream. This homeopathic is for trauma injuries and aids the immune system rather than competing with it. The arnica cream can by purchased in a health food store and in some pharmacies. You can then put on a lightly applied bandage in order to keep out further soil.

Try the above test to convince yourself that it works and then you can become more confident in any healing challenge with which you are faced. The techniques are the same. Do something to improve the immune system then eliminate the waste or toxin that is blocking the healing energies. There are lots of natural healing techniques available to accomplish natural healing, and all are easily available to you before risking dangerous drugs or invasive surgery.

MIND:

> *"The final reality is the idea in the mind of the creator.*
> *Thought forms are the souls of things and matter convolutes to these soul*
> *patterns. So the relation of thought and feeling to health and disease*
> *appears to be not without scientific basis – the physical reverts to the*
> *metaphysical."*
> *Philosophy of Natural Therapeutics* by Henry Lindlahr, M.D.

The mind is a terrible thing to waste – and it plays an important part in any healing challenge. To help control your mind the most helpful technique available to you is hypnotherapy. The nice part of hypnotherapy is that you don't have to have a personal visit to your hypnotherapist, although you may wish to have a good working relationship with one. Learning the self-hypnosis technique is very easy. With a little practice you will become your own healing guru.

The reason it is so easy is because you already hypnotize yourself twice every day. When you go to sleep and when you wake up you pass through the hypnotic state as your brain waves pass through the alpha and theta frequencies. All you have to learn is how to communicate with your subconscious mind. Through hypnosis you can learn to control your energy chakras and auras and thereby the healing energies of your body. Then, as Jesus said, nothing will be impossible to you.

Start by keeping your mind free of trash and toxins and use it for positive, healthy, productive thoughts. You were sent here to learn and life is a never-ending process. It's exciting to become involved and enjoy the energy of life.

SPIRIT:

"Disease is born of us and in us and that is how it should be, because the life of man, and of every other creature, is no more delivered over to chance than the course of the stars. Life would be delivered over to chance if it depended upon primitive microbes germs created for destructive purposes."
Les Microzymes by Professor Antonio Bechamp

If at the confluence of the rivers of Body, Mind, and Spirit, the spiritual artery is clogged or blocked and the healing power of spirit is not available, then the river of life is only running on two-thirds of its potential fuel. So it is important to clear the riverbed and open the pipes to clear any blockages in the form of lack of faith, depression, anger, grief, un-forgiveness and other negative emotions. One method to do this is through the practice of meditation on a regular basis. In an unhealthy situation we need to return to the primitive plane of our origins, to understand how the energy of this life began and tap into the divine plan and how we fit into its purpose.

When it comes to healing I find the affirmative form of healing prayer is the most effective. Affirmations are positive statements that recognize that the divine plan for your highest good is already at work in your life. Sincerely repeating these affirmations will bring your mind into line with your spiritual self in order to manifest these positive conditions in your life. It's the practical application of the philosophy of "as a man thinketh so is he", "think and grow rich", "whatever the mind can conceive the body will manifest", and similar sayings. Since our inner spiritual power will acknowledge only good for us, these positive thoughts go straight to the maker of our reality. We call that healing spiritual power the Physician Within because it is available to everyone – all they have to do is ask and reaffirm.

An easy way to access that Physician Within is through positive affirmations. Develop healing affirmations which you can use numerous times throughout the day. Just say them over and over, either out loud or to yourself. A practical application can be found from my life experience. I was going into a meeting, which I had indications was going to be combative and possibly leading to negative consequences. As I was approaching the building I said to myself a number of times, "I go to meet my good." I wasn't surprised when the meeting went well and the rest of the evening was happy and enjoyable. There was no negativity and the outcome was better than I expected. The reason I wasn't surprised is because I have used that technique so often in my life. It is the reason I've been able to experience the healthy and wholesome life I've been blessed to have.

For your healing challenges you might wish to try some of the following healing affirmations or combinations of them:

Basking in the radiance of God, I experience health and wholeness

I am energized and restored by the ever-renewing life of God

Immersed in the healing grace of God, I am whole and free

The love of God continually flows through me, restoring me to wholeness

I am a new creation through the healing revitalizing life of God

By learning this simple prayer technique you will be able to walk in harmony with the Physician Within you and all your days will be filled with happiness and health.

LESSON: The source of life
"(W)holistic healing relies on therapies that mobilize a person's own powers of self-healing. The person who is ill must acknowledge the power of the vital force that is the true healer."
Wellness Doc

106

We have often heard it said that "we are what we eat." We humans are more than that; we are also what we breathe, what we feel, what we hear, what we say and what we see. We are a whole and complex living organism. In (w)holistic healing individuality and personal responsibility are crucial factors. It is all right to seek aid from experts but the ultimate responsibility for your healing and health are within the person who is seeking the healing. The doctor or drugs do not perform the healing. The whole Body/Mind/Spirit must act in harmony with nature to accomplish the complete healing. The truth of this can be demonstrated with an analogy of the three-legged stool. If we call it the "healing stool" and each leg is called Body, Mind and Spirit respectively, then our stability or healing success is dependent on the number of legs we installed. You can sit very comfortably and securely on a stool that has three legs. If it only has two legs, you could balance on it but would have to keep compensating because you couldn't lean in any direction. If it only had one leg it would be possible to sit on it but it would be very unstable and require quite a balancing act.

In our attempts to return to the source of our life, living plants, we come face-to-face with the ancient art of herbalism. The use of herbs to promote health and well-being goes back thousands of years and was practiced in all areas of the planet. It was only during the last century that science began extracting the active ingredients from the plants to use as medicine. Most of the drugs we use today have their origins in medicinal plants. In recent years the use of herbal medicine is beginning to increase in popularity as we realize they are an inexpensive source of healing medicines as well as being safer than the risk inherent in synthetic drugs.

One of the major differences between synthetic drugs and herbs is that the drug companies have taken what was thought to be the active ingredient in the plant to make its drug. That's like taking a part of your body out and synthesizing it and claiming it is as good as the original organ. Will a wooden leg ever be as efficient as the leg supplied by God? If we want to get closer to nature we need to use nature's medicines to heal the body. The herb works synergistically, meaning the healing properties of the whole herb are vastly greater than the sum of its individual constituents. These herbs have a life force of their own that works complementary to our own life force to bring the body back into balance. No synthetic drug can do that.

Herbs can do more than just alleviate illness. Herbs can also support your health and wholeness as well as prevent diseases from developing. Herbs can help to cleanse the body in the elimination of morbid and toxic waste as a by-product of metabolism. Using herbs in your detoxification programs will help in the elimination of all the body's organs rather than just one organ which most drugs act upon. And of course herbs are used to support the defense mechanisms of the body, the immune system. Herbs will affect the symptoms of the illness plus the origins of the illness.

To use herbs in the process of prevention of disease is not only natural but in harmony with God's plan that everything in nature has a reason for being and is interdependent on every other part of nature. We are all one: plants, animals, humans, the environment, the universe and all living things. Herbs maintain the balance (homeostasis) within our human energy system. As long as we are in balance we will be free from disease. So in addition to alleviating illnesses they can also prevent the illness in the first place.

Tonics, another form of herbal formulation, are herbs that strengthen and enrich a specific organ or bodily system or the whole body. They can do this without requiring a specific physiological response from the body. Prozac may act as a depressant on the body system while St. John's Wort has a calming effect without changing the biochemical reaction of the body. Herbal tonics are gentle and safe to the body systems yet have a mild and significant effect on the whole body. They can aid the body in its normal defense mechanism without depressing these natural responses. Tonics are important to promote well-being so a condition never reaches the chronic stage, at which point the gentler herbs either take longer to work or become ineffective because the body is overwhelmed by the toxic condition that results from the illness or disease. The tonic is able to accomplish these miracles because we are using a whole plant which is in a homeostasis condition to begin with and thereby able to bring the human body back into homeostasis from the interplay of its vital forces.

Helping the body to cleanse itself is another important property of herbs. To do it without harsh chemicals and side effects is the blessing that God has provided us in his plant kingdom. Thus keeping the body free of the free radicals, morbid matter and toxic substances is a major effort in maintaining well being and health. As we have said before, these poisons are the cause of all conditions of illness and disease. They are the cause of the signs and symptoms, not the result of them. The herbal approach to detoxification can be summarized as:

Support: for the whole process of elimination,
Specific support: for overly taxed organs,
Alleviation of symptoms: and addressing any pathologies that may also be present.

The (w)holistic approach to human immunity would be impossible without the use of a medicine chest containing herbals that are effective in helping the body to enhance its natural immune system in the defense against all microorganisms. There are many ways that herbs can be used to improve our immunological responses to invasion. This herbal knowledge has evolved over many geological years into the natural medicines we have today. Much of our current knowledge is based on the work of the American herbalist Christopher Hobbs. He identified three levels of herbal activity, briefly described below.

Deep Immune Activation: herbs that impact the immunological process within the tissue that mediates its work. These plants have an effect upon the cellular foundations of the human immune response. They are not necessarily stimulants or inhibitors but complement the whole complex process of immune response. They also support the whole body systems, which will in turn improve the immune system's efficiency. An example is the bitter tonics.

Surface Immune Activation: This response affects the need to resist pathogenic microorganisms. These herbs do this by stimulating the activity and production of the white blood cells (lymphocytes), which are a major immune cell in the arsenal of the body's Department of Defense. An example would be *Echinacea.*

Adaptogens or Hormonal Modulators: These herbs work through the hormonal response of the immune system. They affect the endocrine glands of the body and are usually specific to the particular gland and its immune hormonal response. An example would be *Ginseng.*

One final and most important comment which needs to be emphasized before leaving the subject of our immune system: We should train ourselves to be sensitive to our body signals. Becoming aware of the feelings and signals the body is sending to us is the first step in preventing an illness from becoming a chronic condition. These signals can take many forms: pain (probably the most common signal), body aches, skin eruptions, bowel and urinary troubles, depression, the loss of a will to live, the feeling that nothing seems to be going right in your life, dreams, intuition, respiratory difficulties, an apocatastasis experience. These are all signals that tell us that something is wrong and needs our attention now. Almost all conditions can be effectively handled if they are recognized in the early stages and corrected by natural means. To return to nature is the tool God had in mind when he created this wonderful, complex, living machine. Too often we are either too busy or fail to notice these subtle body signs among the environmental attacks impinging on our consciousness. When we find anything that is out of the norm we should attempt to identify it and then investigate corrective action. There is no need to cry about the condition or blame it on anyone or anything; it is a message from God to take a healthy corrective action.

BODY:

"Should we be vegetarians? We are placing all sorts of poisons and toxins into our bodies, and eating foods which are not productive of optimum health. Live food leads to more life, dead food to more death. It's as simple as that."

Without a discussion of vaccination no commentary on human immunity would be complete. With the invention and development of vaccines, modern medicine took a big step forward, delaying many deaths. But with the development of these miracle drugs came other problems. The only way to stop the disease was for everyone to be vaccinated. And then it didn't work because the vaccine depressed the human immune system and opened up the human to invasion by other pathogenic organisms. Many of the diseases we vaccinate our children for today, when I was a child we had to live through the disease in order to build up our own natural immunity. We survived because our immune system was stronger than the disease that was trying to use our bodies for its survival. I often wondered if the disease epidemics our planet has had over the centuries aren't a natural population-limiting factor placed upon all living creatures by the creator. Remember the discourse on the bell curve and immunity/survival rates. Even in the face of worldwide immunizations we are still experiencing deadly epidemics, and today they span the globe in a few hours rather than a time frame measured in years.

During the worldwide 1917 flu epidemic the benefits of a natural cure as opposed to the standard medical approach became most evident. At the height of that epidemic the Cook County Hospital (Chicago) treated 300 flu cases and they all died. Across the street in the nature cure sanitarium 300 flu cases were treated with natural methods and they had a 100% survival rate. Had you been there, which type of care would you have preferred?

The power of the modern medical community is so pervasive that people do not question it. Vaccinations are not without risk and impairment of long-term health. Vaccines, after all, are drugs with dangerous side effects. Why wouldn't the modern medical community want to keep those given immunization shots forever on the medical treadmill? In our ignorance, look what the Europeans did to the Native American when they came to the New World.

When you were required to be vaccinated (like before entering school) were you given a choice and provided with pros and cons of both sides of the issue? Can you get a valid research study of the negative side of vaccinations from your physician? I doubt it! In 1909 Dr. W.B. Clark said, "I never saw cancer in the unvaccinated person." In 1909 not everyone was vaccinated. Today it is difficult to find unvaccinated persons so it is difficult to perform controlled studies. If you want to investigate the other side of the story I highly recommend the book: *Vaccination Deception: How Vaccines Prevent Optimal Health;* by Teddy H. Spence, DDS, ND, Truth Seekers Press, P.O. Box 819, Emore VA 23350, (757) 442-3313. The drug-free, risk-free way to prevent disease is to build up your natural defenses!!!!

Some ways to improve and protect your immune system are: Eat organic, fresh whole food; avoid sugar and processed food; avoid drugs, caffeine and radiation; breast-feed your children; determine and avoid any allergenic foods; take vitamin and mineral supplements; get fresh air, healthy sunshine and exercise; and have check-up visits with your naturopathic practitioner.

MIND:

"Every thought creates.
What it creates, of course, is up to you."
Q&A on Conversations with God
Neale Donald Walsch

Listening to your mind also means controlling what your mind listens to. Since within your mind is the transcript of everything you have heard or spoken throughout this and other lives, it makes sense to keep these thoughts pure and healthy. Hypnosis can be used to recall past and forgotten memories. Just as we must monitor our physical body signals to help the immune system, so must we monitor the signals received by our minds. If you live in a negative environment you will become negative. This is why the TV programs I select to watch usually have an educational purpose and provide something to stimulate the mind. I try hard to avoid programs or conversations involving violence as I don't want to manifest violence in my life. What types of programs do you watch for pure enjoyment? In this category I may list sports events or comedy programs. I can't understand why we continue to allow crime, violence and horror shows to be available to young minds. The fault, of course, is that is what the consuming public wants. Then we wonder where the kids get the ideas they act out in their lives. To function effectively you must have complete control of your mind and in order to do that your thinking has to be clear. Therefore, I've always followed the policy not to ever take anything that impairs my mind. Obviously this includes most drugs.

The power of I AM is so important when we are trying to think constructive and pure thoughts. Whenever you think or speak the words "I AM" be sure they are always followed by positive, happy, productive words. Never use the "I AM" followed by any negative statement or condition.

Remember in a previous lesson we talked about getting at the root cause of a situation or condition? This root cause continues to manifest itself in our lives until we are able to understand it and then release it after taking the learning from the experience. The root cause is buried in our minds somewhere and is waiting to be released in order to provide a healing from the experience. The old saying, "If you don't learn from history you will be forced to repeat it," is very true in our lives. But how can we find these root causes of our unhappy experiences? Since hypnotherapy accesses the subconscious mind, while the sentinel conscious mind is temporarily dormant, this technique has proved very effective in calling forth these long-lost memories. Then true healing can take place within all your body, mind and spirit. If you have a need, seek out a qualified hypnotherapist or contact Cosmos Institute of Life's Transitions to see if peace can be restored to your world.

SPIRIT:
"All things in the world of Nature are not controlled by fate for the world has a principle of its own."
Iamblichus, 4th century philosopher

113

How do the spiritual lessons come to us from God and our spirit guides? In order to hear, we must be still and listen. If we are aware, we will hear the call. Many call it intuition - an idea or message out of the blue or in our dreams. Have you ever had a feeling or from intuition had insight into a problem or situation that was bothering you but you weren't thinking about at the moment? Have you ever been struggling with a problem and finally given up with the idea to come back to it later, and while you were relaxed all of a sudden the inspiration came to mind? At such times it is well to write down the inspiration because it might be a fleeting image and gone forever. Sometimes we may dismiss the idea as too far out or impossible. At these times I realize it would be wise to remember these are messages from God or your spirit guide and to pay attention. Many times such spiritual guidance comes at unexpected moments and in strange ways.

Get in the habit of looking at every event in your life from the view of, "Why did this happen?" or "What do I need to learn from this experience?" Nothing happens by chance; there is always a reason or explanation. Inspiration can come when you least expect it. All you need to do is become conscious of your reality and act on these fleeting inspirations.

CHAPTER VI

EVOLVING ON THE PATH OF LIFE

LESSON: Who Am I?
"God, in infinite wisdom, imbued life with no purpose whatsoever, in order that each and every one of us might imbue it with a purpose of our own, thus to define and create, announce and declare, express and experience Who We Really Are."
Q & A on Conversations With God by Neale Donald Walsch

As we approach the sunset of any calendar or fiscal year it is time to pause and reflect on our blessings of the year and the corrections needed in the odyssey of our life. November is the month of thanksgiving and December is the month of rebirth as we celebrate the birth of the Christ child and the renewal of the solar cycle. When last year began did you have a clear understanding of who you were and how you were going to get to where you wanted to be, and what you needed to do to make your dreams a reality? Are you any closer to fulfilling your dreams now? At the end of the year will you be any closer to your dreams if you continue experiencing your life as you are now? Will you make January 1, 20XX the first day of the rest of your life? If you want to take control of your life, now is the time to reevaluate and make an assessment of your life. We are approaching the end of the cycle for this period of our incarnation, evolving into the beginning of the next cycle and we will soon undergo our own resurrection as we grow and experience life to its fullest. *Conversations with God says, "Life proceeds out of our intentions for it."* What are your intentions for the rest of your life? Do you know Who You Really Are?

You must learn how to BE before you can learn how to DO. Many people feel that progress is doing something or that activity is a sign of accomplishment. There is an old saying I remember from somewhere, "If you don't know where you are going, any path will take you there." Who wants to go nowhere? In this lesson regarding this special time of the year (November/December) let's reexamine who we are first; then we can determine the best path to follow to experience the reality that we envision for ourselves. Too often persons and companies make resolutions for the coming cycle with elaborate plans about how to get there. I'm not suggesting that those techniques are unimportant because they are vital to the doing, but first we must know ourselves.

Let's start on the path to finding out "who I am" and "why I am here" now at this time, at this place. I now realize there is no such thing as luck or coincidence, and there is a reason for every event, and my reality is my interpretation of that event. Then it is not important to me what others may do or not do or say; it is only important how I feel about the decisions I make. Before we begin this odyssey of self-discovery I suggest you get hold of an important book to start you thinking of this new paradigm. Many of you may have already studied this book so you are well on your way to discovering who you really are. That book is entitled *Conversations with God: An uncommon dialogue (Book 1)* by Neale Donald Walsch.

In this lesson we will be looking at who we are and why we are here. This, of course, is a life-long effort but all journeys begin with a first step. This Thanksgiving season in addition to giving thanks for God's bounty let us also give thanks for the wonderful ME God created and thanks for help in finding who we are. This wonderful life can only be beautiful if we realize who we are. When we give thanks for our blessings and who we are, we then put our foot on the first rung of the ladder to self-actualization.

BODY:
"All of life is a vibration. An oscillation, if you will, of the divine force. This vibration is the raw energy of the universe. Depending upon the speed, or frequency, of the vibration, a thing is either seen or unseen, felt or not felt."
Q & A on Conversations with God by Neale Donald Walsch

When we consider its simplest form, the body is only vibrational energy. I have always thought of it as the temple in which the soul/spirit resides during this incarnation cycle. So "who I am" physically is nothing more than matter experiencing life at this vibrational level. Your vibration frequency is slightly different from all other souls just as your fingerprint and DNA is unique to only you. It identifies who you really are and your choices determine the conversion of that energy into matter – YOU. Your material body really is of little importance since it is only the vehicle you use to drive your spirit around as it experiences who you really are.

We have been aware of this energy since ancient times. Einstein has shown us that energy and matter are different manifestations of the same force. Matter is the visible expression and energy is the invisible expression of this force. An everyday example of how this works can be seen in the water cycle. In the electromagnetic spectrum we see that as we increase the frequency from invisible to visible and back to invisible we also have an increase in temperature as we go up the scale. As it is in the water cycle, so it is with the cycle of a human life and its spirit/soul. At the cold stage of H_2O we have *ICE*. As we increase the temperature, frequency and energy it turns into a *LIQUID* but it still is H_2O. As we continue to increase the temperature, frequency and energy it becomes an invisible *GAS* and begins to rise into the environment as water vapor. As its temperature and frequency change it takes on energy. As the environment becomes colder it changes form again and we call it rain, snow or sleet (depending on the ambient temperature). It then returns to earth again as liquid rain or solid snow. Thus the cycle starts all over again. The chemical properties of H_2O have not changed; only its physical characteristics have. The Second Law of Thermodynamics in physics validates this whole cycle. See the glossary for an explanation of this law.

We undergo similar changes of form but not of underlying substance as we move through the cycle of life from birth to death and then rebirth. There is no change in the spirit/soul, just its manifestations in the physical visible plane, then on to the invisible plane and return to the beginning to start all over again. This is why there is no true death. Just as energy cannot be destroyed, therefore neither can we since we are the manifestation of matter and energy. This is the wonderful beginning for who we are and how we are made. This body is just a temporary phase of my life cycle. Once I understood this and incorporated it into my belief system there was no more *fear.*

Hence the truth of life-and-death realities is not realized by faith but by the laws of physics, examples of which we see all around us every day.

MIND:
"See each event as an opportunity to recreate and experience yourself in a new and larger way. Make a decision about who and what you are, and who you choose to be."
Q & A Conversations with God by Neale Donald Walsch

In order to know who you are you have to understand your reality. Your reality is produced in your mind and reality is a very personal thing. It is unique to each of us. Any event in your life becomes your reality because your mind says it is real. If someone tells you about an event it becomes a factor in your belief but it is not your reality. A simple demonstration of this is to have two different people witness the same event. Have them recount it and you will receive two different interpretations of that event. If you carry this truth further, whether something is right or wrong in terms of who you are can only be determined by your reality. You have no right to judge whether an event is right or wrong as determined by another's reality. You can never know for sure what their reality is and it is really not your business.

We make errors so many times each day because we don't understand that we can only judge our own reality. When we try to interfere with someone else's reality , problems develop. I admit this truth can become a heavy philosophical inquiry but to improve your life, peace, love and execution of God's plan you need to understand this most important principle. You determine who you are by going to the Physician Within in the quiet of your mind. You can consider the beliefs of others but you must accept responsibility for your own reality.

A part of this odyssey we are taking is to learn to separate our beliefs from our reality. One way to do this is to question every belief you have by questioning where you first received that belief. Be sure you understand that if you didn't experience or receive that truth from the spirit within you, then you are accepting someone else's belief and adapting it as your own. It is not reality until you experience it. I am sure we all know how much trouble we can get into by following someone else's beliefs. History is full of the tragedies of following a false master. This is why the practice of meditation is so important to fulfilling God's hope for you. Notice I didn't use the word plan because your plan for this life comes from you not God. God only hopes you discover your real self and then experience it. Meditation is so important that we will be covering it in more detail during this lesson.

SPIRIT:

"Happiness of any real variety can only spring from beingness. It is what you are being that matters to your soul. For the soul is beingness, at the highest level."
Q & A on Conversations with God by Neale Donald Walsch

Even before you ask I will have answered. (Mat 6:8). This truth is the perfect definition of practical prayer. Effective prayer is about knowing our reality and then giving thanks. In fact, some Native American traditions hold that there is only one prayer: "Thank you." A prayer of supplication (asking God for something you desire) is one of the most ineffective forms of prayer. In St. Matthew just before the Lord's Prayer we are told how to pray. As in the instruction above, if we know ourselves and our reality there is no need to ask God for anything because God already knows our needs before we ask. To do this is condescending. My practice has always been to acknowledge that our needs are already met and then give thinks for receiving the blessing. Nor do we need to have an intermediary between God and ourselves in the person of one of the Masters. None of the true Masters asked to be an intermediary. God is personally available to each of us.

In the instructions for prayer it is said: "But for you when you pray enter into your inner chamber and lock your door and pray to your

Father who is in secret and your Father who sees in secret shall himself reward you openly." (Mat. 6:6). My God is a personal God and one whom I can talk to and when I knock he will answer. But this is the case only if we are receptive to our highest good. So before we can proceed on this odyssey of life we will have to enter into your inner chamber with your God who is throughout the universe in secret and in the silence we will be able to discover who we truly are. This is not a religious quest but one of a personal journey to determine who we really are.

We already have abundant health, happiness, and prosperity; it is only for us to accept these gifts from our Father by giving thanks because we have already received them. To know prayer is to experience prayer. You will experience the benefits of prayer by recognizing that all events are really the result of prayer and looking for the good in every event.

LESSON: Let Go and Let God.
"Your life is always a result of your thoughts about it."
Conversations With God by Neale Donald Walsch

Life is dynamic, constantly moving either forward or backward in the evolution of who you are. You are always growing in maturity and consciousness toward your purpose within God's plan. In order to know whether you are advancing or regressing on your life's path you need to know who you are and where you are going. Remember, there is no such thing as retirement; the spirit/soul is always in motion until your purpose in this life is accomplished. As Charles Kettering said, "The only place to sit down and rest is directly in front of the undertaker's office." As you grow in consciousness the challenges in life become more complex, giving you an opportunity to demonstrate and recreate who you really are.

Most epiphanies and real positive changes finally come about when we reach the depths of depression and realize there is no place to go but up. We recognize that in order for life to get any better we have to change. At this point we either commit suicide or we give up trying to control everything. If we give up then our fears become so pervasive they completely consume us so that we turn to the God of our understanding and ask WHY. It is at this

120

point we then become receptive. God hasn't abandoned us; he has been trying to help his child all along; we just were not listening.

Why do we have to waste all the time and energy in unhappy, unproductive activities and emotions before we give up? We don't have to. Let go and let God! The first step is to acknowledge that your life isn't all that you hoped for it, to know that things could be better. Then you need to spend some time with that Physician Within to understand your awareness of who you are. From that point on it is more serene and peaceful.

When you begin the quest of who you are you should consider the Law of Duality. Life is the sum total of our experiences; the sum of the positive and negative experiences make up who we are. Our experiences, our reality, are the personal interpretation of the events in our lives. We are responsible for the effect that each event in our lives has upon ourselves. We alone determine if an event in our life is good or bad, right or wrong, happy or unhappy, successful or unsuccessful, healthy or unhealthy, . Everything is on a scale; you must experience all of life. You cannot understand good unless you have experience or knowledge of bad. You don't know what tall is unless you have experienced short. Therefore it would be impossible to know who you are unless you know who you are not.

Within this earthly experience all emotions can be divided into only two basic emotions: love and the opposite emotion of fear. Both of these basic emotions relate to your reality of each event in your life. And each emotion results from your feelings about the events in your life. We will go a long way to understanding our lives if we can determine which of the two basic emotions we are experiencing as we go through the events on our path through life.

Just think how much our lives would be improved if we lived them in the emotion of love rather than fear. Neale Donald Walsch has a beautiful acronym for fear – false evidence appearing real. The choice is up to you. Do you want to live in love or in fear, which is manifested as anger, unhappiness, jealousy, indecision, judgment, lack of self-esteem? These negative emotions based in fear are all our opinions of someone else's reality. But we cannot really know or make judgments about some else's life. A lot of our fear comes from just such beliefs.

Karon Korp says in her book, *Remembering Our Spiritual Journey Home,* "In any situation you have two options, one is fear and the other is love." Within that decision lies the power of your choice. In any experience you can choose to believe the illusion (anything that is not in alignment with your Divine Nature is an illusion) or you can choose to believe in the Truth of your Divine Nature. The power of your choice resonates to the very core of your being, into the realms of your multi-dimensional Self.

When we consider who we are we start from a basic premise – we are spiritual beings. The technique we use to access the Physician Within is meditation. The primary difference between mediation and prayer is that meditation is a listening activity, contemplating inward communication. Prayer is more proactive and focuses on sending your desires outward. "Ask and it will be given you, search and you will find, knock and the door will be opened for you. For everyone who asks receives, and everyone who searches finds, and for everyone who knocks, the door will be opened." Mathew 7:7-8. In the Mind section below we will briefly discuss the "how to" of meditation.

BODY:
"Do you know that you are God's temple and that God's Spirit dwells in you? For God's temple is holy, and you are that temple."
I Corinthians 3:16

In our search for who we are, we come face to face with the knowledge that we are spiritual beings created in the likeness of God. Our only purpose for being here is to express the Divine Essence of God. We and God are one. Our body is the temple of God. We came from God as an energized spirit. So in keeping with Bell's Theorem we are the physical manifestation of God. These bodies are only on loan to us during this incarnation and will be disposed of when our mission on this earthly plane is completed.

The body, then, allows us to experience and demonstrate who we really are. It becomes the vehicle we use to manifest and experience who we are. Therefore, by carrying that truth to its natural conclusion, it is our job to protect and maintain the health of our earthly vehicle. If we have a damaged vehicle we cannot express the true essence of God that was our commandment when he sent us here.

If we allow illness, disease or destruction of our bodies, aren't we acting contrary to the hope that God has for us? In summary, we are the product of our thoughts; what we put into our bodies - our hopes and dreams, the doingness of our lives, our relationships - is who we are. So as we become aware of who we are, we will then have the understanding of how to treat our bodies in order to express their Divine essence, the understanding of which will change our lives. Once we understand this it will be impossible for us to abuse our body temples with drugs (both prescription and illegal), alcohol, tobacco, other poisonous toxins, wrong thinking and lack of maintenance and care. Just as your transportation vehicle will stop if not properly maintained, so will your spiritual vehicle stop if it isn't properly maintained. The maintenance man for both vehicles is only YOU.

MIND:

"For the mind is restless, turbulent, obstinate and very strong, O Krsna, and to subdue it, I think, is more difficult than controlling the wind."
The Bhagavad-Gita, Ch. 6, text 34

Learning to be in the silence in order to receive the wisdom of the Physician Within is the foundation of meditation. To hear that still small voice within you need to quiet the chaos in your mind by focusing on one thought or mantra. In Psalms 46:10 comes the admonition, "Be still and know that I am God."

To begin your meditation practice get into a relaxed position, either sitting up straight, sitting in a lotus position or lying comfortably. Then you can go to your Serenity Place and ask the question, "Who am I?" Then wait for the answer. Going to your Serenity Place becomes much easier with practice. The more you practice, the easier it becomes and you will be able to quiet your mind anytime you desire.

To keep your attention focused while you are in your Serenity Place, see and feel yourself sitting comfortably and concentrate on your breathing. Take slow, deep breaths and say in your mind's eye with each inhalation, "who" and with exhalation, "am I." If your mind wanders that's OK; just slowly and gently bring it back to your breathing and the question then wait in the knowing that the answer will come. If it doesn't come during the time of your meditation, don't be discouraged because it will come in its proper time. Remember, God has no earthly time frame in his world. All you have to know is that you already have the answer; you just are not aware of it yet. It may come when you least expect it, in a flash of insight while you are involved in some other worldly activity. Be aware of such intuition so you can recognize it when it comes. It may come in the lines of your reading the next time you pick up a book or magazine; it may come in a conversation with someone. The old adage that God works in mysterious ways is very true and we only need to be constantly aware. God has already told us what we want to know; he is waiting for us to activate our receivers. That is when the "Aha" happens.

Too often humans in prayer, or what they believe is meditation, become discouraged because their supplications are not manifested in their outward experience. They ask God for something, they don't get it and then assume prayer doesn't work. They are like the child who asks for a candy bar and the mother says NO then tries to explain why – "It is too close to dinner", "It will cause tooth to decay", "Too much sugar is not good for you now" . All the child heard was the word NO. God never says no to your needs, and he is a loving father who only wishes the best for his child. He always answers our prayers in a way that is best for us; all we need to do is listen. That is why meditation is so powerful. If I have an infrequent occasion to ask for something from God I may lay out the problem (which he already knows) but want to let him know I'm aware of the problem. Then I give thanks for the blessing which is for my highest good.

SPIRIT:

"The soul conceives, the mind creates, the body experiences. The circle is complete."
Conversations with God, Book I by Neal Donald Walsch

Before you can become aware of who you are you must understand why and how you got here in this form, on this planet, at this time. Your spirit knows the answer – and it will lay out the blueprint of your life if you will ask and then listen. The technique to do this is meditation.

My life began to make sense many decades ago when I settled this issue to my satisfaction. Once I knew there was a blueprint of the purpose for my life, then the challenge was to discover and experience the manifestation of that Divine Plan. That blueprint was not made by God; his divine Plan is very simple. Each of us is to evolve in our soul/spirit until we, as the children of God, have grown to the spiritual level that is God. In order to evolve you must experience. My purpose for this incarnation was developed by me to help me experience what I already knew in my soul. I am to remember and manifest that wisdom. I chose this planet, this time, this place, my parents, and the events as they unfold during this incarnation before I was even born. My soul is still watching over me and guiding me, hoping I will listen so the vehicle which is me will follow the blueprint exactly. I know that I can never progress up the ladder in my evolution during only one lifetime. It has taken at least two previous lifetimes before I finally "got it." I know there will be further challenges left to experience that will give me more opportunities to prove to myself that I have indeed "gotten it." If this were not true I wouldn't be here now. Since I'm not a master yet I know there will be plenty of lifetimes to come that will allow me the experiences of even greater lessons. This is why we never die; the vibrational energy that makes up me cannot be destroyed. My soul will live forever; Jesus and all the Masters as well as the laws of physics told me so.

In the *Positive Quote of the Day, 9/25/00* Harvey Fierstein said, "Accept no one's definition of your life, but define yourself." When we are trying to learn such an important lesson in life as

"Who I Am," don't leave that decision to others. Go directly to the architect of your soul's blueprint – your own soul. This can only be done through meditation and listening to the guidance of your own soul.

Let me leave this lesson with a gift for you. My meditation pamphlet entitled *Daily Word* on Nov. 30, 2003 contained the following message and since it was so appropriate for this lesson I wanted to include it in its entirety:

The affirmation was: "I am growing and evolving spiritually on my quest of self-discovery.

"I am on a spiritual quest – a journey of self-discovery – as I continue my walk with God and discover more of myself and my world.

I am reminded through life's daily lessons that I am part of an ordered plan underlying the events of my life-a divine curriculum of which I am a devoted student.

I desire to grow and evolve spiritually, so I am ready to learn what I can from each experience. I am committed to finding out what I can do to apply my newfound wisdom and to practice what I've learned.

Along my journey, I look forward to each day a gift from God, full of new insights. I welcome each experience for the wisdom and the wonders it contains."

LESSON: How to attain self-actualization.

"All who are on the earth plane at different levels of the earth growth are there for specific reasons of growth. There are no mistakes in the universe; everything happens for a reason."
Cosmic Journeys by Rosalind A. McKnight

In my college psychology class I was introduced to the work of Abraham Maslow (1908-1970) and it was an epiphany experience for me. Suddenly I realized how the purpose of life fit into the scheme of this earthly plane, why we act in specific fashions. Then I realized that Maslow's Hierarchy of Needs (or motives) explained the purpose of our lives: to attain self-actualization. I began to look seriously for the answer of why I was here. It would be impossible to achieve self-actualization unless I had mastered the needs on the lower level of the pyramid. If the lower levels of needs are not met in one's life, then it becomes impossible for one to attain the higher needs. It is difficult to concentrate on intellectual pursuits if the stomach is not filled with food, or there is no roof over your head. Every outdoorsman knows the first act required for survival is to provide for food and shelter, not look at the sunset or you won't see the sunrise.

As you evolve and grow in consciousness you do so by fulfilling your survival needs on the lower levels. It is only then that you can accomplish your full destiny in life. I realized that the world's great masters represented a goal for my life. There was always a higher level to strive toward. Although I don't think Maslow regarded his hierarchy as a spiritual path in life, it sure looked like one to me. If by the time I make my transition in life I could come close to what Dr. Maslow described as the self-actualized person I would at least in my own mind consider my life to have been successful. I offer this idea for you as you contemplate what to do with the rest of your life.

Self-actualization – What is it? According to psychologist Abraham Maslow it is a goal in life, a continuous desire to fulfill potentials. Self-actualization is a process by which an individual becomes the most complete, the fullest: "all that you can be." Simply stated, his hierarchy of needs outlines a level of needs required for human beings and in what order these needs must be met.

SELF-ACTUALIZATION

ESTEEM

BELONGING

SAFETY

PHYSIOLOGICAL

Maslow considered these needs to be survival needs , a requirement in order to maintain health and happiness. Anyone's motivation is also indicated by the level a person reaches in experiencing these needs. Each person's motivation will always be to attain a higher level in the hierarchy. By the time of our transition most of us still have some unmet needs or motives in life that have blocked the attainment of our full potential. Not to worry, though, because striving for self-actualization is a lifelong process of learning and experiencing. We will then have another chance to reach our full potential as a fully self-actualized soul in a future incarnation. By the time we have reached the apex of the pyramid we will have attained self-actualization and reached the spiritual manifestation of a Master and will not need to reincarnate again for this earthly experience.

What does the self-actualized person look or act like? What are the qualities we should seek as a goal in life? Dr. Maslow gives the following description.

1. The self-actualizing person has reached a high level of moral development and is more concerned about the welfare of friends, loved ones, and humanity than self.
2. The self-actualizing person is usually committed to some cause or task rather than working for fame or money.
3. Life is experienced in intense, vivid, absorbing ways, often with a sense of unity with nature.
4. Self-actualizing individuals are not particularly interested in fads, fashion, and social customs, and often appear unorthodox.
5. Self-actualizing people are open and honest and have the courage to act on their convictions even if it means being unpopular.
6. Self-actualizing individuals enjoy friends but are not dependent on their company or approval; they enjoy privacy and independence. On the other hand their feelings for their close friends are intensely positive and caring.
7. Life is always challenging and fresh to the self-actualizing person.

8. They have an accurate rather than a romanticized view of people and life, yet they are positive about life.
9. Self-actualizing individuals are spontaneous and natural in their actions and feelings.

Maslow believed that partially actualized souls get an occasional glimpse of what it is like to be self-actualizing in what he called peak experiences. He described these experiences as intensely moving, pleasurable, beautiful experiences when a person is fully absorbed in the experience, forgets his or her selfish interest and feels a sense of unity with the world. Maslow studied and identified some persons who he felt had attained self-actualization. His list included Albert Einstein, Eleanor Roosevelt and Ludwig Van Beethoven.

BODY:
"Man is the essence of all reality. Man is the product of his own energy
field and consciousness. Man in his wholeness is the complete
integration of all energy flow and the complete
attunement of all elements with its true nature. Man locked into himself
is man. Man released from himself is God."
Cosmic Journeys Rosalind A. McKnight

At this time, when we are searching for the meaning in life and who we really are so we can set the goals for the rest of our life, we should also expand our concept of our body. It is not only a physical body that we can feel and touch and experience pain in, but also the temple of the spiritual essence of ourselves. Within each of us every second of our lives the spiritual energy is at work allowing us to be who we are. This energy is a physical system just like the other body systems(circulation, respiratory, nervous) that are keeping us going and healing the challenges that arise. This system is known as the chakra system. The energy organs are located in seven points along the midline of the body. These chakra centers are located within the glands of the human system that are associated with the medical systems of the body. *Chakra* is a Sanskrit word literally meaning "wheel of light." The light is the energy vibration that operates within the circle surrounding the gland center. The following is the list of the charka centers beginning with the basic and lowest one: First, *Gonads* (physical);

second, *Lymphatic* (emotional); third, *adrenal* (mental); fourth, *thymus-heart* (astral); fifth, *thyroid-throat* (etheric); sixth, *pineal-third eye* (celestial); seventh, *pituitary-top of head* (ketheric). The understanding of how this energy works is very interesting. The energy comes from the ground or Mother Earth up through the feet to the first chakra and travels up the midline alternating in and out of each chakra center until it finally reaches the seventh where it exits out toward the heavens.

Just as the levels of the Maslow pyramid start at the base of the triangle with basic functions and work upward toward more spiritual activities, the chakra centers also move from the basic to the spiritual. Notice, for instance, that the first chakra covers the physical, the second and third cover the mental, and the fourth, fifth, sixth and seventh cover the spiritual aspect of the human experience. The healing of the chakra system works by healing the lower centers before the higher centers can be healed. Just as you can't cure issues of the heart without the gonads and digestive system being in a healthy condition, you must also remove any blockage to the flow of energy beginning at the lowest level. It was most interesting and revealing when I was studying the chakra system in my masters program that I realized the similarity to Maslow's Hierarchy of Needs. I hope this realization is as significant for you as it was for me. If you would like to pursue the chakra system in more depth I suggest the book *Wheels of Light* by Rosalyn L. Bruyere. In this text she discuses the power of the energy system in healing all the dysfunctions of the body we humans are challenged with as well as some of the scientific studies done on chakras and auras.

As both Maslow and the ancients knew, in order to experience perfect health we must begin with healing the basic physical aspects of our being. Thus the only proven way is to get back to the nature cure of good nutrition, exercise and a daily contact with the God of your understanding.

MIND:
"What man conceives of as pain and disaster is only a changing concept in Man's mind, and is not reality in the true sense. The outer

manifestation is only a shadow existence of the real. Everything that
happens is helping to bring all levels of consciousness
back into their own higher existence. "
Cosmic Journeys by Rosalind A. McKnight

In earlier lessons we established that we are what our minds tell us
is our reality. It tells us if we are living in fear or love. The choice
is yours to determine. As you consider who you are, follow each
revelation with the thought, "Does this thought arise out of fear or
love?" If it comes from fear, reject it immediately and investigate
how you could turn it into a situation that expresses love. Then you
will know it comes from the love of the God of your
understanding.

If you make your life a living example of love in which everything
has a divine purpose then you will have faith that everything
happens for your highest good. When you understand this principle
that everything works for good your task is only to find out what
that good is then make your life an expression of that good. In his
book *Questions and Answers on Conversations with God* Neal
Donald Walsch beautifully answers the question, "What can we do
to prepare ourselves for the upcoming changing times?" His
answer began with the assurance that your reality is just what you
thought it was. His how-to advice was, "Go, therefore and be a gift
unto the world. Smile a lot. For a smile is love announced. Love of
whatever and whoever it is you are smiling at." So go and do
likewise and your days will be filled with happiness and love.

SPIRIT:
"If a religious system is not based within the soul it is of man and not of
the God/man relationship. Tapping the soul is tapping the source. Man
was created in the likeness of God; therefore man is God. "
Cosmic Journeys by Rosalind A. McKnight

By now I hope you have a vivid picture of your purpose in life and
who you are. Make sure these images have not come from a desire
on your part of what material wants you feel are important to you.
How does this image of who you are help you climb the steps
toward self-actualization? Once you have this Divine Plan in mind

then start to live as if you already are who you know you are. With this start meditation will become a more important practice in your life to show you the paths to take in your journey. Meditation practice may be a little difficult in its early stages but rest assured that with practice it will become easier and more productive.

LESSON: Alpha > Omega Odyssey – The Pathway to Self-Actualization

"Everything and everyone has purpose and meaning in the universe."
Cosmic Journey by Rosalind A. McKnight

In the last lesson of this chapter it is time to put it all together. We have determined who we are and tested this knowledge through meditation with the God of our understanding. To this information we have searched for the meaning in our lives and incorporated this knowledge into where we are on Maslow's Hierarchy of Needs so we can begin with where we are now in our personal development goals. We have come to realize that life is a journey, an odyssey that will bring us to self-actualization, the goal for all human endeavors. With this knowledge of where we currently are on the hierarchy we can determine what our goals need to be to reach the next level of development. Our personal goals will then design the pathway of our odyssey to the apex of the pyramid.

There are many pathways you can choose on your odyssey. You will always be the architect of your life so consider your choices well. Make this the year when you will evolve toward the person you truly are and want to be. You can become the person you were meant to be. The power and knowledge is already within you. It has often been said that every journey starts with the first step. You have already taken that first step by committing to find out who you really are and why you are here. So now let's find out what to do next to accomplish your mission. If you accept this mission you will become a happier and healthier person who, at the end of the odyssey, can truly say, "I have stood the course and I have accomplished my mission this time around in the service of the God of my understanding."

It helps if we commit these goals to writing. Taking pen in hand first define the following: "Who am I really?" Next make a notation of which level you are at in Maslow's pyramid and how you arrived at that decision. Now what can you do with this information? Establish your goals in small incremental steps so your first successes are not too far in the future.

To illustrate, I'll relate the story with my personal search. It covers too many years to describe in detail, much of which is not important to the lesson anyway, so I'll share a summary. In 1988 at age 52 it was time for my mid-life crisis. Some people have it sooner, some later. Mine actually started almost ten years earlier; I just didn't recognize it. 1988 was the significant time for me, the time I took action. I closed my chemical business, made some positive lifestyle changes, and made a major move to an area where I could do something I really enjoyed while I was searching for what to do with the rest of my life. My wife and I moved to the mountains around Lake Tahoe and I began a second career as a professional ski patroller, also working in the wellness department of a hospital. In addition I worked as a medic for a juvenile detention center in the Nevada desert. All of these experiences were excellent learning times as I realized that life's experiences, though difficult, have a purpose in the learning. The ski patrol experience showed me the pleasure in helping others and I wasn't too old to learn new skills and knowledge. I also did some college-level teaching at the local community college and the private Sierra Nevada College. This experience reinforced my desire to teach and conduct seminars and workshops, which I had always enjoyed during my business/chemical career. During this time I began to understand that I was blessed with good health, my genetic makeup providing a good start, but I was responsible for my own health maintenance. Since I was a walking example of these blessings I realized I could help others to make the lifestyle changes that are necessary so they, too can reach a healthy longevity like what I knew was my destiny.

Most of my experience at the hospital taught me that western medicine does a great job in dealing with trauma situations but most of their failures occur with the illness/disease part of medicine. This was proof to me that total health involved more than just the physical repair of the body. The mind and spirit are extremely important and conventional medicine doesn't apply its expertise in these areas. I realized that the way to maintain health was to control the mind so that the spirit could move and speak to me. I used personal hypnosis as a technique to help control my mind. I learned early that I was the captain of my mind and that I should never put myself in a position where I was not in complete control. This is why I never tried drugs because they altered the control I had over myself. Some of this maturity came from my short experience with alcohol, which provided the motivation to never again lose control. Hence, I knew I needed to become certified in hypnotherapy in order to use and practice this most powerful modality. I enjoyed the academic environment; while I was teaching I was also a student at the college.

The only true path to long-term health is to return to Nature. I started and completed a graduate program for a Master of Science in Natural Health. My plan for my future is to help Alzheimer sufferers through natural methods. My parents eventually succumbed to that dreaded disease of old age.

All of these things were steps in the long but as yet unfulfilled dream. I have been asked why, at the age of 73, do I wish to pursue such ambitious goals at a time when I should be retiring? Learning is a lifelong process and what we think of as retirement is not in my vocabulary. When I stop having dreams and goals I know I have, in effect, decided to return to my heavenly home and that is one decision that is not for me to make.

All these things I've done in the last fifteen years were little steps that were planned to progress toward my ultimate destiny in life. A few years ago I did a past life survey. In that survey a lot of the things I've done in life and the reason I was going down the pathway I was on became very clear to me. At that point my dreams for Cosmos Institute began to clarify. My dream provides motivation. My early goals are the reality steps I need to take in order to make my dreams come true. And my dear reader, each of you is a vital part of that dream – you just don't know it yet because I am on the road to my self-actualization just as you are.

The purpose of Cosmos Institute is to help you in attaining your goals with such activities as goal setting, guided imagery and instruction in self-hypnosis. Learn how to correct the most common causes of poor health with stress management, abuse elimination, lifestyle modification, the relaxation response, nutritional supplementation and education. We help you to access your spiritual guides, learn the impact of past lives on your current challenges, and lessons that can be learned only by understanding why you are where you are. These are just some of the life challenges we all face in this exciting journey as we travel this road of life. These "good" things can be started at any age, and the earlier you begin to make the right decisions the longer you will be a productive partner in this human experience. You are in control of the what, why, and how of your life; we as facilitators can only assist in your journey.

BODY:

"Just as man has a soul the earth and all physical matter have a higher dimension. The soul in tune with its higher self has no earth words to describe its true nature."
Cosmic Journeys by Rosalind A. McKnight

This body we were born with, often called the temple of God, is our vehicle to transport the mind and soul during this incarnation. Hence, the creator of your understanding gave your body to you as a sacred trust. We should not defile, deface or damage it in any way. If you don't take the responsibility to protect your body, remember that the creator who brought you into this world can take you out if you exhibit irresponsibility in your stewardship. These truths are so important to our survival they must be considered in any life plan we may develop. So, our goals must include the lifestyle changes we know are in keeping with protecting this temple from deterioration.

This might include finding your current baseline in your physical health endeavors. What symptoms are you experiencing which you would like to change? Maybe you are suffering from some painful physical condition you would like to change. You need to have a good understanding of any conditions in order to make a plan for corrections. A visit to a healthcare provider may be indicated.

In order to know the nutritional status of your body you will need to start with a laboratory analysis. In fact, I recommend finding out your current nutritional status before starting on any supplemental program. A source for this information could be a nutritional analysis of your body chemistry by www.Bioreport.com or www.directlab.com. Many laboratory tests are available which you can obtain economically and without the intervention of a physician. You can phone these labs and arrange for the type of test you want. They will send you a test kit to take to a hospital and for $3 or $4 you can have the blood or urine samples drawn. The hospital will then send the samples to the lab. The results will be sent to you. You can then take this information to your healthcare provider or natural therapist for consultation.

There is one rule I always try to follow: Do not put anything into me that is not required by my body to maintain life. This is why I always begin any healing efforts with prayer and a search for the best homeopathic or herbal remedies before embarking on drugs or surgeries as my modality of choice. Good, nutritious food is medicine for the body. It is a better therapy than drugs. Remember, PREVENTION is the key since it is easier to prevent an illness than to cure one.

MIND:

> *"Your life work is a work of art.*
> *A craft to be most carefully mastered.*
> *For patience has replaced time.*
> *And you are your own distinction."*
> *Author Unknown*

"Let the words of my mouth and the meditations of my heart be acceptable in thy sight O Lord." Psalm 19:14. Since I was very young the wisdom of these words from the Psalms have been a guiding principle of the power of the mind. The mind controls the body and the source of the inspiration for the mind comes from the spirit. We have only to open up and become receptive to its guiding messages. The use of the words "I AM" will invoke the spiritual into the chambers of the mind. Therefore, it is vitally important that we are careful what we say after uttering or thinking these two powerful words. Whenever you use the I AM the next few words must be words phrased in the positive, not in the negative. Whatever you say must be thought previously in order to be verbalized. The subconscious located within every cell of the body does not discriminate the thoughts coming from the mind. It reacts to every command. But we are in control of all the commands. This is why practical jokes and teasing are such dangerous games to play. It is damaging to both the joker and jokee. To have to say, "I didn't mean that" is to admit your mind was asleep at the controls.

Just as it is important to keep poisons and toxins out of our bodies, so it is with our minds. We must not allow any negativity to slip into our minds. This is why the use of profanity is so dangerous because it conveys such destructive emotions into the environment. Next time you are unfortunate enough to be in the presence of such emotions, pay attention to the reaction within your body. Can't you feel the rise in tension, blood pressure, pulse rate, and the hormonal surge that is so damaging to your long-term health? You don't even have to be a party to the negative scene, but it will affect you anyway. Once you realize how it affects you, just imagine the long-term damage to a very young mind when exposed to such negative scenes. It is the damage to these impressionable minds that is so sad because it becomes a catch 22, a never-ending cycle of violence. These young persons grow up and continue to repeat the negative cycle again. The parent who participates in such actions should be charged with child abuse and have the children taken away. But this doesn't solve the child's problem. The spirit in the child wants the parents to understand. We don't think before we speak because we allow our emotions rather than our spirit to rule our mind. This is the reason why the message contained in our "Go With The Flow" workshop is so vital to the peace and serenity of our lives and world.

In summary we must be constantly on guard not to say or think any thoughts that are negative or toxic to our minds. The consequences for such actions will be manifested in our lives. Since you are embarked on a journey to attain self-actualization such boulders of negativity must be avoided.

SPIRIT:

"There is no other reality than true being. And becoming is the path that the soul takes through earth time to be nurtured and reawakened to its true reality. Each being is the sacred book that contains all knowledge and all reality in and of itself."
Cosmic Journeys by Rosalind A. McKnight

As we search for the meaning in our being we will ultimately come to realize that the purpose for our soul to come to earth during this incarnation is to experience some lesson that can only be had at this time and place. Our spirit made the choice of this time and place as well as choosing the parents we were blessed with to bring us this earthly body. The philosophy contained in the song *I Never Promised You a Rose Garden* has always resonated within my soul. The basic premise of being an American citizen is that only in America are you assured the opportunity to place your foot on the first rung of the ladder and climb as high as your talents, motivation, education and awareness will allow you to go. There are no guarantees of success. With the guidance of your spiritual being, whatever you accomplish or attain in life is wholly your responsibility. You make your successes or failures – I don't believe there is any such thing as luck. I sure wouldn't rely on luck to "bring my ship in." Without a plan in life that includes your spiritual guide, you are doomed to failure. You will be given the opportunity to try to get it right again in another incarnation. Why not resolve to succeed during this earth time experience and save yourself a lot of grief and pain?

Once you accept the fact that there is a divine purpose in everything that happens to us and you see that we're the authors of the plan, life can take on a whole new and wonderful meaning. When there is no room for unproductive requests, we can grow by looking at each of life's challenges as an opportunity to grow in body/mind/spirit, free from the pains of blaming conditions outside us for life. The old Persian proverb that has been a basic tenet of my philosophy has always worked for me. I have found it to be true under the bright light of examination: "Until tomorrow becomes today men will be blind to the good fortune hidden in unfortunate acts." Make this a part of your life and dark clouds will go away and the blessings of a warm sun will shine on your path. There are no guarantees it will be easy but it will be for your highest good. Your highest good is God's only guarantee. As you grow in maturity and consciousness, more complex challenges will be offered. There is no escape from the lessons and no retirement. May God bless you as you embark on this exciting odyssey.

CHAPTER VII

OBESITY DISEASE – TERMINATED WITH (W)HOLISTIC TECHNIQUES

LESSON: What is the obesity disease?
"When our attention becomes fixed on only the diet and its biochemical makeup, or on only the digestive system, pancreas, liver, etc., and their functioning or on only the mind and its conflicts, we see only part of the picture."
Diet & Nutrition – A Holistic Approach
Rudolph Ballentine, M.D.

This lesson will investigate problem that is all too common world-wide and especially prevalent in the United States. More than 65% of the American population is considered overweight, with a body mass index of 25-29 or more, and the percentage of overweight people increases every year. A body mass index of 30 or more is considered obese. The rates for obesity-related disease are climbing at an exponential rate as well. Such dreaded diseases as diabetes, heart disease, cancer, high blood pressure, G.I. disorders and respiratory distresses are among the conditions that result from uncontrolled obesity. Obesity is now considered a serious disease in the US as its long-term effect has invaded our children, with 15% of them seriously overweight. Many of the causes of obesity are lifestyle choices, which if started at a young age are very difficult to change. The cost in healthcare during a lifetime is high, with medical visits to treat the symptoms resulting from the diseases whose genesis is the uncontrolled weight management decisions made throughout your life. [3]

One of the most common excuses used by those battling this challenge is that it is caused by our genes. "I can't help it – it is the will of God. It's not my fault I'm afflicted with this horrible condition." This reasoning soothes our egos because we can blame this unfortunate condition on "George" or some other entity we have no control over. I've seldom heard a seriously overweight person say, "I don't want to be like this; I surely wouldn't weight this much if I could have avoided it." They may think it but seldom express it unless asked. The problem goes deeper into the sub-conscious mind. On a conscious level these people would like to make the lifestyle changes they know are necessary, but on the subconscious level that actually controls our actions, they are not convinced yet. So the very first requirement, in order to heal, is to accept responsibility for our health condition. As soon as we do this we have put our foot on the first rung of the ladder to health. It won't be an easy climb but we have accepted the responsibility and therefore the commitment to succeed. Now we can channel all our energies to making the hard decisions that allow the healing to take place. We must believe we are able to do it but we must also understand that it will take some hard work. Remember, God never promised us a rose garden. He has offered us a lesson to be learned and in the learning, to grow in self-confidence and the awareness of our power to heal ourselves.

The December 8, 2003 issue of *Newsweek* did a feature story on the top 10 health issues of 2003. Number one was on the subject of obesity, though the issues were not necessarily ranked in order of importance. All the stories were important, and possibly another one may be more important to you because you are personally facing those challenges today. I imagine most everyone has some personal issue with at least one of the ten. But for this chapter we will deal with the very difficult challenge of obesity – I'm sure there are plenty of you with a personal interest in this nationally significant killer.

It is customary at the start of a new year to make a resolution of the changes you want to undertake. It is often thought of as a time for new beginnings. Did you know the most popular New Year's resolution is to lose weight? Since the failure rate within the first quarter is so high, anyone can understand the difficulty involved in maintaining these good intentions. This is why I chose this subject for this lesson - to give you encouragement and hope that you, too will be a success.

As with all the stories in that edition of *Newsweek*, the editors began by describing the new drugs that had come out during 2003 in an effort to find the miracle pill that will solve all your problems without any effort on your part. One of the research efforts is trying to determine just how excess weight triggers the development of cancer, heart disease and diabetes. "The hope is that we'll be able to develop a medication that won't necessarily affect body weight but will keep that excess fat from making overweight people sick," says Samuel Klein, director of the Center for Human Nutrition at the Washington University School of Medicine. It seems to me they are still trying to find a solution that is easy and will try to fool Mother Nature, whose laws are inviolate. Nor are there any secrets about the workings of her laws. We just seem to try to find ways to circumvent them. Since you can't violate Mother Nature's laws, each of these attempts comes with it own serious side effects. So aren't you trading one health problem for another? When I see someone who is taking more than three prescription drugs and ask why they are taking each of them, I find that some of them invariably are given to counteract the side effects of the other medications.

In order to combat the serious side effects of these "solutions," the western medical community has devised another technique that utilizes the well-worn knife. When drugs no longer work in a given problem the knife has always been the solution – and so it is with the obesity problem. Surgery for excessive overweight is called bariatric surgery. One type is commonly referred to as stomach stapling, and all the varieties are becoming increasingly popular. But like any surgery the risks are high and the successful conclusion is not guaranteed or easy. Surgery doesn't change the lifestyle issues that caused the problem in the first place. After the long recovery period is over, those lifestyle changes are forced on you because of the physical restraints of the surgery. If the changes are not made, very serious consequences result. Like all surgeries, there are successful ones and some serious failures. The successful cases result not so much from the physical aspects of the surgery but by the mental changes that take place. The patient makes the positive changes because of the fear of what might happen if they are not made.

One of the attempts to avoid surgery is an electrical therapy to the stomach lining in order to vary the hormonal communication between the stomach and the brain. Again, isn't this an attempt to circumvent Mother Nature's law? Haven't we tried this long enough to know it won't work in the long term? The only true healing is to recognize the spiritual source of all healing and return to our nature. This lesson will discuss some of the methods we can use to return to nature and at the same time to accept the beautiful vehicle God has provided us in our odyssey during this lifetime. The next lesson will discuss the energy formula and BMI in more detail.

BODY:

"It must be realized that some of the discomfort experienced by the overweight dieter is a result of nutritional needs that are not being met."
Diet & Nutrition – A Holistic Approach
Rudolph Ballentine, M.D.

The first natural law we must understand is the law of the use of energy. Put another way, it is called the conservation of energy – energy can neither be created nor destroyed. When you were conceived, the single cell from each of your parents combined into the cell that reproduced itself and you grew into who and what you are today. Since the energy of that cell that became you cannot be created, where did it come from? Is this another chicken or egg paradox? Quantum physics tells us that all the energy in the universe came from that single quantum packet when the universe was created by God, at the time the Laws of Nature were put into effect ....in the beginning. God has functioned ever since by his own laws. We only have to understand and apply his laws for a successful life. He didn't create any faulty or defective machinery. So when did the problem start? In many cases it started with our parents and what they fed us. If we chose a healthy mother who was free from toxins like tobacco, alcohol, caffeine, medications and other environmental toxins then we have an excellent chance for a healthy foundation. Then if she breast-fed us for as long as nature provided her milk we inherited her natural immunity. If our parents are knowledgeable and monitor what we eat so we consume only wholesome, healthy, foods and nutrients then we will be able to avoid the diseases of those hooked on soft drinks and junk food.

I would advise having an annual nutritional analysis done in order to monitor if you are achieving a good, balanced intake of nutrients. It is important to correct any deficiencies early before the problem blossoms into a chronic condition.

Our diet throughout life must be a balanced, healthy one, not a crash diet, since this will usually result in deficiencies of some important nutrients. Instead, if we learn to eat a wholesome, balanced diet we will attain a healthy body. Be sure to contact a holistic nutritionist who is schooled in true natural nutrition and is not under the influence of the medical community (an exponent of fad diets), and avoid the dieticians of the food industry who have a cause to promote and were trained in the school of western medicine.

MIND:

"The mind and diet relate to each other in a sort of double feedback fashion... This means that a continuous interplay exists which can, if allowed to run amok, carry one to great heights (or depths) of mental and physical disorder."
Diet & Nutrition – A Holistic Approach
Rudolph Ballentine, M.D.

Since poor weight management is such a significant factor in determining the health of the individual, it is a vital area of effort for Cosmos Institute of Life's Transitions to study and promote with our nature cure enthusiasts, those who are looking forward to a healthy life in the sunset of their years. Remember, we must start when we are much younger. The beginning point of our program is to correct the imagery our clients are using. Without a proper image of how you see yourself then any program or plan is doomed to failure, its resources and time wasted.

We deal with imagery where it resides in the domicile of the mind. The technique we use to communicate with the subconscious mind is called hypnotherapy. Many people are afraid of this technique because they are fearful the therapist will get control of their minds. Please remember, all those shows you see where the hypnotist plants a post-hypnotic suggestion and the subject does some crazy act - in all cases the subjects were volunteers and knew what to expect. A principle and rule of all hypnotherapy is that the subject will never do anything or be made to do anything against their moral code. The therapist is a facilitator who uses positive suggestions directly to the subconscious to help it do what it wants – to act for your highest good which has already been established by your super-conscious (Spirit). It is the clinical hypnotherapist's job to help you, not create a carnival show.

So with that issue settled, let's look at this important concept called image. The image you maintain of yourself should be what you want to look like six months from now. But in order for it work it has to be realistic. This is where the Body Mass Index can be very helpful. Set your goals in 10 point increments. We will discuss how to do this in the next lesson but for now think in terms of losing only one or two pounds per week. This is the only healthy regime that any serious healthcare provider will suggest. Trying to lose 20 pounds in May in order to fit into your new bathing suit in June is unrealistic and unhealthy. This sort of mentality has contributed to demoralization and the yo-yo syndrome with which most dieters are well acquainted. We have all heard that the reason this happens is because we lose a lot of water at the beginning. This is somewhat true, however, we still become dehydrated, and that's unhealthy. Consider working to convert all that fat to muscle. You will become smaller but still maintain your energy. Some of the technique may include the bad "E" word but stick with the image idea for now. You can convert the fat to muscle in your mind. Then hold that image.

One of the reasons it is more difficult to make this conversion of fat to muscle is that it becomes more difficult to maintain or develop new muscle fibers and strength as we age. Look at most athletes and the sports they participate in – don't most of the sports have age limitations when the participants are not as strong as they used to be? You can bet they haven't stopped maintaining their conditioning practices – it just doesn't work as well as it used to.

I have a personal experience in this regard. When I was a professional ski patroller I used to start conditioning in August of each year so I would be in shape by the time the snows fell. If I wasn't, the first two weeks of the season were agony for me with pain and soreness. As I aged, the time it took to recoup my conditioning became longer and the time it took to lose my conditioning became shorter. Experience has its limits when it comes to sports requiring strength and endurance. This is true of life as well.

In our first hypnosis session we use the metaphor of looking at your reflection in a still pool of water. See yourself and feel yourself as whatever you establish as your "ideal body weight." This ideal body image will change over time if you heed the advice to take it in slow, realistic portions. But that is OK. You may change more slowly but you will have more successful goal attainments and will be considerably healthier. For now start thinking about what your ideal body image should be.

SPIRIT:
"Inherent within each of us is a self-regulating mechanism whose job is to adapt and maintain the best of health."
The Weight Is Over by Dr. Jack Tips, CCN

Hypnosis, meditation and prayer are all techniques for communicating with your super-conscious (Spirit). When we accept and believe that the true path to all healing begins with the spirit that controls the mind which in turn controls the body, then the importance of the involvement of our super-conscious becomes obvious. In order to understand how spirit works in our world we need to get back to the fundamentals of nature. Science has established that all activity in the body takes place at the cellular level within the body as well as in the energy fields outside our bodies. The strength of the energy which influences us is directly proportional to its distance from the body. The energy force never reaches zero, just as gravity has an influence on all the matter in

146

the universe but in a diminishing effect with distance. Hence, its influence is infinite within the laws of quantum physics and is termed a nonlocal correlation. I first realized the significance of this as it relates to our spiritual life when I read about Bell's Theorem (see glossary). It was then I understood that all life is related and we are all ONE with God. Since we are all made up of energy we all came from that single quantum packet of energy that God released in the Big Bang (see glossary). This energy force is the reason prayer, without the limitation of the cosmic speed limit (speed of light), works so well - why prayers are answered instantaneously even if the subjects are on opposite sides of the planet.

How can this help us with the influence of spirit on our ability to control our weight challenges? Within the last couple of decades much research has been directed toward what is generally referred to as "consciousness" studies. The world of the nonlocal (see glossary) has entered into that effort with a significant influence. Consider the principle of the hologram which has come out of the work of the quantum physicists. The principle behind the hologram is that you can consider it as a single picture, but if you take a section out of the picture and project it, the resulting picture will still contain everything contained within the whole picture. This part of science evolved when it was determined that all our memories are contained within each cell of our bodies, not within the geography of our minds. In other words, each cell is a subsection of the hologram of our minds. Therefore, each cell contains the spiritual self from which we all sprang. Since our spiritual self and all our memories are contained within each cell then it is possible that the cause of our obesity may come from a prior life and some unresolved karma.

LESSON: The Energy Equation

"The basic equation that relates caloric intake to weight is very simple. If caloric intake consistently exceeds caloric expenditures, the body will tend to store excess calories as fat. The simple fact is that so many Americans are fat because they are eating far more calories than they expend."
Eating Well for Optimum Health by Andrew Weil, M.D.

147

Its' all about energy. Energy is all there is in the universe. Everything in the universe, including life, is made up of energy which is vibrating at a specific frequency depending upon the function and needs of the situation. There is a basic law of science: in order to maintain homeostasis (balance), energy in must equal energy out. See the glossary under the Second Law of Thermodynamics. It is impossible to violate this law of nature. Dr. Weil advocates that we should always be consciously aware of the calories we consume. The amount of calories we need is dependent upon the activity level we experience in our daily life. This is one of the reasons obesity has become such a problem in the US, as we have reduced our exercise and increased our sedentary lifestyle. Children today are not required to have physical training on a daily basis in school nor do they play as I did as a child before the advent of TV. TV has done a lot to improve our lives except in the realm of our health. This is why searching for the magic pill to keep us all thin and still allow us to do whatever we desire is a pipe dream. There is no way we can violate the laws of nature. So remember the formula for obesity: energy in = energy out + excess fat (which we hope will be 0).

All living organisms require energy to live. We all know this and it is easy to prove. Just stop eating and breathing and you will experience what happens if you stop taking in energy. All our living cells require the energy they obtain from the foods we eat and the air we breathe. Any unnatural or toxic ingredients in the food we eat or the air we breathe will cause some damage to our system.

We don't always have complete control over the toxins that are in our food or the pollution in the air we breathe. We do have some control over the choices we make; where we obtain our food and what kind of foods we eat; we can filter the water in our homes and purify the air we breathe in our homes and offices.

When we are thinking about the amount of energy we consume, we need to understand that different foods supply different energy levels. Energy comes to our muscles and brain in the form of glucose; it is the fuel our bodies need for their energy. Our bodies are bio-chemically designed to utilize glucose as energy. Our bodies are able to convert glucose into fat but it is more difficult to convert stored fat back into usable glucose. Calories are what we call the energy measurements and are defined as the amount of heat (energy) required to raise the temperature of one gram of water 1° C. The chemical makeup of fats allows them to produce more energy than carbohydrates, hence we receive more than twice as many calories per gram from fats than we do from carbohydrates. The body can also obtain glucose by making it from proteins, which is a complex chemical reaction in the liver (ketosis) that rarely occurs except under great nutritional or medical stress.

You can gain fats very easily and quickly by the consumption of fats. Remember, there are many forms of the fats, carbohydrates and proteins. They each have different properties and all three are required for a healthy body. This is why, to completely understand nutrition you need to have the guidance of a holistic nutritionist. As an example of how easy it is to consume too many calories and thus exacerbate your efforts of weight control, consider that nutritionists generally believe the average daily caloric requirement of someone with an average activity level, depending on sex and body size is 2,000 to 3,000 calories per day. If you consume the average American breakfast you will eat approximately 1,500 calories. That only leaves 500 – 1,000 calories left for two more meals. Obviously it is easy to gain excess calories which are stored as fat. You can see why it is important to be aware of what you are eating and how it impacts your total caloric intake.

To determine your BMI use the following computation:

$$BMI = \frac{weight\ (lbs.)\ X\ 0.45}{(height\ (ins.)\ X\ 0.025)^2}$$

For example, consider a 150 lb. male who is 66 inches tall. His BMI would be: 150 X 0.45 = 67.5. 66 X 0.025 = 1.65^2. 67.5/2.7 = 25. He is at the upper limits of the standard and then, considering his body frame he could be considered within a good healthy weight. The larger the body frame, the higher the side of the standard you can be on and still be healthy. In order to determine your body frame size, take the thumb and middle finger on one hand and wrap it around the wrist of the other hand. If the thumb and finger overlap you have a small frame, if they meet you are medium, and if they don't meet you have a large frame.

Be careful judging the body frame size by a person's appearance. I am personally 5'6" and weigh 147 pounds. When people look at me they think I am a small frame, however, using the above scale I am a large body frame, meaning my healthy BMI is 24 to 25. In this case 'small' and 'large' don't refer to size, but rather, to the thickness of the bones and 'stockiness' of the skeleton and, therefore, the amount of muscle that can attach to it.

Once you have determined your current BMI you can use this information to help you determine your weight goals. If you have a BMI higher than 30, by definition you are considered obese. Then you know you are potentially going to be a victim of all the unhealthy conditions that are the result of obesity. The sooner you are able to correct this condition, the better your health will be. You can also use this formula to set goals for your ideal body image. Let's assume you are a female of medium frame. Your goal should be to have a BMI ratio of 20. Since your height will probably not change if you are past 20 years of age, you can determine the ideal body weight that will give you your BMI goal by solving the formula for the unknown weight. As we learned in the last lesson, set short-term goals of 8-10 pounds per month.

Be aware that a BMI below these standards is also unhealthy. The nice thing about using the BMI scale rather than the insurance rate scale is that the BMI is related to health, unlike the outdated life expectancy charts of many years ago. The determination of the BMI scale was based on measuring the effect of the relationship of height to weight and how it manifested in unhealthy conditions over time. The original study took place over a 20-year period in which the participants were followed up, based on science, with consideration for the body frame size factored into the equation.

In the next lesson we will tackle the glycemic scale and caloric restrictions.

BODY:

"Eat a balanced and varied diet. Avoid obesity and fad diets. There are no magical guidelines for good nutrition. Patients should resolve to plan their diet around the watchwords variety, moderation, and balance."
The American Council on Science and Health

Your metabolism is the rate at which you are able to utilize energy and the efficiency with which your cells are able to use that energy as food. Obviously your metabolic rate is a very personal thing and there are many individual factors that go into determining how your body utilizes the food you eat. But it needs to be considered when we are looking for the things that will keep us healthy. Unfortunately, this is a complex subject and a detailed investigation is beyond the forum of this book. There are times like during sleep when the metabolic rate is slow and times like during heavy activity when the metabolic rate is rapid. When we are healthy the rate we are functioning at will take care of itself. The quality of the food we take in, the source of our energy, is a consideration each of us must make.

The field of nutrition, while extremely important, is a very complex subject and one that is full of rumors and false information. A number of years ago I remember reading that the knowledge in the nutrition field doubles very six months. That is a lot of information to keep up with so the availability of a holistic nutritionist to monitor your program could be very important. Notice I said holistic nutritionist. We should be dealing with the whole body and how it is affected by natural laws rather than trying to find ways to circumvent the laws of nature and synthesizing our foods.

The hormonal and chemical supplementation given to animals used for meat and dairy products is an attempt to improve on nature's process. However, the chemical compounds in this supplementation are detrimental rather than beneficial to human health when they are carried forward in the food supply. The environmental toxins we place on our fruits and vegetables to improve their production are extremely toxic to our human bodies. The slogan "everything is better through modern chemistry" is not necessarily true. The holistic nutritionist believes that the closer we can get to the source of our food supply the healthier will be the result. In order to increase our food supply, farming has modernized the methods of production. This has improved efficiency but lowered the quality of our food. I guess it depends on which side of the equation you are standing on. Even the excellent food derived from fish has become contaminated by the pollution of our streams and oceans. Fish raised in hatcheries are contaminated with the added toxins used to increase production. The chemicals added to foods to improve their color, taste, and freshness are extremely detrimental to our health. The idea of local cooperative food sources and farms is a good one and I recommend you consider them if they are available to you. Your health will thank you for it. Another healthy option is to grow your own garden, either in your yard, in containers on your patio or in a community garden plot. Not only will this provide you with healthy food to eat, it will also give you exercise and fresh air.

As a first step in making changes in your nutritional/health program you might consider swearing off food items like soft drinks, red meats, junk foods, trans fats, food additives that do not come from a natural source (like artificial sweeteners), any food that has the word "refined" on the label, alcohol and tobacco products. Refined foods have had the nutritional value processed out of them. Tobacco products are 18% sugar (and don't forget the nicotine and other dangerous substances in them). Alcohol, especially beer, will increase your weight rapidly. Ever notice the beer gut? At one time in my past I couldn't see my feet until I stopped drinking beer. In about six months the beer gut was gone and I could see where I was walking. Don't try to eliminate all these food sources at once; it will be too difficult on the body and mind at one time. Learn to eliminate one item at a time by substituting a healthy alternative instead. As an example, eliminate all soft drinks and substitute pure water, caffeine-free teas and fruit juices.

152

MIND:

"The mind and diet relate to each other in a sort of double feedback
fashion... This means that a continuous interplay exists, which can, if
allowed to run amok, carry one to great heights or depths of mental and
physical disorder."
Diet & Nutrition – A Holistic Approach
Rudolph Ballentine, M.D.

A significant problem with most obese persons is the damage obesity does to their self-esteem and therefore their mental health. When a person is unhappy with their personal appearance they lose their interest in social interaction. Social interaction is a requirement for a healthy life and the lack of social opportunities will have damaging effects on your well-being. This cycle becomes a catch-22 situation causing your obesity to increase; then your social interaction will continue to decrease.

Dealing with the challenges of obesity is hard work and requires a lot of willpower and motivation. It is never as easy as those ads lead you to believe. There are no magic pills nor will there ever be any way to control your weight without a lot of effort on your part. The sooner you can accept and acknowledge that fact, the sooner you will be able to take responsibility for your health and begin to make progress in your effort.

The first step is to find the motivation within your own mind and spirit to begin the long, difficult path to optimum health. Once you have the motivation, you can begin talking with your mind to accomplish the goals you envision. There are three techniques available to you to make these goals possible. They are prayer, imaging and hypnotherapy. Pray to talk with your spiritual guide and ask for help to accomplish your goals, recognizing that nothing is possible without the help of your spirit. Then use imaging and affirmations to train your body to accept the accomplishment of your ideal body image. Realize that your goal is already met – all you need to do is accept the divine image. It was your mind that got you into this condition and it will be your mind that will lead you out. Learning the techniques of self-hypnosis is a method you can use to bring your mind into agreement with your desired image.

SPIRIT:

"When we pray we are talking to God.
When we meditate we listen to God."
Wellness Doc

There are many conditions that have a spiritual foundation which results in obesity. Many are what we call "false Gods." A false God is the worshiping of some wrong emotion or condition that is believed to cause all your problems. In other words, not taking full responsibility for your thoughts and actions. Some of these false Gods are depression, selfishness, hate, revenge, stress, anxiety, personal conflicts, an 'it's not my fault' attitude and fear. You get the idea. All of these false Gods will result in increasing weight if not brought under control. To many people, eating and inactivity is the reaction to these false Gods. The solution to these problems is not drugs; they don't address the cause of the problem. You may see your medical doctor but his or her solutions deal only with eliminating the symptoms with drugs. The one you need to see about the condition is always available.

In order for any solution to work you must first discuss the problem and ask for answers from the God of your understanding. The technique to access this source is called meditation. When you meditate you are talking directly with the spirit within each of the cells of your body. The spirit is always available and wanting to help. All you need to do is listen. It is during meditation that we are listening to our soul/God of our understanding. Meditation becomes easier with practice so if meditation is not a familiar procedure to you, consult one of the many good books on the subject.

If you listen carefully you will find out many of the causes of your problems and discover the best approach to get back onto the correct path of life. Many of these causes can also be learned from a hypnotherapist by a technique known as Time Line Therapy. It is a rapid and efficient method to find the original event that causes

154

these detrimental false Gods. Once you understand yourself better, solving the problem is very easy.

LESSON: The Fallacy of Die-Ts
"Change is life's characteristic; commit to making perpetual positive changes and go with the flow. When we cooperate with natural law the rewards are profound."
The Weight is Over
Dr. Jack Tips

"Nutritionists say it's calories not the carbohydrates that count."

That was the headline above the cover story in *USA Today*, February 11, 2004. As most of us are aware, Dr. Robert Atkins, the author of *The Atkins Diet*, passed away on April 17, 2003 at the age of 72. The cause of his death was not his diet but a fall on the ice resulting in head trauma. The event did provide ample opportunities for experts on both sides of the diet issue (those for or against a low carb diet) to square off against one another. Advocates of vegetarianism were quick to bring up the prior heart disease issues that Dr. Atkins had been fighting the previous year. His wife denied he was overweight and that his heart disease had anything to do with his slipping on the ice, but it had everything to do with his passing. What else could she say? I personally doubt the heart disease had anything to do with his slipping on the ice, but it had everything to do with his health condition at the time. The headline in the current issue of *USA Today* said: "Atkins wasn't obese..." By definition he wasn't. When he checked into the hospital he weighted in at 195 and was six feet tall. Based on the BMI scale he had a body mass index of 27.1 which made him overweight but not obese by definition. If he had a medium body frame, which his pictures seem to indicate, he would be 29 pounds overweight. If he had a large frame he was 15 pounds overweight. Remember, BMI is an indicator of health and is a tougher standard for healthy longevity than the probability charts of the insurance industry.

The reason this hit the press almost a year after the accident is that some of the long-term studies which caused the headline mentioned above are beginning to come in. There were a number of interesting articles on diets in that issue of *USA Today* and the following day's issue, and they would be well worth reading if you can get a back copy from the internet. My purpose here is to point out that the conclusion reached by most of the experts is the same as I've been advocating all along. I have no quarrel with Dr. Atkins personally; I'm not jealous of his fame or riches; I only question the gullibility of the public that is still looking for the secret to the weight management challenge without accepting the law of energy which Mother Nature has made inviolate.

Energy is required for life and you cannot violate the fact that energy must be properly utilized. Because of our modern lifestyle, activity usually amounts to that dirty word that begins with an "E" - Exercise. As the headlines note, we still need to balance calories with our activity rather than reducing the number of food types that are required to sustain life. If you try to eliminate any of them then you will suffer the consequences of poor health. A diet should only include the elimination of excessive amounts of foods that are not required by the body, or for which the requirements are so low that they are automatically supplied by what we eat anyway. These include simple sugars, caffeine, animal protein, additives like preservatives and "refined" ingredients, trans fats and fast foods. Dr. Andrew Weil, in his book *Eating Well for Optimum Health,* had this to say about diets: "Although low-carbohydrate diets may work for short-term weight loss they are not the healthiest strategy for losing weight and I do not recommend them as an everyday way to eat. That does not mean that I endorse low-fat diets, either. Those regimens present different problems."

As indicated in the previous section, the study of even one of the food types is very complex and it seems nutritionists have favorites whose merits they are prone to advocate over the others. This is why I advocate for the programs promoted by Dr. Weil. He is more concerned with the idea that we are a product of Mother Nature. Without getting too complicated and confusing, we can consider the two basic types of carbohydrates: simple and complex. Our body handles these carbohydrates in many different ways and their effect may vary by individual. A simple carbohydrate is not stored

156

in the body and must be used immediately by the muscles and brain in order to avoid raising the blood sugar beyond healthy limits. Complex carbohydrates are stored in the body and are used by the body when the simple sugars are depleted, but complex carbohydrates require a complex route of biochemistry. Dr. Weil has a very clear discussion of these matters in the chapter entitled *The Basics of Human Nutrition* in his book. It would be well worth investing in his most informative and helpful book.

One of the tools available to help us determine the best carbohydrates is called the glycemic index (GI). It is an index of how the different carbohydrates affect the blood glucose levels. The higher the glycemic index, the faster the food causes glucose to increase in the blood and therefore the higher will be the insulin production and the greater the risk of the body's response to the harmful effects of the insulin. To arrive at the GI, subjects were fed a measured amount of a carbohydrate and tested for an increase in glucose in the blood. This method has allowed the individual variations of the subjects' predisposed insulin response to creep into the final result. This is why the index may vary depending on the author of the table you are using. Remember that the GI tables are only approximate. They should be used as a guide only. As an example, take the vegetable carrots. In some studies the GI of carrots was as high as 95 while in others as low as 42.

Some nutritionists and M.D.s have advocated that one should not eat carrots. This shows a misunderstanding about the nature of GI. The volunteer subjects are fed fifty grams of a carbohydrate. Carrots contain only 7% carbohydrate so to get fifty grams of a carbohydrate from carrots alone you would have to eat a lot of them. The test amount of carrots was one and half pounds! No one eats that many carrots at a single meal (except maybe Bugs Bunny); in reality, a much smaller serving would be a part of a complete meal. The full meal should have some low GI items in it also; the end result is a balanced meal. So if you are consuming a high GI item, also include a low GI item to balance it out and keep your blood sugar within manageable bounds. As many Type I diabetics know, consuming a high-protein food along with a carbohydrate will slow the release of glucose and help maintain a balanced blood sugar level.

BODY:

"The health conditions must first be established in the mind before they can be conveyed to and impress upon the cells. The well being of the human body as a whole depends upon the health of the billions of minute cells which compose it."
Philosophy of Natural Therapeutics
Henry Lindlahr, M.D.

Most nutritionists recommend you get between 50 and 60 percent of your calories from carbohydrates. Dr. Weil also agrees with this assessment. To help you get started with a plan, I'm going to list the other strong recommendations Dr. Weil makes for an optimum healthy diet.

1. The majority of carbohydrate calories should come from less refined, less processed foods with low glycemic index ratings.
2. It is desirable to eat some low-GI carbohydrate with most meals such as whole grains, beans, vegetables, and low-GI fruits (temperate fruits like berries, apples, and cherries as opposed to tropical ones like mangoes, papayas, and pineapples).
3. If you eat high-GI foods, eat them in moderate quantities and balance them by adding some low-GI foods at the same meal.
4. Reduce the impact of high-GI foods by eating them as part of missed meals that include fiber and acid.
5. Minimize consumption of foods and beverages sweetened with high-fructose corn syrup. Do not use pure, granulated fructose as a substitute for table sugar.
6. Make an effort to replace white and whole-wheat bread with dense, chewy, grainy breads whenever possible.
7. Learn to like firmer-cooked pasta rather than longer-cooked.
8. Eat more small, waxy, new potatoes and fewer large, floury potatoes.
9. Eat more basmati and converted rice and less regular or sticky rice.

10. Eat more beans. They are high-quality foods providing low-GI carbohydrate along with other nutrients.

MIND:
"Our lives and affairs are completely influenced and shaped by the character
of our thinking."
Eric Butterworth, spiritual author and lecturer

One downside of our modern scientific food production methods is the ability to formulate foods with ingredients that the consuming public likes but that have an insidious tendency to become addictive. Their use starts out very pleasant but as you enjoy eating them, your body requires more of the substance in order to maintain the enjoyment. As your consumption increases, your health declines. Simple sugars and trans fats are an example of such addictive substances. The fast food industry picked up on this fact very early and continues to cause harm to the public. It is very difficult for the public to return to nature when there are so many unhealthy options available to them. There is only one way to change how your body reacts to food and that is a change in your mindset.

The way to do this is to talk with the controller of the mind – the subconscious mind. The technique usually relied upon is hypnotherapy. One of the most common and earliest uses for hypnotherapy was to help change addictive behavior. It has proven itself over quite a long time, going as far back as the sleep temples of ancient Egypt. If we can reinforce some positive affirmations that can speak to these poor additive behaviors numerous times each day, positive results will come about. You cannot just say not to do something; that is not a positive affirmation. You must replace a poor behavior with a healthier, more positive one. The mind does not accept negative statements like, "I will not consume any more chocolate cakes." It is better to replace the statement of addictive behavior with a more healthful one. Instead say, "I will eat more fruits and yogurt for desserts." In each section of the Cosmos Institute of Life's Transitions weight management CD (image, nutrition, exercise, cravings), the post-hypnotic suggestions are made in the form of positive affirmations. We suggest you post these affirmations where you will see them regularly so you can reinforce them in your mind throughout the day, as you replace the addictive behavior with more healthy choices. All you do is resolve to put your mind to work for you rather than to support a momentary pleasure.

A healthy diet does not have to be devoid of pleasant foods. There are many books written with recipes that can be very tasteful. It does take a little creativity on your part, but with the mindset to improve your diet to one of health, this is possible. Dr. Weil's book mentioned earlier has many healthy recipes and includes what he calls The Optimum Diet.

SPIRIT:

"Truth is the reality we each place upon a question. Truth may be different to separate individuals and is yet the truthful reality to each or maybe the same reality?"
The Wellness Doc

There have been numerous instances when, while the client was in a Time Line Therapy session with a hypnotherapist, the original root cause event of some other issue turned out also to be the cause of the client's obesity. Obesity is often a secondary gain for clients to receive attention and love. The conditions that brought on these negative attributes may have started in this lifetime or in some cases they may have begun in a previous lifetime. There have also been cases in which the original event happened during multiple succeeding lifetimes. There is a lesson to be learned and challenges to overcome in each life experience. If you fail to learn the lessons then you are doomed to repeat the experience until you finally have that "ah, now I get it" event.

If you feel you are doing all the right things: good nutrition, exercise and good mental attitude, but you are still unable to conqueror the obesity problem, it is time to look to the spiritual self for an answer. Your spirit is the one common denominator through all your lives. It holds the secret to your life's successful accomplishments.

A Time Line Therapy session with your hypnotherapist can usually get to the root cause of the problem in a very short time. By short I

160

mean a single one-hour session. Once you know the root cause, you can take the lesson to be learned and let go of the event. Your spiritual self is then satisfied you have learned the needed lessons and you can go on to another lesson and never have to worry about obesity again. It sounds so simple but if you have tried everything else without results then this might be the answer you need. So often obesity begins with the unhealthy emotions of anxiety, anger, depression, greed and fear, . When you turn these emotions into love, your unhealthy emotions and obesity disappear.

LESSON: The Search for the Fountain of Youth
"Keep the faculty of effort alive in you by a little gratuitous exercise every day."
The Principles of Psychology
William James

It would be impossible to conclude the lesson on obesity without a discussion of exercise, or physical activity if you relate better to that term. I hope by now you are convinced that no weight loss program can be ultimately successful without exercise being a part of the formula. In fact, exercise can mask many of the defects of a poor diet because of its ability to reduce the effects of poor nutrition by improving elimination of waste and toxins, controlling stress and converting fat to more efficient muscle, . Do not misunderstand me; complete disregard for a healthy diet will have long-term effects on your overall health which will not be pleasant. God can do all things but he will not make you thin by just imaging alone. God will not violate his own physical laws. God only helps those who sincerely wish to help themselves. So imaging cannot in itself substitute for good physical exercise. Once we realize this, then we can become successful in our weight management activities without the wasteful efforts of searching for that fountain of perfect weight in a miracle pill. Ponce de Leon wasted a lifetime in such a search because there is no such thing; that is in violation of natural law. He thought he found it in the sulfur water of Florida only to die anyway. So don't waste your life on the misconception that you can be healthy without physical activity.

Let's embrace the concept that physical activity is a requirement for a healthy life and first consider why we don't like it. The biggest blockage we use as an excuse is TIME. I know because that is the excuse I personally have to battle daily. Maybe your excuse is, "I'm too big to exercise because I don't have any energy." In reality, you are too big because you don't utilize the energy your food is providing. This is a catch-22 situation in practice. Or the excuse might be, exercise is too expensive to belong to the gyms or invest in the equipment. "I can't afford it." These seem to be the main excuses I hear. If you look at each one realistically and honestly, you can find a solution. If not, send me an email with your favorite excuse and I'll see if I can help.

A word of caution to everyone: Before attempting to embark on an exercise program I must suggest you consult with your healthcare provider so any program can be compatible with whatever physical limitations you are currently experiencing. The medical community has accepted the necessity for physical activity. It wasn't too long ago that heart and other surgery patients were encouraged to rest. Now they get you up walking within 24 hours of most surgeries or as soon as possible thereafter.

Let's take a look at the time issue first. One of the reasons this is the top excuse in the US is that exercise is not high on our priority list. This is a problem you have to work out for yourself. Once you accept the proposition that the solution to your unhealthy condition requires physical conditioning, you will place it higher on your time list if you truly want to improve your long-term health and longevity. Do you know how much time you need to commit in order for the activity to be beneficial? First, you do not need to be in training as an athlete would. Unless you are a professional body builder, spending hours in the gym is not necessary. All you need to do is gradually raise your pulse rate to your training level. How do you determine your effective training heart rate? It is very simple and has been established by experts in the field of physical training. Subtract your age from 220 to arrive at your ideal pulse rate. To get the maximum benefit you should maintain an exercise for 10 to 15 minutes at your ideal pulse rate. Then stop! If you are healthy your pulse should return to normal within 5 to 10 minutes.

The law of diminishing returns goes into effect after the above time limits. This means that the incremental increase in benefit decreases to zero very rapidly and is proportional to the effort being expended. In other words, keeping your pulse rate up for more than 10 to 15 minutes doesn't gain you any extra benefit. Also remember, DO NOT try to reach this pulse rate on the first day or even the first week of starting your program. Only work out until you become winded, then stop. With each passing day and with patience you will eventually reach your effective workout level.

Look for ways to increase your physical activity in everyday life: walk the dog; use the stairs rather than the elevator; park near the end of the parking lot so you have to walk farther; when you are walking somewhere, walk faster and with purpose rather than with a slow, leisurely gait. You may have to substitute time for exercise by not sitting in front of the TV, which in most cases is unproductive time anyway. Maybe you could place your stationary bike in front of the TV. I've been known to read while on a stationary bike, which helped my mind and body at the same time. You may also plan a meditative walk on a daily basis. With a little creative thought I'm sure you will find a way once you are committed to health. Experts agree that 20 minutes of exercise at least three times a week is all that is needed for a healthy body. Surely everyone can find one hour spread across a week somewhere in their busy schedules.

The energy issue is really a result of not sticking with the program. It's the most common result of someone who, instead of following the advice of the experts to start off slow and maintain persistence, wants immediate results. When they don't achieve their
hoped-for image within a week or two, they give up. It is impossible to achieve results overnight and the sooner you accept that fact, the more successful you will be. All good things come to those who are persistent and patient.

Earlier we indicated that to lose more than one or two pounds per week is folly and unhealthy. When you expect to achieve your goals immediately you are setting yourself up for failure. I'm sure you have heard of the person who decides to start an exercise program, signs up with a gym and immediately starts on a strenuous exercise program of one to two hours. The results are that after a couple of days they are so sore they can't get out of bed. No wonder they stop the program out of necessity and the desire to reduce the pain. Their goals are discarded as unworkable or bad for them. When exercise is painful you should drop back to a level that your conditioning indicates is proper. There is a lot of error in following the advice "no pain, no gain." While that was useful for boot camp recruits, that made for a painful experience and few of them continued the program after their required time was up. As everyone knows, nature will rapidly de-condition you if you don't play by her rules. It doesn't take long, as anyone who has ever been in good physical condition and then decided to take a holiday can tell you. Then they must endure the pain all over again. The successful programs are those that become a life-long experience, an integral part of your normal schedule. As you slowly maintain your program your energy will increase to meet your conditioning needs. See the example of the student described below.

While joining a gym or health club may be nice, it is not necessary to meet your exercise goals. Many people spend thousands of dollars on exercise equipment that collects dust in a corner after the first month. The problem is not with the equipment but with the motivation. If you can afford it and have determined that you are going to follow through with your program then I recommend you invest in good equipment that can be used to exercise all the body muscles A stationary bike and a piece of rubber to stretch the muscles will do wonders. We all have the equipment needed to begin an exercise program. All you need is your shoes and a little motivation. It has been shown that walking at a brisk gait will provide the exercise benefit of running without the impact problems on your skeletal system or excessive stress on your heart.

In July 2000 the Trevose Behavior Modification Program released the results of an obesity study that began in 1970. This was a long-term study to determine how to lose large amounts of weight and keep it off over the long haul. To participate you had to be at least

100 pounds over your ideal weight and maintain the program or you were removed from it within the first year. After five years 10% of the participants stayed within 95% of their original weight goals. This program encourages gradual weight loss through good nutrition, constant calorie counting, exercise, weekly weighing and support groups. This study is significant because it covers a long time frame and proves the theory that gradual weight loss, even though the starting condition is over 100 pounds overweight, is the best way to set goals. Isn't this what weight management experts have advocated for decades?

I used to work as a medic for a juvenile detention program in the desert of Nevada. It was a last-chance program for juvenile delinquents before they would be placed in the correctional system. It was based on an athletic program and completing their schooling. For those who successfully completed the program, 99% stayed out of law enforcement involvement, which is a very good record. I remember one fifteen-year-old who came to the program weighing in at 316 pounds. He couldn't do one push up and had difficulty getting up off the ground. The boys had to run a timed three-mile course twice a day in order to maintain the standard. This boy had difficulty walking 100 feet. The program wouldn't allow him to quit so he had to keep trying. He took a lot longer than most of the students but he finally was able to maintain the standard exercise protocol after about a year and a half. He took over three years to complete the mandated program, which was his court sentence. During his stay his parents never came to visit but when he graduated they came to pick him up and they did not recognized him at 195 pounds and well over six feet tall. He loved to eat and because he required a lot of calories to maintain the physical demands of the program we let him eat whatever he liked, but no bread or desserts. He could eat whatever he could pile on the plate but could not go back for seconds. I had to keep my eye on him as he tried to sneak in seconds and dessert whenever he thought he could get away with it. Near his graduation he finally became proud of his accomplishments and the way he looked so that I'm confident he probably continued his conditioning at home. I was extremely pleased with the results of what exercise and restricted caloric intake could accomplish and it made a believer out of me.

BODY:

"If it is possible thus to control by the power of will the vital functions in the body of another person it must be possible also to control these functions in our own bodies. We can learn to dominate and regulate the vital activities and the life currents in our bodies so that they will do their work intelligently and serenely even under the stress of illness or danger."

Henry Lindlahr, M.D.

Exercise can have a positive effect on a body system that is often misunderstood and rarely appreciated. It is also important in the physiology of weight management. That system is your lymphatic system, which is a vital part of your body's detox and immune response. It is very similar to the circulatory system except it doesn't move blood around nor does it have a pumping mechanism to move the fluid. The lymphatic vessels move hormones and excess fluids from the tissues of the body, fluids that are not returned to the blood supply. So the lymphatic system removes toxins and other waste from the tissues, thereby helping to clean out and purify the fluids in the body. Since the lymphatic vessels have no pump to move the fluids they require the muscles of the body to move the fluids through the system. Hence, it is important to maintain an exercise program that will keep the muscles healthy and move the fluids along rather than allowing the toxins to stagnate and build up deposits. Many of the hormones that are so important to our organs use the pathways of the lymphatic vessels to move about the body and accomplish their missions. With poor muscle tone the movement is slowed and becomes inefficient, leading to illness and overweight. Now you know why it takes so long to get into shape and why you can get out of shape so fast when you stop exercising. The lymph channels are not clear and it takes time to get the stale fluids moving again. So even the lowly lymphatic system will thank you if you maintain a healthy condition. Exercise and movement has a beneficial effect on our lymphatic system that is one of the major health issues of a sedentary lifestyle.

MIND:

"If the mind could not exert such absolute control over the cells and cell groups, it would be impossible for us to walk, talk, write, dodge danger, etc. with almost automatic ease."
Henry Lindlahr, M.D.

You can exercise your mind while you exercise your body. The whole body/mind/spirit is exercised at the same time. What a beautiful opportunity to practice holistic techniques in one event: a three-for-one program. Often, while riding on the stationary bike I've used that time to do some reading or meditating. Since the bike is stationary you can even daydream. Close your eyes and transport yourself to your secret place and thereby activate the relaxation response and all its stress releases that are possible. You can do the same thing during a yoga posture. If you are walking or running you could use a walkman to play some self-improvement tapes, or maybe some tapes you make yourself that will implant positive affirmations and suggestions into your subconscious mind as your body is getting its workout You could use this time to mentally work on a problem you may currently be wrestling with. This time could also be used to work on your ideal body image and visualize the new you. There are so many constructive mental activities you can do while your body is getting its workout. The point is to put your mind to some constructive, positive purpose.

SPIRIT:

"Don't try to solve the mysteries of life with your mind. You can't apply logic and reason and ordinary linear thought systems to this stuff. Stop it. Go to your heart. Get into your feelings. Don't look for answers; seek instead wisdom. Wisdom and answers are not necessarily the same thing."
Holographic Universe
Michael Talbot

There is an ancient exercise program that is at least 4,000 years old and can be practiced by the elderly, those with stiff, creaky muscles and bones, the ill and disabled, and the young with developing bodies. It is called Yoga. The practice has now spread to an international forum performed by all age groups and cultures, and in the western world the practice is based on Hatha Yoga. Yoga comes from the Sanskrit word for union. It is a gentle exercise system that benefits the whole person in the union of body, mind, and spirit. This union is accomplished by practicing correct breathing, postural exercises and meditation. Yoga must be practiced regularly to be effective. The breathing exercises encourage us to expand our lungs, increase our energy and vitality, and improve circulation - just the benefits we are seeking in an exercise program. Yoga is safe for anyone to practice but until you become proficient you should seek the advice and support of a professional yoga instructor. Should you have any current health challenges, be sure to inform the instructor so they can be sure to suggest the proper postures that will not impact your medical conditions. Yoga has been successful at dealing with a long list of problems so everyone can benefit from its practice – even into old age. There are many classes going on in most cities so it shouldn't be difficult to find one in your neighborhood.

What a wonderful program and one that will impact all the phases of body/mind/spirit and still be a great addition to your weight management goals. If you are not into developing a body-builder's physique, alternating between days of walking and then yoga will work miracles for your body no matter what it looks like now.

CHAPTER VIII
The Nature of Spirit/Soul

LESSON: An Explanation of Terms
"I recognize the wide variety of ways to understand and access the God
of my understanding. There are many paths to the spirit/soul, each
directed to the one universal Spirit/God; we share
a common bond of divinity; we are diverse in our beliefs. "
The Wellness Doc

The Ancient Hawaiians had a wisdom of spirituality that is resurfacing on the planet today, whose tenets form the basis of what I like to describe as the New Spirituality – A Return of Nature. Their belief system is called KAHUNA (*ka* meaning "to keep" and *huna* meaning "secret"). It taught that everything and everyone in nature is a manifestation of MANNA (eternal energy). This ancient Polynesian wisdom says that we and everything (organic and inorganic) are part of a living energy system that evolved from one source. Everything is related and will always be inseparable. The Nature Cure doctors of 250 years ago believed and demonstrated that each of us is born with a vital energy force that is the real healing source for all the ills of nature. Their medicine works to allow this energy force to do what it was designed to do as it heals the human and animal spirit.

Einstein spent his life searching for that fundamental law of nature that can be expressed in a unified theory of everything, but was not successful. Today as the complex principles of quantum physics become more fully understood and the laws of nature unfold in its beauty, we are experiencing an evolution in spiritual/soul understanding. Doctors Gary E. R. Schwartz, PhD and Linda G.S. Russek, PhD in their book, *The Living Energy Universe,* have a wonderful name for this: "Spirit-Assisted Medicine." In this lesson we will explore the nature of this vital energy force, Spirit, soul, God, which is required for our healings. Too often we look at this as the protected field of our religious leaders rather than the vibrant and living entity that is within each of us and accessible to all of us if we but call on it. Healing cannot be accomplished by our medical doctors without this vital force. Nor can our spiritual leaders heal without the acknowledgement of the laws of nature that allow the vital force to do its work.

Because of the depth of this area of inquiry it requires an understanding of terms that may seem foreign to some of you. To be sure we are all on the same wavelength let's start with a few definitions. Throughout this chapter we will be using a number of technical concepts which I won't be defining within the text in order to make the reading easier. However, for your use the explanations of the following terms can be found in the glossary at the back of this book: Spirit, Soul, Bell's Theorem, Vital Force, Energy, Religion, Sectarianism, Denominations, Karma, Reincarnation, Angels, God, The Physician Within, Ghost, the Hierarchy of Souls, Death.

BODY:

"Pain in life is especially insidious because it can block the healing power of our souls, especially if we have not accepted what is happening to us as a preordained trial. Yet, throughout life our karma is designed so that each trial will not be too great for us to endure."
Journey of Souls by Michael Newton, Ph.D.

We now know that our bodies are composed of energy at the cellular level. Einstein has also shown us that mass and energy are different manifestations of the same force. We are, in reality, little energy machines. As long as we are fed a diet of good healthy foods our machines will work for 100 + years. Before the soul chooses a body for it to incarnate in, careful consideration is given to the attributes of the physical body. The purpose is to experience the many lessons to be learned so that we may evolve through higher dimensions within the spirit world. Only through living and surviving many different challenges in the physical world is our soul's purpose strengthened, because the real lessons in life are learned from recognizing and overcoming the challenges of being human. It is only through these lessons that a soul can evolve in the spiritual world and ascend to a higher plane so that physical incarnation is no longer required. All these spirits and souls are

170

parts of the electromagnetic spectrum that have different properties depending on the frequency of their being.

Let's review the physics of this electromagnetic wave force that plays such an important part in the divine plan. As we increase in our energy frequencies we are elevated to higher and higher energy levels within the spirit world. This process can be explained through the workings of quantum physics. The various types of electromagnetic waves were predicted by Maxwell's equations and were later verified by instruments and observation. Electromagnetic waves carry energy in space and can transfer energy to any object in their path. Starting from the long wavelengths with the lower frequencies (the distance between the waves and is measured in Hz – Hertz), we have Radio Waves (approx. $10^5 – 10^8$ Hz) > Microwaves (approx. $10^9 – 10^{11}$ Hz) > Infrared (approx. $10^{11}- 10^{15}$ Hz) > Visible Light. Visible light is composed of a number of frequencies around 10^{15} Hz and is the only electromagnetic force visible to the human eyes. This small range of light is seen by us as seven basic colors > Ultraviolet (approx. $10^{-15} – 10^{18}$ Hz) > X-rays (approx. $10^{16} – 10^{20}$ Hz) > Gamma rays (approx. $10^{18} – 10^{23}$ Hz). As you can see there is some overlapping of the frequencies. Why is this important to us relative to the spirit world? I believe the frequencies of the souls/spirits in the next world are somewhere between $10^{25} - 10^{\infty}$ Hz. I see nothing in the science to indicate this is not possible. Our understanding of the electromagnetic spectrum is based on only the observations and measurements we can make. The scientific foundation for the spiritual world is easily made if we can extend the laws of physics beyond that which we understand in this three-dimensional world we are confined within. The thought of spirits being a higher frequency is easy to understand and makes perfect sense when viewed in this manner.

MIND:
"I consider human ideas and imagination as emanating from the soul, which provides a catalyst for the human brain."
Journeys of the Soul
Michael Newton, Ph.D.

Telepathy is the technique used by spirits to communicate among themselves. Spirits are not physical and hence do not have vocal cords, so they talk with their minds. They are resonating at a higher frequency than the spirits in physical form (us!) that are stuck in this three-dimensional world. How many times have you had a thought or inspiration that popped into your head and had nothing to do with what you were doing or thinking at the time? I'm convinced these intuitive moments come from the spirit world and it is important that I stop to ponder the meanings or lessons. It is when we disregard such moments that the future doesn't turn out as productive as it could. Often such inspiration comes at a time when we are stumped on a problem or debating a direction in our lives. I know it is my spiritual family trying to direct me in the right path and they ask only to be recognized. Be aware of when those moments come; take the lesson that is being communicated under serious consideration.

This is why I know that at the moment of transition of the spirit, our minds also go with the spirit. They form the memory bank of the spirit. Science has now shown that the mind is not physically located in the brain; holographically it is a part of every living cell in our bodies. I refer you to Bell's Theorem (see glossary) as the foundation for that idea. You can also go to your Serenity Place and ask for the spiritual family member by name to come to you; then close your conscious mind so you will not be analytical at this time and wait. They will come to you – they are just waiting to be asked. I have talked (telepathically) with my brother and parents with this method. Since you will be communicating telepathically, don't be concerned if, when you ask a question, the answer does not come back verbally as if you were involved in a human conversation. You can ask a question verbally and the spirit will hear or be aware of the question but you will probably receive your answer intuitively. Sometimes the environmental conditions will change and force a decision in some unexpected direction. Just wait patiently and the answer will come. It may come while you are fully awake and involved in something else at the moment. It may be a flash of insight. If something comes into your mind that has nothing to do with what you are thinking about at the moment – write it down so you won't lose it then give it serious consideration. My experience indicates that these events are the ways our spirit guides communicate with us. Gary Zukav says, "Intuition is the voice of the nonphysical world."

Here is a scary thought. Because your family members who have already made their transitions are omnipresent, all-knowing spiritual beings, they no longer think or understand as we humans do. Love and forgiveness are a part of their nature now. Hence, while they see all that you do, they realize that you are still a mortal being who is still evolving and learning. Your challenges and problems are lessons you are still learning but they are standing by to help you with the correct choices. If you don't listen, they know you will have another chance to experience the lesson and you are forgiven your fault this time around. Your spirits have already made peace with their own transgressions from their physical lives and they DO NOT JUDGE. Judgment is a human emotion and one we should constantly be on guard to avoid. Hypnosis and meditation are the modalities used to access your spiritual family. The technique is to clear your mind and wait for the inspiration to come to you. It will happen with practice. Don't give up if it seems hard or even impossible at first.

SPIRIT:
"It has been hypothesized by many spiritual/energy healers that people who live their lives with Love generate a higher frequency of energy/vibration than people who live their lives with hate."
The Living Energy Universe
Linda G.S Russek, Ph.D.

One of the natural characteristics of spirits is in the way they communicate both among themselves and with us. This brings up the question of psychics and mediums. Personally I believe the world is full of fraud in these two areas of inquiry but I also believe there are legitimate souls working to help us in this physical plane. The problem is that we must distinguish between the fraudulent and the sincere. I'm not sure I can separate the truth from fiction in this field but there has been some scientific inquiry into this area that has convinced me of the possibility of real communication between humans and the spirit world. I know this because I've personally communicated with my spirit guides and family members. I also recognize that intuition is the form in which my spirit/soul communicates with me; all I need to do is become receptive to their efforts. Dreams are a form of communication and often require experience to delve into their interpretation. I'm not an expert in that area, however, there are people who are.

These methods of communication suggest a modern day analogy: our trusty cell phones that have become a necessity to everyone. As we carry our cell phones with us imagine all the energy waves that are constantly bombarding our bodies from calls to and from other people's cell phones. We are not aware of these attempts to communicate because they are the right frequency for someone else's phone, not ours. However, when the proper frequency comes it resonates with our receiver, the cell phone, we answer and open the communication channel. The one vibration we are tuned in to gets answered among all the millions of other vibrations that are not recognized. So it is with our attempts at spiritual communication.

LESSON: Our Spiritual Essence

"To know ourselves spiritually means understanding why we joined in life with the soul of parents, siblings, spouses, and close friends. There is usually some karmic purpose for receiving pain or pleasure from someone close to us. Remember along with learning our own lessons we come to Earth to play a part in the drama of others' lessons as well."
Journey of Souls
Michael Newton, Ph.D.

As we begin our odyssey into the realm of spirituality we must learn to step outside of the three-dimensional world we can touch, feel, see and hear. Most humans can believe only in things they can verify with their senses. Because this is their belief system they easily become fearful when they observe phenomena they don't understand. When we realize there is a purpose to everything, there is no need to become fearful when things go bump in the dark. FEAR (False Events Appearing Real) does not exist in reality; when you truly believe in a personal, protective God nothing can happen to you that is not for your highest good. We can infer the existence of non-physical phenomena by the results. Creation is the result of God – there can be no other explanation as we look around us. We can't see energy but we can infer its existence by observing the manifestation of energy in the form of matter. Science can prove the existence of energy by inference and

174

mathematics. Have you ever seen gravity? Yet we know it exists as an invisible force, inferring its existence by mathematics. We all know gravity is there; we believe in it and its power, so why not extend that thinking a little further to the world of the invisible spirits? Therefore, let's resolve to step out of our three-dimensional box and see another world that is evolving all around us, a world of spiritual beings who are waiting for us to open up the channels to their world so they can communicate with us.

Another difficult concept we humans invented that does not exist in the spirit world is that of TIME. Linear time is a concept we invented to help explain the physical world of our existence. Since time is a linear concept, the spirit world is omnipresent (everywhere at once) and time is a space measurement, there can be no time or space in the spirit world. This is why a universe that spans 13.7 billion light years is incomprehensible to us but the spirit can traverse it in the blink of an eye. (See Big Bang in the glossary) This is why there is no such thing in the spirit world as zero time. Science has tried to reach T=0 to fully define the origin of the universe and has reached back to T^{-42} seconds (that's a one with 42 zeros and a decimal point in front of it). I submit we will never understand T^0 until we, too, make our transition home. So let's remember that in the spirit world we have no use for the clock that controls our earthly lives.

In an article in the December 2003 issue of *Spirituality & Health* (see how important time is to us to stay legally/politically correct?) Louise Danielle Palmer defines spirituality as "an inner resource that helps us make sense of a world that is sometimes cruel and usually chaotic."

I agree, if we view the world as cruel and chaotic then we are not functioning from the true source of our spirituality. When I finally understood and grasped the Law of Karma (see glossary) then I understood life and my purpose in it. It was the proof that everything happens for the best. It is the basic law by which the principle of apocatastasis (see glossary) is a living philosophy in my life. When we look at life as an apocatastasis experience then all the events in our life become crystal clear and we are face-to-face with the Law of Karma. Incidentally, I don't believe the Law of Karma says we will come back to earth in some lower life form. I believe we come to this earthly existence to learn and thereby experience the lessons the soul needs for its continued evolution to higher planes (frequencies) in the spirit world. This conforms to logic as the only reason for life and is intimately intertwined with the Law of Karma. We sit at the apex where the laws of nature, apocatastasis and karma meet and determine who we really are.

When things are going well for us it is easy to believe these laws are at work in our lives. However, when things are not going so well we want to blame someone else or even the devil for our misfortunes. Our soul understands what is happening as a part of the divine plan which it created, even if we don't want to believe it is a part of the divine plan. It is for us to search for the lesson in each of life's experiences and then grow from that experience. In the next lesson we will take up the question of why bad things happen to good people, why people are born with disabilities and why small children who have not experienced life yet should be called back home as a result of disease or accident.

BODY:

"A national survey in the US indicated 90% of both males and females were dissatisfied with the physical characteristics of their bodies. This is the power of conscious amnesia. Much unhappiness is created by society stereotyping an ideal appearance. Yet this too is part of a soul's lesson plan."
Journey of Souls
Michael Newton, Ph.D.

After tens of thousands of regressions to the time between lives, Dr. Newton has developed a very detailed description of the spirit world and its functions within the divine plan. Dr. Newton was a skeptic, the typical reaction of a scientist until he was overwhelmed by the regressions that slipped into the spirit world. The similarity of these experiences forced him to accept a new paradigm. Other researchers in the field, such as Sylvia Browne, confirmed these basic visions. My grandmother taught me many of the same ideas and Dr. Newton's book, *Destiny of Souls,* helped me crystallize my beliefs. In the lesson we learned earlier that everything happens for a purpose and so it is with the choice of our earthly body. Many people are unhappy with the bodies they feel they were given. The grass always seems to be greener on the other side. Since we chose this body and our parents while our soul was planning the next incarnation, there must have been a reason. Wouldn't it be better to find meaning in this body rather than spend a lifetime in regret because we are envious of someone else's body? Each of us has talents and beauties and the odds are they are not represented in our external body form. Beauty isn't necessarily a skill or talent.

An interesting theory that has always attracted me and makes perfect sense is that the spirit that was incarnated in this body and mind of Bill Warner is only a fraction of the soul which is still located in the spirit world. This idea is all in keeping with Bell's Theorem. When I was born and my spirit was manifested in this life there was also another birth somewhere else that was also a part of the soul of this earthly Bill Warner, another duplicate of me in a different environment but with the same divine plan. We both had the same plan but were put in different circumstances which meant our experiences might be the same but handled differently. The universal divine plan says we all have free choice so what each of our spirits experiences may approach life's lessons from a different viewpoint and thereby have an entirely different experience that results from the same event. The common soul will still learn the lessons, only from two offspring making different choices.

The truth is there are no good or bad, successful or unsuccessful lives, just different lessons along our spiritual odyssey. This is referred to as parallel lives and explains why, in regression, we sometimes find lives that overlap in our time frame but have no contradiction in reality for the soul. The scientific proof that these duplicate lives are possible is found in the physics of the hologram (see glossary). What a great day it will be when my soul mate and I return home and compare notes. I wouldn't be surprised if it turned out to be someone I have had relationships with in this life. It is interesting to realize when we do a past life survey how, in each life there are significant persons who are also significant in current life. In my case I've discovered my father, mother, brother and even my old scoutmaster in previous lives, not in the same relationships but they're there, nonetheless.

It is a comfort to me to know my spiritual family will be with me for an eternity as we walk the spiritual path together. In fact, most of the persons you are involved with today have crossed your path somewhere in the past. Once you learn to access your Akashic Records (see glossary) you can find out how these spirits are interwoven with you. As we continue this journey we will explain the "book of life" in more detail. In the meantime, just be thankful for the body and physical characteristics you now have. Look for the good rather than the blemishes.

MIND:

"It is difficult to tell a newly-injured person trying to cope with physical disablement that he or she has an opportunity to advance at a faster rate than those of us with healthy bodies and minds. This knowledge must come through self-discovery."
Journey of Souls
Michael Newton, Ph.D.

Many of us, in our search for the meaning of life and what our divine plan is, say we are on a quest to understand the Mind of God. There was even a book written by that title which is a search for the Mind of God within the principles of the scientific method. Since it is difficult to manipulate the parameters of the spiritual mind, we must accept the nature of the spiritual mind on faith tempered with logic. The mind is the mechanism the spirit uses to communicate with and influence the body. The mind is not located within the brain, as most people believe, but a holographic part/whole of it is located within each cell of our body. Modern research has shown this to be the case. Each cell contains all the memories of all our incarnations as well as the memories of this current life. Drs. Schwartz and Russek, in their book *The Living Energy Universe,* develop the controversial theory that energy carries the memories of the universe and that energy is stored in every atom and cell in the universe. They ask the questions, "Is it possible that everything that has happened in the universe is ultimately stored everywhere in the universe?" and "Is this universal living memory what we mean by the evolving Mind of God?" It seems to me that life would be more productive if we learned to read the Mind of God rather than pursue the scientific logic to prove the answer to that question is "Yes."

We have mentioned the strange phenomenon when ideas "pop" into your mind. They always seem to come at a time that has no relationship to the thoughts preceding or following the current thinking. This special time is what I call the Mind of God. It is not for me to understand it, just to recognize it and give it serious consideration. Many great scientific discoveries have come to the scientists involved this way, when they were working on other problems. It is said that the theory of quantum physics and its quanta of energy came to Max Planck in an intuitive inspiration. This idea led to Bell's Theorem and the crumbling of the cosmic speed limit as it applies to the spirit.

Why should I worry about reading the Mind of God? All we need to do is have faith in the Mind of God. The spiritual part of me already understands the principles. It just says, "Listen up, dummy, you don't need to understand – just listen." So in our meditations, let's just listen for the Mind of God. My grandmother called it the still small voice within.

SPIRIT:
"A soul is largely influenced by cultural conditions and events, as well as by the participants in these events, during a span of chronological time."
Journey of Souls
Michael Newton, Ph.D.

Dr. Herbert Benson, M.D. of the Mind/Body Medical Institute has hypothesized that the placebo effect (see glossary) is a natural bodily reaction similar to the fight-or-flight response triggered by the master gland, the hypothalamus. The placebo effect rejuvenates and restores the body's innate unconscious evolutionary reaction to establish health and well-being whenever it is in danger. The placebo is not just a dummy pill but must involve the mind and the patient's belief that the pill will work. In addition, the physician must also believe in the power of the medicine to heal, otherwise it is doomed to failure. The existence of the placebo effect was established when an anesthesiologist, Henry Knowles Beecher at Massachusetts General Hospital, postulated that 30% of a drug's or doctor's treatment success was due to the patient's expectation of a successful outcome. This became know as the placebo effect and the drug companies have been trying to prove their products can beat the placebo effect ever since, often without much success. Let me quote from Dr. Benson when he established the neurochemistry link to the placebo effect: "The placebo effect is triggered by nitric oxide made by the sympathetic bundles of the brain producing a flow of endorphins, cannabinoids, and estrogens with various effects: getting rid of pain, reducing inflammation, killing viruses and bacteria, and even defending us against chronic conditions."

Dr. Benson claims the development of the relaxation response as a significant healer of disease. He wrote a wellness book outlining the benefits of relaxation. While I agree with the benefits of the relaxation technique, it is not new; its origins began with the Egyptian Sleep Temples centuries ago. This is also the technique used by hypnotherapists for over 200 years. Dr. Benson says, "The relaxation technique response brought about through prayer or meditation is thought to trigger the same healing effect which would explain the relation between spiritual states of higher consciousness and the qualities of healthful living often associated with the goals of spiritual practice." Thus, another M.D. has asserted the value of spirituality in healing, albeit through the back door.

The theologian Matthew Fox says, "We need to create a Creation Spirituality, a spirituality that is as creative and evolving as the universe itself, a spirituality that not only keeps up with science but informs and inspires it as well." Spirituality as taught by our spiritual institutions has failed to demonstrate and inspire universal Love and acceptance of each other. From ancient times the old Masters like Buddha and Jesus, right up to the modern Masters like the Dalai Lama and Mother Theresa, have failed to convince us of our common purpose and the Laws of Love which the soul needs for universal peace and life.

LESSON: A Description of the Spirit World

"The lesson we must learn from human relationships is accepting people for who they are without expecting our happiness to be totally dependent upon anyone."
Journey of Souls
Michael Newton, Ph.D.

In the last lesson we discussed aspects which are part of our earthly experience but are not a part of the spirit world: time, space and the law of karma. In this lesson let's look into the spirit world of my understanding. Much of my belief system comes from the work done by many hypnotherapist who have, by accident or design, regressed persons to the time between lives. One such author/scientist, Dr. Michael Newton, has made a special study of the spirit world. A common thread among all these reports is that the descriptions of the spirit world are very similar, even with persons whose belief systems were contrary to what they found when they made the journey. I have not read or met a single person who has had an out-of-body experience or intentionally regressed to the period between lives who has not benefited by an epiphany due to the information they received. As we discuss this realm of the spirit, keep in mind that we are talking about a dimension of energy and space that we do not experience here on earth. You will have to step out of the box of comfort your common sense tells you about reality. Also, remember that spirit is a frequency of energy that is beyond the known frequencies of the electromagnetic spectrum.

Within the spirit world we find different levels of souls, from young ones to older souls. The spirit functions at higher frequency levels as one becomes older and more evolved, with the one spirit - God - sitting at the apex of the hierarchy, waiting for all of us to come to him/her. A spirit is omnipresent, omniscient, omnipotent and a member of a soul circle comprised of 10 to 20 souls, all in the same stage of their evolution. We often refer to these as our soulmates. Each travels the same path we do as we evolve from one life to the next. Many of them are important to us in our current lives and are often in some relationship to us in our lives on earth. Take any member of your biological family and it would be a safe bet that you have been the father, mother and sibling of that person in other lives, usually still working on the issues left unfinished before. In previous lives we have all been both the murderer and victim; each has a lesson to teach, and if we don't learn it we will be forced to repeat it again.

The goal of this family of souls is to evolve up the hierarchy together. They help each other to learn the lessons that each needs. The objective is to evolve to the point that you no longer need these earthly experiences. As you evolve to higher spiritual levels you become a teacher and leader for the other, younger souls. Occasionally you may choose to come to earth or another physical dimension (another cosmic body) in order to demonstrate to other souls how to choose the proper pathway of life. These older souls are manifested in the persons we call Masters because of their extensive earthly experiences. At any point in time there are many such Masters currently on earth, performing their divine plan to help everyone come into oneness with God.

When you make your transition from this earthly life you can be assured that your family soul circle members will be there to welcome you home and get you through that difficult time of adjustment until you feel comfortable with your spiritual family again.

Then comes the critical life review period with the support of your other spiritual family members. This time may be a year decades or centuries – there is no linear time as we know it on earth in the spirit world. It is now that you can enjoy the happiness and joy you receive from your family as it is placed in your memory bank. It is after the review, when you understand all the decisions you made in life and how they impacted your divine life plan, that you can begin to plan your next incarnation. You make this new divine plan in cooperation with the other family members so you can continue your evolution. This 'time' in the spirit world is really a time we don't want to leave, but we recognize that incarnating in an earthly body is important in order to experience all the lessons. Only on a physical plane can we experience the challenges that are necessary to become a spiritual teacher and Master, the ultimate destiny of every soul.

When we come to earth for our next incarnation it is with a divine plan in our soul. However, there is a catch - each of us also has complete freedom to choose while in the physical dimensions. Every day of our lives we are given challenges by our creator and an opportunity to make the proper choice either to grow in spiritual consciousness or to regress. No one can stand still. This is why we are responsible for our actions; we made the plan, we made the choices, hence we also must accept the consequences of those choices. There is no true good or bad. We experience every event in our own lives as either good or bad when we interpret the consequences of our actions on earth. You cannot experience good unless you have experienced bad. There is no such thing as bad until you have experienced it. There is no such thing as fast unless you have experienced slow. Everything in life is relative and its reality is dependent upon our interpretation. There is no reality except that which we give it, the understanding of which determines the experiences in our perceived world.

There is no good or bad – there just is! Hence, if there is no good or bad, by extension there can be no judgment. God does not judge our actions and neither should we judge the actions of our fellow humans. What we may consider good or bad in another person is probably not what they consider good or bad. So how can bad things happen to good people? Who determines who is good or bad? In whose eyes are they the way they are? These judgments are only important to the one who is experiencing the event. After all, he developed the plan and made the choices that brought him to this point in his life. Only he can determine how he relates to those consequences. So really, bad things do not happen to good people. What happens has already been planned.

How can this apply to the small child whose life is cut short before it really gets started? In the first place, there is nothing sad about a soul that is called home. That soul had planned the incarnation for a reason that we are not privileged to understand. The pain of the passing of a loved one only exists in those who are left behind, not for the one called home. It is very possible that such a transition may be a part of the karma (see glossary) of the parents. There may be a lesson for them to learn.

Those who are born with disabilities or deformities are another issue. Some people believe that God couldn't produce such an imperfect child, while for others it seems to be a wasted life. Others have turned their infirmities into positive rewarding lives. Remember, their incarnation was planned before returning to the challenge of being earthbound. A disability at birth could well be a karmic act for the parents or the child to learn how to create a positive, rewarding life out of a negative start. Helen Keller is probably one of the best-known examples of someone who turned a negative into a positive.

BODY:
"By the time you are five years of age most of the old you, the previous lifetime you, will have dropped in favor of a more appropriate you of the current time and space."
Your Book of Life, Accessing the Akashic Records
Gary Bonnell

When I was boy I was told that St. Peter stood at the pearly gates with a big book which he would consult when I presented myself at the gates of heaven. I was told that if I had any bad notations in the big book next to my name then I would be turned away. What a horrible thing for a Sunday school teacher to tell a small boy. Later I learned that God does not make judgments or punish his children. I eventually realized that we developed these stories in order to keep the faithful in line through fear. It didn't take long for my parents to convince me that my God was a loving God and didn't condemn or punish his children (me). They helped me understand that there is no one to keep score. My beliefs and actions in life will determine how I fare. Life after death is a nice place to go and the only judgment will be my own evaluation as I review what I did while I was incarnated. My parents helped me realized that if I want to be happy I can save the self-incriminations because I am responsible for the bricks I lay for my house in heaven. If I want a big house I need a lot of good bricks with which to build it.

It was much later, somewhere around thirty years ago, that I learned there really is a big book in the spirit world. It is called the Book of Life or the Akashic Record (see glossary). I also learned that everyone has access to this book anytime they want. By consulting the records of our incarnations in this book we can positively react to the challenges and pressures of life with the confidence of one who is fully aware of his/her soul's purpose. We are able to respond to life naturally without fear of the past, present or future. We are able to understand and remember past life events in terms of their influence on our current life experiences. This ability helps us to release our fears and then grow from our life experiences. Gary Bonnell says in *Your Book of Life,* "If we remember that it is our response to events that determines the outcomes we remain sovereign souls." We are therefore responsible for all the events in our lives because of our responses to the events. In fact, death is a response to life, not an event in life. If we can remember this truism then we can continue to grow as spiritual beings.

The Akashic Record is the recording of all the actions we have made in our past and current lives. We add to the record every second of the day by our responses to events. The record is a historical compilation of events but a non-judgmental recording of them. In addition to our personal records, all the responses from the beginning of time everywhere in the universe are also recorded. When we are making our between-life assessments and plans we rely heavily upon the Akashic Records as we make adjustments to our divine plan.

The earliest known historical evidence for the Akashic Records is from Tibet around 7500 BCE. It is believed that the awareness of the Akashic Records predates this ancient time but when oral traditions are the method of recording history it becomes difficult to establish the reality of the events. In spite of this drawback, these events are not lost to history and are still accessible to our collective souls.

Each and every being within the universe is a part of the Collective Mind of the Universe. Our personal records are one cell within the Collective Mind of the Universe. All we need to do is know how to access them. It is like having an active library card at your local library.

MIND:
"Everyone accesses the Akashic unconsciously through intuitive feelings, sudden urges, vivid dreams, inspirations, spiritual insights or just plain gut feelings."
Your Book of Life: Accessing the Akashic Records
Gary Bonnell

We do not need to wait until our own transition in order to see into our personal record. As the quote above indicates, we do it unconsciously every moment of our existence. The trick is to realize that these moments of insight and inspiration are coming from the Akashic Records. It is wise to pay attention.

Your Book of Life is a single cell within the Akashic Records that shares its information with the Collective Mind. Your Book of Life is also available to those able to access the data. There is nothing wrong with this because in the spirit world there are no private agendas to worry about. There is only Love for all souls. There are conditions and protocols for accessing the Records which you can learn if you wish to delve deeper into the mysteries. As we move from the micro of life to the macro of spirit WE ARE ALL ONE. We are also all one in this physical plane, whether we like it or not. Yes, we are all keepers of our brothers and sisters. The more we demonstrate this truism of life the further we are along our spiritual path. If you could look at the chronology of your record you would notice a steady improvement in your soul's evolution from a primitive to a highly-developed spiritual being.

Linear time is a function of the human mind. In an earlier lesson we said that in the spirit world we must have a different concept of time. Linear time as we know it exists only in the Collective Human Mind; it is manifest within the cellular portion of the mind

186

and the physical body. However, the Collective Animal Mind, Collective Plant Mind and Collective Mineral Mind are not aware of linear time, as their consciousness exists in simultaneous time. As you delve into the Akashic Records you will need to become familiar with the difference between linear and simultaneous time because different records are expressed in one or the other of the time references. Simultaneous time is past, present, and future expressed as one. This is difficult for most humans to grasp but is important as you read the records. As you begin to realize that the spirit exists in a world of omnipresence, it isn't too difficult to understand that simultaneous time can be possible.

A friend of mine told me that when her daughter was 2 or 3, she regularly made comments about events in her past lives, but she always made those comments in the present tense. Somewhere around age 4 or 5 she changed to past tense. My friend feels that over time her daughter became more firmly entrenched in the apparent linear time of the physical world. Isn't it sad that most parents discourage their children from believing in such revelations instead of encouraging them to learn when these recalled events come forth so easily? Some past life investigators specialize in children under 6 years of age because their past memories are often so vivid and honest. Just think what we as parents could learn and what our children could learn about who they were and why they were born if they were encouraged to develop rather than suppress these memories. One of the leading researcher in children past lives is Ian Stevenson, M.D. if you are interested in investigating the case studies of these subjects.

SPIRIT:

> *"All the cosmos is a single substance of which we are a part.*
> *God is not an external manifestation but everything that is."*
> Spinoza

Stepping outside of the box is not as difficult as it seems at first. Everyone has the intuitive power to access his personal Book of Life. Your spirit is in and out of the Records often; you simply need to expand your consciousness in order to open the channels of communication. Rest assured that your soul will welcome the opportunity to reveal all the mysteries that have been a part of you over so many eons.

If you are motivated to pursue reading your own personal Akashic Record then with a little effort, study, and patience you, too can look and comprehend your record. Just think what wonders this information will provide to solve many of the challenges you may be facing today. Gary Bonnell's book is an excellent starting point for beginners in their search. The first half of the book explains in detail the Akashic Record and what to expect when you delve into your personal record. If the brief discussion of Time above seems confusing to you, Gary devotes a number of pages to helping you understand Time as it relates to consciousness. To help you develop the skills required to access your record he includes a number of different techniques you can choose from as well as the detailed scripts you can use to access your journey into the records. With some patience and practice you will soon be able to access your record without external mechanical aids. Gary Bonnell can be reached at the following postal address: c/o Richman Rose Publishing, 2295 Towne Lake Parkway, Ste. 116-306 Woodstock, GA 30189-5520. The publishers of his book can be reached at the following email: RRose8@earthlink.net. *Your Book of Life: Accessing the Akashic Records* can be purchased in book form; it is also available in audiotape sets. Good luck on your adventure! If you care to share your journey, we welcome e-mails of your experiences, and with your permission we would love to publish your adventure.

LESSON: The Physician Within

"Where there is doubt also restore faith; where there is indifference, also sow love; where there is injury, also grant pardon; where there is darkness, also command light; where there is despair, also impart hope; where there is sadness, also bring joy. Do not seek so much to be consoled, as to console; to be understood, as to understand; To be loved, as to love, for it is in giving that we receive. And it is in receiving that God shares creation with us."
St. Francis of Assisi

The water cycle in nature is an excellent analogy of the spiritual aspect of the soul. At its lowest temperature and energy-free frequency water is a solid mass. We call it ice or snow. As the energy frequency increases, water takes on its common state of a liquid. It then is able to provide hydration for our bodies and become involved in almost every useful chemical reaction on earth in order to sustain life. It is a vital ingredient to all life forms on earth. It becomes the standard by which all other chemicals are compared in many physical characteristics (for instance, distilled water has a specific gravity of 1). I think we can all agree we would not be alive if it were not for water. As water's energy frequency increases and the subsequent increase in temperature continues, water changes its form again to a gas or vapor. Many times this vapor is invisible, as is the spirit/soul. As water vapor ascends toward the heavens, the reduced atmospheric pressure results in decreased energy frequency and thus lowered temperature, causing the vapor to change back into a liquid or solid we call rain or snow, which falls back to earth again to start the cycle all over.

Isn't that description of a natural law just like our own eternal spiritual being? Our bodies die but our spirits move on through the spiritual realm and back to earth in another physical being, to start the cycle of eternal life all over again. The Law of Conservation of Energy (see glossary) is confirmed as active and real in our personal lives as well. The trilogy of life/transition/rebirth illustrates there is no such thing as death, a word that should be eliminated from our vocabulary. The spirit is eternal and isn't affected by the physical body. It can reside in the body but is not a permanent part of the physical life cycle, only a common thread among the parts.

Consider another analogy from the field of chemistry. Take denatured water and add some salt, another substance very important to life. Shake and allow the salt to completely dissolve into the water. The resulting substance has different properties from either of the individual starting substances. If you put the solution out in the sunlight and remove any sealing top to the container so the essence can escape, in time we notice the water

189

has gone, leaving behind the salt crystals. The crystals are considered waste and are disposed of or in some instances reused if we are environmentally correct. But the water has become invisible again only to return later. The essence of the water has not changed when it starts a new cycle over again. The crystals are a representation of our physical bodies and the water is a representation of our spiritual essence, to be reborn in another chemical mixture that will perform some needed purpose. When that purpose is completed it is disposed of, as the spiritual essence is released intact to again participate in another purpose. Recycling is found in most of nature's laws so why should we humans or animals be any different? Once I recognized this life cycle, the meaning of life became crystal clear to me. The essence of God is manifest in all of nature and its beauty is profound. The ancient Hawaiians knew that all things are connected and saw no need to separate them; everything is a condition of spirit.

Native Hawaiian spirituality is called Huna (in western terms) and their principles are important to us because they offer a spiritual practice based on the unity of mind, spirit and body. The Hawaiians weren't affected by the separation of science and religion during the European Renaissance. Their principle philosophy is concerned with the three selves and their relationship to one another. This allows the person to gain personal balance, optimum health and general well being. The Huna religion doesn't teach a judgmental or revengeful god but allows you to manage your own energy to direct its power to serve your needs and desires. You can transform your life and realize the peace that is always within you. The three selves are represented by: loving yourself, nurturing other beings and the land, and living in harmony with all of life. So why did we Christians think we had to send missionaries to change their belief system? What we did was bring entropy into their peaceful lives. If you would like to investigate this form of spirituality in more detail they have a very educational and informative website: http://www.hunalife.org.

What do I mean by returning to nature? If I have a health challenge I do not think of drugs and surgery as the solution to the problem. I first access the Physician Within and then search for the solution to the problem in the homeopathic and herbal remedies. They are faster acting, you will know within the first day if you have the correct remedy, than the chemical solutions of drugs plus with none of the side effects or toxins. And they usually provide a complete cure rather than just the easing of the symptoms.

BODY:

"The Universe adores you for it knows your broadest intentions."
Jerry & Esther Hicks

My Mom was an angel on earth. I know to many of you, you would say the same thing about your Mom. Yes, I believe in angels just as my Mom did, but she lived her angelic life. I'm sure your Mom was the same to you but I can't leave the spirit lesson without commenting on my Mom. My mom collected angels of all kinds from everywhere in the world. She received her first angel from her cousin the day I was born, a beautiful blue glass one. Deciding on presents for her was easy. She was called the angel lady of St. Petersburg, Florida because she had a collection of a couple thousand angels which she displayed to the citizens every Christmas holiday. The citizens of St. Petersburg gave her that title, but I call her an angel because that's what she was. She is still my guardian angel watching over me from on high. I never heard her say a cross word to or about anyone. She loved all whom she met and my brother and I knew we were surrounded in love when we walked into our parents' home. Yes, I had a blessed upbringing for which I am truly thankful. Mom touched many people's lives and made the world a better place for her having been here. The quote above surely applies to my Mom as she did cast Love upon the Universe.

I also know she is an angel in her heavenly home watching over me as I'm still experiencing the lessons of life. My Grandmother, Dad, Brother, and Mom are all gathered together in the challenging work of trying to keep my life on its divine path. So do I believe in angels? Most definitely yes! They are always watching over me and will communicate with me to help solve challenges. All I have to do is be willing to listen, just as I did while they were here on earth. There are no bad angels or ghosts in my life. I just won't let them in. I'm confident that all the good things that happen in my life are because of their benevolent care.

Your life can go just as smoothly if you open it up to your guardian angel. You have one, you know. Isn't it time you introduced yourself to them? Remember, you came to earth with good intentions and your spiritual guides are waiting to help you to realize them.

MIND:
"You are choosing your thoughts, your emotions are guiding you."
Jerry & Esther Hicks

As a man thinketh, so is he. I believe most of my readers will agree with that ancient truth. We know that what we think will manifest itself in action and then in our reality. Within the body and spirit our thoughts are expressed as emotions. I think our emotions are a function of our spiritual essence, an expression of our spiritual beliefs. Emotion may be defined as spirit made manifest. This is why I've always believed that violence on TV or any other public media is not a healthy situation. It's why many health promoters advocate a 'news fast' – a complete escape from the negativity of the world so the spirit/soul can be refreshed with the positive aspects of life. It's no wonder depression is so universal in our modern world. Depression is negativity taking control of your spirit, resulting in a loss of positive emotions and will to live. Our emotions are an expression of how we feel about a particular event or life in general.

These are important concepts regarding how we can control the way we view and experience life. By understanding how this process works we can truly become the architect of our own lives. Once we realize that bad things happen to us as a result of our emotional state and that the genesis of our emotions is in our thoughts, each of the factors in this flow equation is completely under our personal control.

THOUGHTS > EMOTIONS = GOOD OR BAD EVENTS

Try this experiment for yourself. Think about some bad or depressing event or something negative someone said to you. Contemplate for a few moments on the thought or emotion that created that unpleasant situation. See and feel the negative event as you experienced it. Observe how you feel and what happens to your pulse rate and blood pressure. Now say to yourself, FORGET THIS! I DON'T NEED TO FEEL LIKE THIS! Turn your thoughts to a pleasant or happy event, maybe something a person said to you today that made you happy or thankful to be alive. As you can feel and experience this positive emotion, notice how your other emotions and outlook on life improve. You have just proved to yourself that you can control your emotions through your thoughts. Be aware that good, positive emotions open the gateway for your spirit to come into your body and mind. For a couple of decades now, hundreds of scientific studies have demonstrated that laughter always improves the emotions and becomes a vital aspect of healing, including healing that emotional disease we call depression. And it doesn't cost anything for the medication (laughter).

SPIRIT:

> *"We are spiritual beings having a human experience,*
> *not human beings trying to have a spiritual experience."*
> Dr. Wayne Dyer

To accept the truth that you are a spiritual being logically leads to the only possible conclusion: that everlasting life is your divine legacy. The beauty of the divine plan is that everlasting life means we will never die. Death by definition means that our spirit/soul has left the body vehicle it used during the current incarnation in order to express its divine essence. That's why I try never to use the words death or die in my vocabulary. They have no meaning because when my spirit is finished with this body it will leave it and become transformed into my eternal spiritual body. Hence, as long as I've accomplished my divine goals in life, my transition is the opportunity to rejoin my spiritual/soul family. When all my lessons have been learned and my experiences completed then I can stay in my spiritual home for an eternity.

The basic emotional problem facing human beings with the transition of the spirit is the fear of what is on the other side. The beauty of the model I've presented in this lesson is that you can be sure the time (remember there is no time beyond this three-dimensional sphere) spent with your soul family is one our spirits welcome and anticipate with joy. The reason I try to stay away from funerals is because it should be a rejoicing occasion for the one who has passed yet there is so much unhappiness present. Isn't that unhappiness an emotion that results from the fear of being left behind and the attendant loneliness? Isn't that fearful emotion an expression of selfishness instead of expressing joy for the deceased who has returned home? One's transition should be a celebration of a life of one who has contributed and produced joy for their family. Our divine life's plan was made before we were born so we realize the deceased's spirit was a willing participant in this transition to a higher dimension. We should experience joy rather than sadness. The only transition I can think about that was not planned was one resulting from suicide. Such a situation is a cop-out from the lessons of life. It's like the child who quits school because he hasn't learned his lessons or doesn't want to accept the responsibility of life.

CHAPTER IX

God's Perfect Creation: You

LESSON: You Are What You Eat

"Although man might build a better mousetrap, nature always seems to build a better mouse."
Author Unknown

When I realized that everything in life happens for a purpose I became aware I was responsible for any condition in my life. Then the floodgates opened and my life took on a new meaning. I knew I was made in God's image and therefore a spiritual being traveling in a unique piece of equipment called a body.

My body was created perfect in every way – there may be some features I'm not happy with, but that's my problem in perception. My job is to take the gift of life and preserve and protect it for the duration of whatever time God has allotted for me to learn my lessons. For every challenge sent our way, God has already programmed the defense measures we need. This can be seen in the wonderful workings of our bodies. So often when I contemplate how the body works I'm often amazed at the magnificent machinery that can automatically correct any challenge that comes our way.

The natural healing ability of our physical body is an example. How could God have built such a complex but perfectly functioning piece of equipment? No matter how advanced the computers become, our engineers cannot improve on the human and animal brain. When we try to improve on Mother Nature we get into deep trouble. Every day there are numerous commercials on TV exhorting the benefits of some prescription drug to ease our conditions, but each one has a shopping cart full of side effects that are often worse than the original condition. Our bodies are a product of Mother Nature so why not let Mother Nature do the healing?

When God created us the plan was perfect but because we are living systems we have to abide by the Laws God created in physics and biochemistry. Hence, our living cells have to respire and as a result, the by-product of respiration is the waste that is generated. In the macro example of our living system we experience that fundamental law every time we take a life-giving breath. We breathe in air and extract the useable elements like oxygen, water vapor, and a few other trace elements. We then exhale the carbon dioxide (which the plants use) and other toxins. When we consume food we extract the valuable nutrients and expel the waste products which are organic in nature. Nature recycles them in the water cycle and the soil. Our microcellular body does the same thing. The problem lies in the waste products of cellular metabolism. We call this waste molecule a FREE RADICAL.

These free radicals are chemically active and are searching for an oxygen molecule to steal or absorb in order to become neutral or in balance. Because they are active it is difficult for the body to excrete them with our waste products through the usual channels. Free radicals find the oxygen atoms from among our cells. When a free radical attacks a healthy cell and steals an oxygen atom in order to be in balance, then the attacked cell is no longer healthy because it is no longer in balance itself. As it continues to be bombarded by free radicals it becomes more and more unhealthy, eventually resulting in sickness and disease. When the free radical and its family find a juicy feast in a DNA molecule and it destroys one of the complex chains, then we are really in trouble. This is a big problem because the cell will replicate a damaged DNA that alters our body code. As this process continues we fall further into ill health.

The early pioneering Nature Doctors were aware of this process and the cause of disease, though they didn't have the modern name of free radicals. They called the damaging molecules 'toxins,' which they obviously were. The "how" behind the science hadn't yet been discovered.

Why would God create such a damaging process to the health of his offspring? This is a challenge for all living systems. As in all of God's creations he did provide a defensive mechanism in the foods we eat to sustain life. We call these miracle foods fruits and vegetables. They are the foods your wise mother told you to eat. The ingredient in these foods that protect us is called an anti-oxidant molecule.

As long as we animals and humans lived close to our food supply and the population stayed within the limits of the food supply everything was working according to God's plan. However, we started violating natural laws and we created many more sources of free radicals because we tried to improve on Mother Nature. Cellular metabolism is the one source for free radicals built into our living systems by Nature but we created many more sources, i.e., tobacco, stress, sunlight, pesticides, pollution, airline travel, medications, processed foods, food additives, X-rays, exercise, chlorine in treated water, mercury in seafood and teeth fillings, and many more body stressors. As you can see, in an attempt to sustain wellness we have actually created the conditions for ill-health.

There are only two sources for the miracle antioxidant molecules: they are found only in fruits and vegetables and natural supplements. Most people feel if they consume a healthy level of fruits and vegetables they don't need supplementation to maintain health. But how do you know for sure? The usual way to determine the level of antioxidants in your body is by a blood test. The downside to this measurement is it shows the level at the time the blood is drawn within the circulation system. Since your blood is a dynamic system it is constantly changing. Hence, we need a protocol to measure the antioxidants in the tissues of the body in order to get a more accurate measurement. A piece of equipment called the Bio-Photonic Scanner does just that. It measures the antioxidant level in the tissues with a non-invasive, rapid, painless beam of light aimed at the fatty tissues in the hand. In the validation of this equipment they found that the average level in millions of people measured throughout the world was only 19,000. To be considered at a good healthy level you should have 30,000. And if you are doing a good job with the proper supplementation you could reach into the 50,000's.

I was first introduced to the scanner at a health conference back in 2003. One of the lecturers at this conference was Elson Haas, M.D., the author of the textbook *Staying Healthy with Nutrition.*[4] He advocates the use of supplementation but he personally does not use supplements as he gets his antioxidants from food only. He volunteered to be scanned and we were excited as this would show if he practiced what he preached. He scored 84,000, which was the highest I've seen in my two years conducting scanning in over 300 persons. It proved that if you know what you are doing and are consistent in your program you can maintain health with diet alone. Most people in the world can't do that.

An interesting fact that should provide motivation for the smokers is that ONE cigarette will load your body system with 10^{15} free radical molecules. It takes a lot of antioxidant molecules to overcome that level of toxins. This is why even light smokers have a difficult time staying healthy and why smoking is guaranteed to take years off of your life.

If you want to investigate the scanner in more detail just Google "Bio-Photonic Scanner" to learn about the science and how you, too can find out your score.

BODY:

"Most people do not consume an optimal amount of vitamins by diet alone. It appears prudent for all adults to take vitamin supplements."
Journal of the American Medical Association 2002; 287:3127-3129

In January 2002 the AMA finally admitted what many of us have known all along – that a nutritious diet of fruits and vegetable plus supplementation will keep us healthy without the damaging effects of invasive surgery and potent drugs. I'm sure they came to this conclusion because our food supply is continuing to deteriorate. Last month I attended a conference where one of the speakers said,

198

"In five years 100% of America's food supply will be genetically produced." That is really a tragedy because then there will be no vitamins and minerals in our food supply. Then even our supplements will have to be imported. And we do this to ourselves in the name of the advancement of science.

Let's move forward a few years and in 2009 100% of our corn supply is GMO produced (unless you can find truly organic crops) and much of our produce is now raised with the aid of Monsanto's GMO seed. Every couple of years there is another effort to pass legislation to adopt CODEX in the U.S. as it is already adopted in the EU. While it did not completely eliminate over-the-counter sale of vitamins and minerals, it established maximum allowable concentrations so low that all therapeutic values are lost. Of course, Big Pharma and Big Agri are the forces behind these efforts and only massive letter writing to our legislatures keeps these forces at bay.

Since it is the objective of a good life to be happy and healthy at the time of our transition, prevention of sickness and disease has to begin early. This is the purpose for our advocacy and teachings at Cosmos Institute of Life's Transitions.

Since we now know that vitamins and minerals are required to maintain our health, let's take a look at the vitamins that our bodies need every day to survive. Following is a partial list of some of the vitamins and what they do for us. Vitamins are natural substances found in living materials such as plants.[4] They must be obtained via the food chain or supplementation. They are usually not produced by the body, though there are a few instances in which vitamins are produced as a result of the body's natural biochemistry.

Vitamin A - Prevents skin disorders, enhances the immune system, maintains and repairs mucous membranes, and is important to the functioning of certain organs.

Vitamin B Complex – Enhances memory, concentration, judgment, learning ability, and prevents mental deterioration. Helps in maintaining the health of the nerves and is active in anti-stress mechanisms.

Vitamin C – Protects against the harmful effects of pollution, helps to prevent cancer, protects against infection and enhances immunity. Reduces levels of bad cholesterol while increasing levels of good cholesterol. Promotes the healing of wounds and bruises. Helps maintain growth of teeth, bones, gums, ligaments, and blood vessels. Aids in the production of anti-stress hormones. Required for at least 300 metabolic functions in the body. Works in conjunction with Vitamin E and beta-carotene to enhance the anti-oxidant properties of all these vitamins. Since the supplies of vitamin C are immediately consumed and excesses are flushed from the system, supplementation needs to be in divided doses at least twice per day. This is one of the problems with one-a-day supplementation.

Vitamin D – Supports bone and tooth formation, muscle function, and thyroid gland function and it is necessary for the absorption and use of the minerals calcium and phosphorus. Involved in the regulation of the heart beat. Important in the prevention and treatment of breast and colon cancer, osteoarthritis, osteoporosis, and hypocalcemia. It is important to realize that the absorption of vitamin D can be interfered with by the use of some cholesterol-lowering drugs, antacids and steroid hormone drugs.

Vitamin E - Important in the prevention of cancer and cardiovascular disease. Retards aging, improves circulation, reduces blood pressure, reduces scarring from wounds, necessary for tissue repair. Aids in prevention of PMS, cataracts, and tissue healing. Promotes healthy skin and hair. Protects against approximately eighty (80) diseases. Essential for normal cell structure. Involved in the formation of red blood cells. Protects the lungs against injury from air pollution and helps preserve tissues.

These vitamins are by no means all the necessary vitamins to life, but are included in a group called antioxidants that are a part of our vital defense mechanism .

MIND:
"A deficiency of a vitamin or mineral will cause a body part to malfunction and eventually break down – and like dominos other body parts will follow."
Prescription for Nutritional Healing
James F. Balch, M.D.

Lifestyle change is really a function of your mind. Before you can make positive changes in your life your subconscious must convince your conscious mind that it is the best thing to do. Most of the time this is a hard sell for the subconscious to accomplish. Our conscious mind has trained the body that what it has been doing all along is both worthwhile and pleasurable and doesn't need changing. You must first be motivated to change because how you envision the future or the pathways of your goals will determine your success. From this motivation the subconscious mind can take action. You get this motivation from knowledge and experience in which you can visualize what you want to happen.

When I was a child we learned a technique they called "treasure mapping" in Sunday School. When you have a goal or sincere desire you want to work toward, you can either draw or cut out pictures that describe what that goal is then paste those images on a piece of paper and put the paper where you can see it everyday. Usually this is on the bathroom mirror or dresser. Many times we carried the pictures in our wallets or books so we could look at them frequently during the day. Today we call this technique visualization. So the psychological community took what I thought was a Warner concept and found the science behind it. Because any good book on healing, stress reduction, or psychology advocates it.

In one of the many books I have on the subject in my library, visualization is defined as the conscious use of your imagination in order to create attractive and positive images that can be used to heal or change aspects of your life. All children have an active and productive imagination. Why? I guess because they are closer to heaven. Then as their life unfolds, we adults teach them that imagination is childish and not appropriate for adults to involve themselves in. If you wanted to relax or get your anger under positive control you can mentally visualize transporting yourself to your own secret place. Your secret place (or some call it "my serenity place") is a place which represents peace, calm, quiet, beautiful, and all those other adjectives that calm your mind and soul. Wonderful things happen to you while you are in your secret place.

While watching the 2010 winter Olympics it was interesting to note that the U.S. female skier Lindsey Vonn had drawn a picture of herself as a downhill racer when she was very young and kept it up on her bedroom wall so she could visualize her dream daily. She won the gold at 20 years old.

SPIRIT:
"When you fear illness and disease you will manifest the very condition you fear in your life. So acknowledge daily the beauty of health your life is manifesting and God will provide what you seek."
The Wellness Doc

As time passes and the oxidative damage to cells continues, the toxins begin to build faster than our defenses can be marshaled to defeat them. But, the spirit still has some armored forces to throw into the battle. I call this the Physician Within, a powerful force within you that can help to clear the battlefield of the enemies' dead and wounded. To access this Physician Within we need only to communicate with our spiritual self. We can do this by utilizing the power of visualization and meditation. Cleaning up our body is a common objective for this type of spiritual access. It is really a form of self-hypnosis, which is the technique used to access your spiritual self. Since illness and disease are the result of free radical damage to healthy cells then all we need to do is eliminate unhealthy cells from our body and allow the healthy cells to grow and propagate.

Let me give you a brief summary of how the technique works and those of you familiar with meditation should have no difficulty practicing it.

202

Become very comfortable, arms and legs uncrossed, and take a few deep slow breaths. Close your eyes. You may want to travel in your imagination to your secret place if you have already established one. Now when you are completely relaxed roll your eyes up (under your closed eyelids) so you can see above your head. Notice that very white soft cloud floating just above your head. It is the most beautiful white cloud you have ever seen. It is also a healing cloud, leaving behind a healing energy to protect the healthy cells. In order for it to do its healing work we must allow it into our bodies so it surrounds each cell and tissue as it travels throughout the body. Now allow the cloud to float down and fill up your head while you visualize the white cloud turning darker as it absorbs the dead and unhealthy cells. Allow it to continue through the throat and down each of the arms and when it reaches the fingertips it fills up the space in both arms until it spills over into the chest cavity. Down into the abdominal cavity, the genital organs, and into each leg. When it reaches the toes, spigots at the ends of each toe and finger allow the dark cloud to escape and float into outer space, leaving behind a clean and healthy body. If you have any health challenges during this meditation just let the cloud spend some extra with that organ as it passes through the whole body.

You can perform this exercise upon waking in the morning and just before going to sleep at night. I've also used the visualization of lying at the edge of the waterline on a beach. As the wave comes ashore it washes over the body, absorbing the unhealthy cells and taking them with the wave as it recedes. The next wave repeats the process.

LESSON: The Mineral World
"Your journey has brought you to the sunset of your life over the sea of your creation."
The Secrets & Mysteries of Hawaii
Pila of Hawaii

To most people the idea of becoming a vegetarian has no appeal whatsoever. Are not fruits and vegetables a sustainable and renewable life-form in which humans are not required to intervene in order to utilize them as a food source? The other two sources of food are the killing of live animals, including fish, and dairy products from the milk of female animals. I must admit that I enjoyed a good meat product as long as I didn't have to do the killing. I used to partake of this food frequently in my earlier years. However, with increasing knowledge and a desire to insure a healthy longevity I have consciously attempted to significantly reduce my consumption of animal products. I haven't converted yet to a total vegan but would like to become one as I'm sure it is the healthiest diet available.

For me personally I have never tried to hunt, as the only purpose I can see for hunting or fishing is to kill a life form that I never enjoyed. I recognize that there are people who can live with this activity. In fact I've eaten the deer meat killed by my son or brother-in-law without complaint or debate. I don't know what I would do if faced with having to kill in defense or if I were starving. Fortunately for me, God has not placed me in the position to have to make that decision. Assuming it was OK with God to utilize live animals and fish sources for food, such sources passed on their life energy to us. We still know that utilizing range animals for food is healthier than from industrially-farmed animals. Here again is an example of trying to manipulate Mother Nature and in the process creating unnatural health challenges for us. Because we add hormones and antibiotics to the animals in order to increase production we have changed the natural benefits to our detriment. These hormones and antibiotics are then consumed by us and become toxins to our bodies. In addition to the toxins we add to the animals their food source is also controlled with additives and poisons which we also consume increasing the free radical and biochemistry of our own biology.

Then what has happened to our fish population? It has become contaminated by the poisons from the chemistry we have allowed into the waters that is their home environment. We then ingest these toxins when we eat the fish. Mercury is an example of a poison that has become widespread and particularly dangerous to us. In fact, the majority of our water supply has become so contaminated that the only possible safe source of water for our

204

consumption is by filtration of the water before utilizing it. Even the chlorine used to disinfect the water is a significant free radical coursing through our bodies, attacking our healthy cells.

FRUITS:

Nature's perfect food (irrespective of the dairy industry's claim) is fruit, as it can be eaten right from the tree. Fruits are natural and very healthy. They have a very high water content just like our bodies. Their seeds contain the sparks of life to insure the continuation of the species. Fruits contain a wide variety of important vitamins and minerals and are low in fats and high in fiber - an excellent combination for a healthy human life cycle. They are low in calories and sodium, making them the natural weight management staple. Most fruits are sweet and their colors cover all the colors of the spectrum, again an example of natural law at work. One of fruit's most pleasing attributes is that they contain natural sugars, making them sweet without the higher calorie refined sugar contained in processed food. Eating whole fruits is a better choice for our sweet tooth and supplies just the proper amount of sweetness we require.

The juice made from the whole fruit is an excellent choice of beverage as it contains many of the vitamins and minerals the body requires, much more than do alternative beverages. This is particularly true of the soft drinks which have been so popular and yet such a common cause of the obesity problems in the world today. Fruit juices are also an excellent choice in the detoxification and cleansing process so vital to maintaining health. Fruits can be frozen fresh shortly after harvesting without losing much of their nutrients.

VEGETABLES:

Vegetables are the other ideal food. Fresh vegetables are the life force provided by nature to sustain the life force within our own bodies. The Latin root for vegetable means "to enliven or animate." Just as with fruits, vegetables are high in water content and the necessary vitamins and minerals, and low in fat and protein. Because we often cook or boil vegetables some of their nutrient value is lost in the process, so the closer to the natural state the vegetable is when consumed, the better the nutrient value. It is best to thoroughly wash the vegetable in order to remove the environmental toxins that can be on the exterior. Consuming organic vegetables is a better solution if you are able to obtain them. So fresh and raw is the ideal in the preparation of vegetables. If you have difficulty in digesting raw vegetables the next best choice is to lightly steam them. Vegetables can also be frozen without too much loss of nutrients and can be stored for quite a long time.

Juicing of vegetables is an excellent technique to obtain a healthy beverage used in a liquid detoxification or cleaning program. Vegetable juice is an excellent source for obtaining antioxidants because juices are easily and quickly absorbed by the body.

BODY:

"The next generation of Americans may be the first to have a shorter lifespan than their parents chiefly because of their growing weight and sedentary lifestyle."
New Balance Foundation Advertisement

In the last lesson we discussed some of the important vitamins. In this lesson we will take on some of the important minerals.[4]

MOLYBDENUM:

This mineral is one of the lesser known, probably because its importance was only recently discovered. It is considered one of our essential minerals. Unfortunately it is scarce in our soils and hence in our foods. Deficiencies are usually caused by crop overproduction and soil depletion. In the soil molybdenum serves as a catalyst to the nitrogen-fixing process and its decreased presence can cause a reduction in plant growth. Because of these conditions and its recognition as an essential mineral to life and growth, the concern about deficiencies in our diets has generated more effort in recent years. This mineral is important to the enzyme systems of our bodies. These systems play a vital role in uric acid formation, iron utilization, the metabolism of

206

carbohydrates and sulfite detoxification processes. Molybdenum may play a role in the prevention of some cancers because of its action in the prevention of known carcinogen compounds, but research hasn't yet established this connection. Like most trace minerals its beneficial quantities are in a narrow range of daily intakes and hence there may be higher levels that are toxic to humans. This also means molybdenum deficiencies are common. Since our food source of molybdenum is decreased due to industrial farming practices, proper supplementation becomes extremely important. In humans and animals deficiencies may cause weight loss, visual problems, rapid heart and breathing rates, lowered levels of consciousness and reduced life span. It is recommended that our source for molybdenum be from a multi-vitamin that also contains some copper because the body loses some copper in natural reactions with molybdenum.

PHOSPHORUS:
Phosphorus is the second most common mineral in our body after Calcium. Our bodies spend a significant effort to keep a balance between the competing minerals of phosphorus and calcium. It is necessary to keep their ratio in homeostasis for good health. Phosphorus is found in all of our cells and is a part of many biochemical reactions. It is vital to energy production and exchange, particularly as it relates to the utilization of carbohydrates and fats and the synthesis of protein. Hence, it is important to bone and tooth growth. There are many other functions of our bodies that require phosphorus. The all-important acid-base balance requires phosphorus. It is used by the muscles, including the heart, to regulate the heartbeat and nerve conductivity. It is used by some of the vitamins in their conversion to the complex, useful compounds required for life. There are no known toxic levels for phosphorus, however, high levels of dietary sources of phosphorus from meats, soft drinks and prepackaged convenience foods can interfere with calcium metabolism, causing a serious calcium deficiency. Could this possibly be a cause for the high rate of osteoporosis from our love affair with these fast food sources? Because of its prevalence in our diets, phosphorus deficiency is rare but when present may cause symptoms of anorexia, weakness, weight loss, irritability, anxiety, weak bones,

stiff joints, skin disease, tooth decay and arthritis. Its prevalence in our foods generally means that in a multi-vitamin the concentration of phosphorus is low and in seniors' supplements the ratio to calcium is usually low (1:5 compared with the usual 1:1).

SILICON:

Silicon is low on the periodic table (13). It is the most abundant mineral in the earth's crust and as such is not only abundant but important to us as an essential nutrient. Silicon is found in our bones, blood vessels, tendons and cartilage, adding strength to these tissues. This nutrient represents about 0.05 percent of our body weight. Because it is so prevalent in the soil it is a significant component of our food. It may also play a part in the transmission of energy within the body just as it does in its original rock quartz crystals. Some scientists believe silicon plays a part in ridding the body of stored toxins and promoting the elasticity of the skin and thus may be thought of as an anti-aging mineral. "Silicea," a homeopathic remedy, is described as functioning as a "microscopic surgeon." It can help the body rid itself of foreign substances such as splinters and abscesses. Some believe silicon can help to heal fractures and plays a role in the prevention of osteoporosis. The studies of the effects of deficiencies and toxicity of this mineral in humans are still on-going. The over-production of crops on our soil without replenishing the lost silicon could cause a reduction in our silicon intake from food. This may result in increases in disease and loss of strength in our tissues.

CALCIUM:

Calcium is the most abundant mineral in the human body and one of the most important. Approximately 98% of the calcium in the body is contained in our bones, about 1% in our teeth and the remaining 1% in other tissues and the circulatory system. Many other nutrients and some hormones are involved in calcium absorption, function, and metabolism. Maintaining a balanced blood calcium level is essential to life, particularly the cardiac functions. Calcium deficiencies are more common in the elderly and postmenopausal women. Poor calcium absorption is a major factor in osteoporosis and is one of the reasons the quality of the mineral source is so important for dietary and supplemental calcium.

Other vitamins and substances are necessary to transport the calcium to the intended needed site in order to effect absorption. Because of the various factors affecting absorption, anywhere from 30 – 80 percent of the calcium the body takes in may be excreted. Excess salt and sugar will also reduce the absorption of calcium. Calcium plays a role in cell division and is essential to blood coagulation. Abnormally high intake of calcium for brief periods is not a problem because excess calcium is usually excreted through the urine and intestines. As you can see, the body's use and toxicity of calcium is very complex. Diet and supplementary concerns should be under the control of a medical or healthcare specialist rather than self-medication. The concentration of this mineral and its small window of availability within the body's biochemistry makes calcium a very important mineral which should be used with professional advice.

COPPER:
Copper has been known as a very important trace mineral for a long time now. Copper is present in all our body tissues in small amounts. The amount of copper in our bodies is approximately 75 - 100 mg, less than the amount in a copper penny. It is a catalyst in the formation of hemoglobin, the molecule that carries oxygen to our cells. It is also involved with respiration, the oxidation of vitamin C and biochemical reactions with Zinc. Being a metal it is a conductor of electricity, making it a vital part of the nervous system's function as well as numerous other biochemical reactions.

The major concern with copper is the narrow line between therapeutic and toxic doses. This means it is easy to avoid deficiencies of copper because it is so widespread in our food sources but with uncontrolled supplementation it is easy to reach toxic levels. The recommended dosage for copper in adults is 2 mg., and lower in children. Excess copper will interfere with the absorption of zinc. Zinc deficiencies can cause a number of serious problems. In dealing with copper or zinc you should enlist the aid of your healthcare provider in making decisions to change your diet or supplementation.

IRON:

Iron is a very important mineral which can affect a number of physical problems. It is found in every cell of the body and is vital to the transportation of oxygen to the body tissues. It is the main mineral that is at the center of the hemoglobin molecule. Deficiencies in iron are more common in women in their reproductive years, requiring at least 18 mg of iron daily because of losses in the menstrual blood. Pregnancy requires increased levels of iron as the fetus needs about 7-8 mg per day. Iron is also stored in the liver, spleen, and bone marrow, where it can be drawn on to supply the body in case of temporary low iron supplies.

There are a number of sources and types of iron, each with different absorption rates, so it is also important to be informed as to the chemical form of the iron we consume. There is a long list of factors that affect iron absorption both positively and negatively. While deficiency of this mineral is more common, there are also toxicity levels for iron overload that may be an individual sensitivity factor. Many different symptoms may arise from iron deficiency; they are too numerous to mention in this venue. Iron is another mineral that you should discuss with your healthcare provider to insure you are maintaining adequate levels of dietary and supplemental iron as well as choosing the proper form for your needs. This is a case where just any iron will not do.

MAGNESIUM:

Magnesium is an essential macromineral as it is involved in several hundred enzymatic reactions dealing with energy and cardiovascular functions. Decreases in magnesium in the diet have been exacerbated with the wide spread use of supplemental Vitamin D and calcium, as well as high dietary phosphorus intakes from refined and processed foods. The drinking of soft water decreases magnesium intake while diuretic drugs cause magnesium loss. Alcohol, caffeine and sugar also decrease magnesium levels. Decreased blood and tissue levels of magnesium have been related

210

to high blood pressure, kidney stones, heart disease and heart attack caused by coronary artery spasms.

Most of our dietary magnesium comes from vegetable sources and seafood. Since the magnesium comes from soil that the vegetables are grown in, the concentration in vegetable products is dependant on the soil and can vary from place to place. The processing of foods prior to consumption can also cause a loss of magnesium.

Magnesium is often thought of as the anti-stress mineral as it is a natural tranquilizer. It relaxes muscles and the gastrointestinal tract. While calcium stimulates muscle contractions, magnesium relaxes muscles. Magnesium is primarily an intracellular nutrient. It activates enzymes that are important for protein and carbohydrate metabolism and is used in DNA production and function. It monitors electrical potential across the cell membranes, allowing nutrients to pass into and out of the cells. It is essential in many metabolic functions such as the production and transfer of energy, muscle contraction and relaxation, nerve conduction and protein synthesis. It also functions as a cofactor to enzymes in many biochemical reactions.

There is a long list of problems that may be helped by magnesium so supplementation is a good consideration as a therapeutic or preventive remedy. Toxicity is relatively uncommon as excesses are usually eliminated in the urine and feces. However, magnesium needs to be taken along with appropriate doses of calcium or overload could be possible with unpleasant results. Magnesium deficiency is fairly common and more likely in people who eat a processed food diet, in people who cook or boil all foods (especially vegetables), in alcoholics, those who drink soft water and those who eat food grown in magnesium-deficient soil. Magnesium absorption is decreased due to burns, serious injuries or surgery and in patients with diabetes and liver disease. In situations where the elimination of magnesium from the body increases, i.e., alcohol use, caffeine intake, excess sugar, excessive sweating or dehydration, or the consumption of diuretics or birth control pills, calcium and magnesium must be kept in balance or a long list of symptoms may occur. Supplements of calcium and magnesium should be taken in a 2:1 ratio, with magnesium one-half the dosage of calcium. Because of all the problems listed above, before changing diets or supplementation you should consult with your healthcare practitioner.

POTASSIUM:

Potassium is very important in the human body, especially in cellular and electrical functions. It is the main positive ion found within the cells. The balance between sodium and potassium is finely tuned and can easily get out of balance if either is deficient or over-consumed. As an example, a high sodium diet (such as modern processed foods) combined with a low potassium intake (from lack of fresh fruits and vegetables) causes vascular volume to increase and tends to elevate the blood pressure. Then doctors may prescribe diuretics that can cause even more potassium loss, exacerbating the underlying problems.

The natural diet of fruits, vegetables and whole grains is rich in potassium and low in sodium, helping to maintain normal blood pressure. The typical modern American diet is therefore counter-productive to maintaining a normal potassium/sodium (salt) balance. When replacing fluids during exercise it is healthier to use orange juice or vegetable juices rather than salt tablets. The kidneys are the regulators of the body's potassium levels, however, alcohol, coffee and other caffeinated drinks, sugar and diuretic drugs cause potassium loss and the lowering of blood potassium levels. Because potassium is highly absorbable in water, it is easily lost in the cooking and processing of foods. It is also rapidly lost with vomiting and diarrhea. Elevations or depletions of potassium can cause problems, as maintaining consistent levels of potassium in the blood and cells is vital to bodily functions. A change in diet and supplement programs should be undertaken with the consultation of your healthcare practitioner.

ZINC:

Zinc has so many important functions and uses that it should be considered when dealing with many of the daily problems encountered in modern life. Zinc depletion in the soil and in food processing makes food lower in zinc levels, which can produce a

212

large number of symptoms due to deficiency in the diet. Zinc is now known to be necessary in the production of more than 100 enzymes and is probably involved in more body functions than any other mineral. To list all of the functions is beyond the scope of this brief summary; suffice it to say that it should always be considered when investigating any body functions.

As with the other minerals, cooking and processing cause a great loss of this vital mineral. Zinc absorption rates within the body will also vary depending on bodily needs and stomach acid concentrations. Alcohol increases the urinary loss of zinc, though the most common route of zinc loss is through the feces. Sweat, stress, burns, surgery and weight loss also increase loss. Zinc lozenges may be an excellent source to help abate any suspected zinc deficiencies. Zinc lozenges are also an excellent treatment for a lowered immunity. They help the immune system by increasing T lymphocyte production and other white blood cell functions.

Zinc is generally non-toxic in amounts less than 150 mg of elemental zinc. Overuse by excessive supplementation may cause some gastrointestinal irritation, nausea or diarrhea. Other possible overuse symptoms may include mild immune suppression, premature heartbeats, dizziness, drowsiness, increased sweating, muscular coordination problems, alcohol intolerance, hallucinations, and anemia. However, these symptoms may mask a copper deficiency. Zinc may interfere with copper absorption so zinc should be taken along with copper. Zinc deficiency is common as we age due to low intakes. Serum levels of zinc do not take into account the stored levels in the tissues so blood tests may not be a perfect indicator of total zinc levels in the body. However, trying elemental lozenges may be an easy way to test if certain symptoms are relieved by increases in supplementation. Again, you should consult your healthcare practitioner when making diet and supplement decisions.

This list is by no means complete; it is just a summary of the common essential minerals. There is a lot more that can be said about each of these minerals. My intent was to indicate the complexity of vitamins and minerals so you won't be too influenced by media hype. Obviously your healthcare practitioner should be a part of your considerations about your health, diet, and supplementation.

MIND:

"When you change the way you look at things – the things you look at change."
Author Unknown

If we are serious about improving our chances for a healthy longevity we must therefore re-evaluate our mental attitudes toward our dietary intake. It is really true that we are what we eat. As we recognize that truism, we come to the full realization that the closer we approach the vegetarian diet (the absence of meats and dairy products) the better will be our long-term health. For most of us that requires a change in our mind-set. This was confirmed to me a few years ago when I met a nice young couple at our annual health fair where I was introducing the Bio-Photonic Scanner to the citizens of Rabun County. As mentioned earlier, the Scanner measures the antioxidants at the tissue level and is an excellent, economical, non-invasive and rapid technique. The woman scored 18,000 and the man scored 74,000. The higher the score, the better is the body's defense mechanism against free radical damage. While both were consciously trying to maintain their health, the woman was obviously concerned about the great difference in their score. She was experiencing some minor chronic health challenges but they were not serious enough to justify the disparities in the score. Then the man told me that he had been juicing each meal for three weeks. Since juicing is an excellent source of antioxidants, his score and health results were significantly improved. The essence of the juiced food is in a liquid form that is readily absorbed by the body; little digestion is required.

I had the opportunity for a follow-up scan on this couple about three months later. They said the husband had quit juicing because the cost/volume benefit seemed to increase beyond their budget. The results were predictable - the husband was only about 10 points higher than his wife. It did prove a point, that if you juice or

214

supplement you must continue the program because in a very short time the free radicals will take control of your health. In order for a juicing-only diet to be completely healthy you would need to consume a wide range of fruits and vegetables in order to obtain the required nutrient amounts needed by your body. So while juicing is an excellent technique it needs to be combined with other techniques in order to provide all the body needs. Likewise, the combined techniques of Body/Mind/Spirit are required for complete health – no one technique alone will work.

So a proper diet needs to begin with a mindset change at the subconscious level in order to accomplish the goal of creating a new and healthier YOU. The one overriding principle is that the closer we are to the source of our natural food the healthier that food will be for us. All "fad" diets violate that principle. Everything in moderation is the secret. Since our bodies build a "craving" for certain food groups we tend to overdo our consumption of certain food groups, thereby creating a toxic buildup. One of the worst examples of this is the sugars. There are a number of different types of sugars which are required by our bodies but because of their prevalence in all our foods we can consciously eliminate them and still receive enough for our cellular energy maintenance. But for anyone who has tried to improve their diet, they know how important it is to have a heart-to-heart talk with their subconscious. This is why self-hypnosis and meditation are such valuable techniques.

SPIRIT:

"All things spring from a spiritual source."
The Wellness Doc

I was always impressed with the idea that plants and fruits were placed on this earth as the food source for humans and animals. They are living entities and as such have a spiritual foundation as their source of power. This spiritual power is transferred to our cellular structure that provides for growth and nurtures our lives. The Native Americans recognized the souls of the animals and plants they killed for their food by giving thanks to the spirits for the sacrifices made by these animals and plants. Don't religious

215

peoples of the earth also give thanks to their creator for the bountiful food provided by their spiritual source?

I believe that since our creator set up the free radical problem as a result of the biochemistry of our bodies, the creator also provided the antioxidant solution in our fruits and vegetables to counteract the toxins thus created. The problems with our food source were created by humans and are being repaid with our ill health.

So juicing provides an excellent way to consume the spiritual essence of our foods quickly and efficiently. As you decide on a juicer please remember that all juicers are not made equally. If you lose much of the benefit (the nutrients) from the food in the process of juicing then the value of the technique will be lost and money spent on the equipment will be wasted. If you compare the nutrient loss of different machines you will notice that you really get what you pay for in juicing equipment. Price, therefore, should not be a consideration in the purchase of your juicer any more than it should be with vitamins, when you might purchase low priced vitamins and not get the nutrients you believe you are paying for. Just as heat will destroy nutrients in our cooking process, so will heat generated by the juicer destroy the value of the juicing process. So while some heat is necessary to extract the juice, look for a juicier that produces the least amount of heat in its operation. Then you will obtain the greatest benefit from the spiritual essences of your food.

LESSON: Supplementation for a Healthy, Nutritious Diet

"The types and forms of nutritional supplements will change during our lives depending on increasing age, gender, health conditions, and food sources. Before starting on any changes to your supplemental program consult your healthcare practitioner first."
The Wellness Doc

When God set the Laws of Creation into motion the plan was perfect – untouched by human hands. As man evolved and the human population grew in number stress was placed on the Divine Plan. Thinking man began to manipulate his environment to suit his needs. He forgot a basic rule of life: If you attempt to change

216

Mother Nature you will lose. You must learn to cooperate with Mother Nature to have a sustainable future. Humans were given free will that works beautifully as long as you follow the rules.

Cracks in our defense mechanism began early as our population outstripped the sustainable food supply. Then we added over-production of arable land, pesticides and other additives to food to increase production and profits, and chemicals to preserve foods as the population moved farther from the source of food production. Increasing the exploitation of productive land for uses other than crop production caused more and more erosion and depletion of water sources. Failure to use adequate crop rotation methods further depleted the soil's natural resources.

In the early history of man when populations were small, as the food supply was consumed the tribes or groups of humans could move to find more. The North American Plains Indians were an example of this. They followed their basic food supply, the buffalo or bison. Their houses were made from the skins of the buffalo so they were easy to erect, dismantle and transport when it was time to move to follow their food sources. When humans found there was food all around them in the form of vegetation and plants and they realized their seeds could be recycled, providing a renewable supply of food, their wanderlust stopped. However, as populations continued to outstrip the available sustainable food they had to find ways to increase production. Thus they created the catch-22 situation outlined in the paragraph above. Our attempts to manipulate the laws of nature create a never ending cycle in order to satisfy this essential basic need – to sustain life - creates the problems facing us today. In a small community specialization of tasks can be productive but as the population again increases, the number of producers of food becomes smaller in relation to the total ability to supply the larger group.

Humans also realized that God provided us with another vital source in the plants – the natural medicines to repair this human machine we call a body. For centuries we looked to the plant world to produce our medicines. But then in the nineteenth century a few people began to realize that if they took the active ingredient God supplied in the plants and mass produced this ingredient, there was a profit to be made. "Poof" - the pharmaceutical industry was born. They also found that the production of synthetic chemicals could increase the food and medicine supply. The problem with this "solution" is that the vital force or spiritual essence (there are many names for this essential ingredient) cannot be reproduced synthetically. To do so would violate God's laws of nature. Our problems and illnesses began from that point. Remember, organic production contains the life force of nature. However, chemical manufacturers have already found ways to skirt the laws so their production falls within the legal definition of organic. When will we learn that the return to nature is the only survival technique allowed by God's plan that has been in effect for 14 billion years?

Humans had learned, but not always applied, the fact that a varied and healthy diet rich in natural ingredients was required for good health. Hence, early health therapies began with a healthy diet with the integration of natural elements as medical therapies. In the 19th century the Nature Doctors used nutritional diets, fasting to cleanse the body, and natural medicines to help the body heal itself. See chapter 4 for a review of these doctors. If you were able to obtain such a program of health you would not need nutritional and medical supplementation. The reality of the world today is that it is nearly impossible to obtain these ingredients directly from your food any more; therefore supplementation is the only available path to have the life you were ordained to experience.

"Macrobiotics" is based on the fundamental belief that everyone should be healthy enough to enjoy life to the fullest. This idea originated in early Tibet and China and is based on the idea that humanity is part of the environment and the cosmos and that our health, both physical and psychological, is determined by our appreciation, connection and intake from the world around us. George Ohsawa in 1945 synthesized all the beliefs of this system and adopted the term "macrobiotics." Ohsawa wrote over 300 books, which dwelt on the importance of a healthy, balanced diet, seasonally and individually adjusted. Remedies and first aid were drawn from Japanese folk medicine and practical guidelines for a healthy lifestyle were drawn from *The Nei Ching,* a comprehensive

218

study of anatomy, physiology and diagnosis. This book also held a cosmological view of human beings, derived from the major world religions.[18]

The macrobiotic philosophy reconfirms the idea of being responsible for your own health, your aspirations and your actions. Ohsawa and the early Chinese doctors made it clear that the job of the physician was to prevent illness rather than fixing things later when they were not working properly. In fact, I found it interesting when I learned that early Chinese physicians were compensated when they treated their patients and kept them well but had to treat them without compensation when they became ill. If that was true in western medicine, our physicians would realize their job was prevention, not treatment, and we would all be better off. There would be no incentive for prescribing a toxin with side effects which only treats symptoms instead of treating the whole body to help it heal itself. As an Emperor said thousands of years ago in the book *Nei Ching*, "It is hardest to treat someone who has become rebellious (sick) – a wise doctor helps those who are well and have not become rebellious."[18]

The problem with diets is they tend to eliminate some important food group or other from your consumption. Since a nutritional diet means consuming ALL of the vital nutrients, then to eliminate any one of them means your body is lacking in some important nutrient, thus leading to a condition called malnutrition. In time death is the only result. So if you are unable to obtain some essential nutrient, you must use supplementation in order to maintain health.

The government has established what it calls a "recommended daily allowance" (RDA) for supplements of vitamins and minerals and for the basic nutritional components carbohydrates, fat and protein. You see these as a percentage on labels of foods, vitamins and minerals. These are the minimal dosages necessary to avoid malnutrition and deficiency diseases. There is a wide difference between avoiding malnutrition and having good health. Of course the government gives no consideration to situations in which therapeutic doses are required or desired.

The amount of the various nutrients listed in the nutrition panel of a supplement label is the amount in a single dose. To calculate the daily dose you must multiply the amount on the label by the number of times you take the supplement per day. Also bear in mind that the dosage on the label may not be the amount your body actually receives – this difference is tempered by your ability to absorb the substance, which depends on your digestive system and the particular ingredients of each supplement.

When dealing with multivitamins a single dose per day, while convenient, may not be healthy and may be wasteful. Taking such a large dose of so many different nutrients all at once is a shock to the system. It is difficult for the body to absorb so many different concentrated nutrients at once, and some nutrients may actually block absorption of others. The body will get rid of many excess vitamins and minerals so if the body doesn't need or can't absorb the full dosage at the time it will excrete the excess. Vitamin C is a perfect example of this so it should be taken in a minimum of at least two dosages daily. When your immune system needs a boost you can supplement with larger doses temporarily. At least one dose of calcium should be taken before bedtime as bone growth and repair is performed during sleep cycles. An added benefit is that calcium is a natural relaxant and can help you sleep.

Ever since the Dietary Supplement Health and Education Act (DSHEA) became law in the United States in 1994 Big Pharma (with the assistance of the FDA) has been trying to get the law repealed. This is a U.S. law that classifies supplements and herbs as foods. Because they are legally classified as foods, no upper limit can be set on their dosage. This law was passed by unanimous Congressional consent. This act has protected the availability of nutritional supplements and herbs sold over the counter in the United States. Without these supplements, those wishing to maintain their health would have to rely solely on the food supply, which is woefully inadequate in most nutrients. This law is also what is keeping CODEX from our shores, while this horrible piece of legislation is eroding the health of the Europeans. See the information on CODEX below. Only a grass roots swell

220

every couple of years keeps DSHEA from being repealed. If the public becomes complacent we may lose that freedom because Big Pharma is very persistent.

If you would like to join the millions who are actively watching over our health freedoms, consider joining the Health Freedom Alliance (www.healthfreedoms.org). Their current demographics are: 3,361,598 members and 12,339,752 petition signatures. They claim to have diverted $17,57,785,510 from the coffers of Big Pharma. This organization is the watchdog over our health freedom.

Safety is the issue many opponents of supplements and herbalism bring up as a reason supplements should be under the control of the FDA. The reliability of the FDA is suspect when it is funded by Big Pharma, so why should we countenance to their council? Let me relate a story from 2004 that dramatizes the safety issue. I call this: "If two is good – three is better."

That saying may apply to a hug but not to anything with the potential to harm. The popular press reported on a tragedy which has happened all too frequently. Because a professional baseball player misused an herbal product and died, the medical examiner took that occasion to launch a crusade of negative indictments against the use of supplements. Steven Bechler of the Baltimore Orioles died after a heatstroke episode, which in itself is often fatal during a workout in the hot Florida sun. The medical examiner blamed a weight loss supplement found in Bechler's stomach as the cause of the tragic incident. The active ingredient in the popular supplement was the popular herb *EPHEDRA*. But we shouldn't indict the whole herbal supplement industry, and particularly a perfectly good herbal remedy, without first looking at what happened and putting the blame where it belongs.

"The fault, dear Brutus, lies not in the stars but in ourselves that we are underlings." This is again a case of not reading the cautions on the label. When will we wake up to the knowledge that the recommended dosage on any drug/herb/vitamin/supplement means just what it says? The fact that something is natural does not automatically make it safe at any dosage. Arsenic and uranium are completely natural but we treat them with the appropriate respect. The same respect should be accorded to all supplements, even the apparently harmless ones. Arsenic is a safe, useful, and important compound when used in its homeopath form, yet deadly otherwise.

Bechler took three pills of his diet supplement rather than the recommended two. But even if he had taken only two pills, he might not have avoided the unfortunate incident because Bechler was aware of two other medical conditions he had that were contraindications for using ephedra. They were possible high blood pressure and liver disease. He had already been warned of potential problems in these two areas as late as two days before his death. In defense of the herb, there were eighteen conditions listed on the label as cautions which potential users should discuss with their doctors before taking the herb. Apparently Bechler chose not to do so. Also included in the ingredients of most weight loss supplements is caffeine. The combination of ephedra and caffeine for someone with high blood pressure is very risky.

The philosophy "if X is good then 2X is twice as good" is not only a fallacy but in many cases could be fatal. The basic principle to carefully follow label directions applies in all walks of life. Consider the case of cleaning compounds where the label says two ounces per gallon of water yet many people just pour from the jug or use the concentrated product to clean. You can bet that all manufacturers will produce a product that will perform at its optimum best. The days of the producers putting silver dollars at the bottom of the drum has long since vanished. Could ephedra be getting a bad rap? Since 1994 only about 100 deaths have been reported from ephedra-based supplements, most of which were weight loss formulations, which generate $161 million in annual sales. In comparison, aspirin and similar drugs account for more than 16,000 deaths each year. I admit the sales of painkillers are much larger than weight loss drugs but so is the incidence of misuse. But isn't any of these deaths a waste? The responsibility for these deaths lies within ourselves.

So let's not throw the baby out with the bath water. There are some important principles to keep in mind when using any drug, supplement, or chemical. If you follow these simple rules religiously you will receive the greatest benefit for your dollar and will live to be a healthy centurion.

These simple rules are as follows:

1. Discuss with your healthcare provider anything you are planning to put into your body. Be honest with them and tell them everything you are using. Many simple-over-the-counter drugs can be very deadly in the wrong combinations.
2. NEVER mix chemicals or drugs unless you are confident you know the reactions.
3. Be sure to read the label or instructions on anything you are putting into your body, including the ingredients and the caution messages. Then follow to the letter all dosage recommendations. If you don't understand the cautions on the label – ASK. Most labels even supply an 800 number.
4. Don't start a supplement program because of media hype. Consult with your healthcare provider first. The supplement might not be right for you. Your healthcare provider can only be of help if you are honest with them.

The American Association of Poison Control Centers published in the Journal of Clinical Toxicology the new 174 page annual report collected by the U.S. National Poison Data System the following conclusion:

THERE WERE ZERO (0) DEATHS CAUSED BY DIETARY SUPPLEMENTS IN 2008.

That should put a fine point on the safety issue of supplements.

There were ZERO deaths in 2008 from multiple vitamins, any individual B, A, C, D, or E or any other vitamin, amino acid or herbal product, blue cohosh, echinacea, ginkgo biloba, ginseng, kava kava, St. John's wort, valerian, yohimbe, Asian medicines, ayurvedic medicines, or any other botanical or homeopathic remedies. ZERO deaths from any mineral supplement. Two children died as a result of medical use of the antacid sodium bicarbonate, and one man died from accidentally drinking sodium hydroxide, a toxic degreaser and drain-opener.

No man, woman, or child died from nutritional supplements!!

Over half of the U.S. population takes daily nutritional supplements. If each of those people took only one single tablet daily, that makes 154,000,000 individual doses per day for a total of over 56 billion doses annually. Since many persons take more than just one vitamin or mineral tablet, actual consumption is considerably higher and the safety of nutritional supplements is insured with such a record.

Hence, if the FDA and news media claim nutritional supplements are allegedly so dangerous, then where are the bodies? If you don't think the media is involved in this cover-up, consider how many of the media even reported that no one died from nutritional supplements. [19]

Since 1962 Big Pharma, and Big Corp, and the rest of the sickness industry has been working with the United Nations, its WHO (World Health Organization) and WTO (World Trade Organization) to establish World Food Code standards throughout the world that will benefit only their own products and exclude all others like nutritional supplements. This code also includes a mandate that all foods be produced by GMO seeds. [20, 21] This regulation was finally enacted, with the U.S. delegates voting for it, last year. What it did for nutritional supplements was to establish the policy that "nutritional supplements are dangerous to people's health." With this policy in mind they set such ultra-low permissible dosages that the supplement has no chance to maintain health. Thereby the services of the sickness industry will become required by everyone in the world since therapeutic dosages of natural supplements will become unavailable because they would be illegal.

224

The name of this code is Codex Alimentarius. It has nothing to do with consumer protection as the promoters try to make us think. Instead it is about the economic ambitions of multi-national corporations, especially the pharmaceutical industry. An example of their power in the EU (European Union) countries in 2009 and 2010 was the swine flu hoax. Their coffers were overflowing from that one.

The DSHEA is the only protection Americans have from the Codex Alimentarius becoming the law of the land, although there is a push to try and repeal the DSHEA at almost every session of congress. With all the other significant changes taking up Congress's time we must be vigilant to see that Codex isn't pushed through in the confusion. So far the will of the people has prevailed but we need to keep a watchful eye on this issue. America wants to remain a member of the WTC so they are still applying pressure to America to adopt Codex or suffer trade restrictions with the EU countries.

With so much misinformation about supplements, how is John Q. Public supposed to separate fact from fiction? First, don't be influenced by media hype – consult with your trusted healthcare provider. Second, investigate the manufacturer of the supplement you are interested in and be sure you are satisfied with their research, quality control and manufacturing processes. They should be able to tell you the references for the research used to develop their products. They should be able to tell you the source of the raw material they use in their production. And last, you can verify their claims and determine if the products contain what the label says by consulting two independent testing organizations, Consumer Lab (www.consumerlab.com) and Supplement Watch (www.supplementwatch.com).

Their test materials are not sent to them by the manufacturer but are purchased from the manufacturer's distribution outlets (stores). The manufacturers do not pay for the reports produced by these organizations. If the products do not meet the claims by the manufacturer after testing by the organization, they do not receive the certification stamp to place on their label and literature. The organization websites will provide you with information on how products fare from their tests. There is a small fee for this information as this is the only source of income for the organizations, which are supported by the services they provide to their subscribers.

The slogan "Buyer Beware" is very appropriate for the supplement industry. Remember, there are quite a few really good companies that supply high quality products. However, your health is no place to pinch pennies or take bids on low quality purchases. A pill that costs 1 cent is too expensive if it doesn't work for you or increases toxicity in your body.

BODY:
"A healthy diet is one in which the food you eat contains all the nutrients needed by the body to exist."
Note #18, pg. 83

I hope I have convinced you with the above discourse that supplementation is vital for you to consider when developing your health plans and programs. The first step, though, is to be sure what it is you need to correct. In other words, before you can begin to improve you need to know where you are. Just as it is wise to have yearly physical checkups and some regular tests, I would recommend a "wellness panel" be performed as well.

Should you wish to bypass the medical doctor visit because you believe yourself in excellent health and want to just run laboratory tests without the doctor visit and expensive lab test fees, there is a cheaper way which I use myself. There is a company called Direct Laboratory Services, Inc. You can purchase the tests you want online at a far lower cost than the doctor's office or hospital. Just like buying about everything else these days, you simply go to a website, order what you want into the shopping cart, insert your secure credit card and push the send button. The home office of Direct Lab will send you a lab test kit order with the signature of an MD at their company along with the vials they will need for the blood sample, plus instructions of where you should go to get the blood drawn. This is usually the closest hospital. Go to the lab there and pay about $4 (this might vary by hospital) for the blood draw. They will draw it in the vials you give them. Then you send the samples off to the testing facility. In a few days you will receive the results of the test along with an explanation by an MD from Direct Lab. If there is anything problematic in the results they will advise you to make an appointment with your healthcare provider and you can go from there.

Their website is www.directlab.com, phone 1-800-908-0000. They even have a phone number that is easy to remember. If you have questions, I've always found their operators to be very cooperative. I just looked at the website while typing this and I see they even have a special on their DLS Wellness Report and a video you can watch that tells you about it. It says this is a complete body scan. They also have a comprehensive wellness profile which should be run prior to starting a vitamin/mineral program, as this will give you your vitamin/mineral status as it stands now. Wow, such a deal! This month's sales include a Women's Health Check, regular price $179, this month only $107. This test would cost over $700 if ordered by your physician. Examples of these savings are found throughout their site. They say they are also on Facebook and Twitter, for those of you who use these social networking tools.

In any discussion of supplementation, the use of herbs must play a part. When I have a therapeutic problem herbs are one of the choices I look into when investigating a solution.

HERBALISM, or the study of herbs (plants) has been used as a healing art for thousands of years. It has been part of the Indian Ayurvedic medical system, the Chinese medical system and the Native American spiritual healing system. In fact, all cultures, current and past, have used herbs as the medicines of their traditional healing arts. It has been reported that Cleopatra's famous beauty treatments were based on the popular herb *Aloe Vera.* Our modern prescription drugs have their roots sunk deep into the arts of herbalism.

From ancient times until the mid-20th century, pharmacopoeia descriptions of medicines all had herbal foundations. Because plants are biological life forms, they are not patentable. Hence, the whole plant is of no interest to the pharmaceutical companies since they can't make a profit on it. To create our modern prescription drugs the pharmaceutical companies look at the medical properties of plants that are effective for treating specific symptoms. They extract what they believe are the active ingredients then attempt to formulate those ingredients synthetically in a lab. They combine these synthetic compounds with other chemicals to offer to us a speedy remedy for our ills. They believe that the whole is equal to the sum of its parts, not realizing that this geometric theorem does not apply to biological systems. Because they try to manipulate Nature, she withholds the spiritual essence of the plant which in combination with the other plant's chemistry is what heals the whole body, not just alleviating the symptoms.

Herbalism works because it applies to the (w)holistic approach to healing. For healing to be a cure in any living system, we must recognize that the spiritual qualities of the living system contain the vital force that only Nature can produce. So the remedies recommended by the herbalist are designed for the individual and support the whole body, mind, and spirit of the client, rather than just relieving or suppressing symptoms of the illness or disease.

HOW ARE HERBS USED?

Herbs are a safe and effective choice to alleviate illness and disease. But they can accomplish so much more to keep our human system in a state of homeostasis (all human systems in balance). Tonic herbals play a vital role in the maintenance of health and the prevention of disease. They can do this through prevention, detoxification, elimination and supporting the body's natural immune system. Tonics are herbals that will strengthen and heal either a specific body tissue or organ or the whole body system. These tonics come from the whole plant so are the gifts of health to the suffering humanity by Mother Nature. Tonics are mild and gentle and when used properly are safe and have a profound effect upon our bodies. They have a normalizing and nurturing effect on

228

us because when properly used they can keep us in the peak of health and wellness. Tonics can be used as a shield to protect us from known or inherited health problems as well.

Of course, not all herbals are tonics. Some have powerful and specific effects upon a particular body organ or system. Some act to cleanse and detoxify our bodies. In the view of natural practitioners, all illness and disease have their root causes in toxins in the body. These can be a product of natural metabolism or they can be external toxins that enter the body from numerous sources including opportunistic microorganisms, chemicals in the environment, . All of these toxins generate free radicals and other negative effects in the body. This is why it is so important to remember that our bodies require *Fresh Foods, Fresh Air, Fresh Water, Good Nutrition, and Rest* to sustain a healthy life. A basic premise of the Wellness Doc is that if your body doesn't need it to complete the biochemistry required for life then you shouldn't put it into your body.

Herbs come in many forms: infusions (herb teas), decoctions (a more concentrated infusion, used with hard or woody herbs), tinctures, capsules, pills, lozenges, baths, douches, ointments, salves, creams, poultices, hot and cold compresses and suppositories. The particular form of the herb will depend on the specific reasons for the herbal therapy. This is one reason why the most effective remedies will come from a consultation with an herbalist practitioner.

MIND:

"Most people do not consume an optimal amount of all vitamins by diet alone. It
appears prudent for all adults to take vitamins supplements."
Journal of the American Medical Assoc. 2002; 287: 3127=3129

Our bodies have an amazing ability to heal themselves. For hundreds of years medical science has known about this power yet it has never really been understood. This mysterious power was known as the placebo response (see glossary), the mind's powerful influence over bodily illness and healing. One of our Founding Fathers, Thomas Jefferson, wrote of this power in 1807 when he said, "One of the most successful physicians I have ever known has assured me that he used more of bread pills, drops of colored water, and powders of hickory ashes, than of all other medicines put together."

The Placebo Response[22,] written in 2000 by Howard Brody, M.D., is one of the most interesting, informative books that I've ever seen on the placebo response. It presents the experience and study of his physician–patient relationships and his discoveries of this mysterious healing phenomenon. The book is so filled with useful information about this power of the mind that I recommend it to those of you interested in how you can incorporate this healing power in your own life. The thought occurred to me that if we knew how to utilize our minds to take advantage of these techniques we could improve our own healing efforts. The placebo effect can be used for positive or negative results, so if we understand its workings we can utilize it for positive manifestations in our bodies.

For the purposes of this venue let me summarize a few interesting points made by Dr. Brody to get you started on your odyssey. Dr. Brody solved the mystery of the placebo response by combining three essential theories as follows:

Expectancy – changes in bodily health occur because we anticipate them.

Conditioning –past experiences create a pattern of bodily change and may be repeated in the present.

Meaning -the way we interpret and make sense of events.

The book deals with these aspects and provides new clues as to how the connections work through his many stories and research. Dr. Brody examines phenomena such as:

➢ You'll heal faster after surgery if you see trees and grass outside your window than if you're looking at a brick wall.

➢ After asthmatic children were given vanilla aroma to use with their inhalers, their asthma eventually improved in response to the vanilla alone, even when the inhalers contained no active drug.

230

- Some patients who had sham angina surgery performed in a double-blind experiment showed improvements lasting six months or more which their physicians could not distinguish from the results in patients who had had the real surgery.
- When people watched a movie showing Mother Teresa taking care of the poor in Calcutta, their bodies secreted extra amounts of salivary immunoglobulin A, a major germ-fighting chemical.
- When Japanese teenagers who were allergic to a tree similar to poison ivy, were touched with leaves from a harmless chestnut tree but told those leaves were from the poisonous tree, they developed severe rashes. When touched with the poisonous leaves, but told they were from the harmless chestnut tree, they had no reaction whatsoever.
- When a new medical treatment is introduced with much excitement and hope, the first patients to receive it typically show a seventy percent positive response rate even in cases where the treatment − on more careful study − is shown to be medically worthless.

This book presents a convincing case that we can harness our inner pharmacy for better health and healing. I highly recommend it to you for study.

SPIRIT:

"One growing area of modern health research is the link between health and spiritual activities; scientists are finding that prayer and religious dedication can actually make a difference in one's state of health."
The Placebo Response by Howard Brody, M.D., PhD. Pg. 165

Whenever I'm searching for an answer to a physical challenge I begin looking at my diet, then lifestyle, then herbalism, then my medicine of choice − homeopathy. I have always solved my health challenges without resorting to prescription drugs. This is why I have refused to participate in the government's drug insurance program. Natural methods have always worked for me. So let's look at the last of the supplemental programs, homeopathy.

HOMEOPATHY is based on the belief that everyone is an individual and should be treated accordingly. This method does not use drugs or surgery and was first pioneered in the 19th century by the German physician and chemist Samuel Hahnemann (1755-1843). However, way back in the 5th century BCE Hippocrates, the father of medicine, used homeopathic remedies in his medical tool kit. His understanding of disease and its effects on the body is what made his practice homeopathic. His understanding of the individual patient and their powers of healing remains the basis of homeopathy today, although this method is not recognized or practiced by most modern day MD's. The violence and invasiveness of early modern medical practice was unacceptable to Hahnemann. He fought against the use of brutal practices and strong medications that caused terrible side-effects. He began investigating alternative practices, beginning by experimenting with remedies on himself first.

Chapter 4, Lesson 4 has a description of the workings of homeopathy so you might want to review it again.

When I was studying homeopathy for my masters degree there was one question that bothered me about homeopathic remedies, something that just didn't seem to compute in my scientific mind. I couldn't find a satisfactory answer from the texts, the instructors, or emails to practicing homeopaths. That question was, since homeopathy is based on the idea of assisting the body in its efforts to heal, and the dilutions of the remedies are so great that there is virtually no trace of the active compound left in the remedies, how can they possibly work? .

I've used the remedies myself and am aware of their powerful effects but I couldn't understand the mechanism because there couldn't possibly be any of the active compound left in the remedy. This is the main reason allopathic medical people don't believe in homeopathy, because it doesn't make sense with the currently-known laws of chemistry. I wasn't satisfied with the standard response that it works, so don't worry about the how or why. Then when I came upon Bell's Theorem (see glossary) I felt like I was hit by a bolt of lightning. The answer lay in the theorem and what I had learned in my herbal studies. There is a life force in everything on the planet, a force that is omnipresent and affects every connection in the universe. This is why we are all connected as one, a concept scientists have a hard time understanding because it isn't visible or measurable and therefore, in their view, doesn't exist. Their narrow scientific ideas work in a material, three-dimensional world but not in a world beyond the fourth dimension, which is the home of the spirit. Such a world can only be proved by mathematics and faith, as in the proof of Bell's Theorem. Since every planet and every animal on the planet has a life force working within themselves, the ultimate answer is to just let go and let healing happen. I know it works so I give thanks that the physician within me is always standing guard.

The truth of this concept can be seen in the indigenous natives from the story of the Cat's Claw herb. Here is a summary of that story. The references are in the notes section.

Cat's Claw might be one of the most confusing and effective nutritional supplements available today, but with good reasons. Currently there are at least 16 plants in the world that are called cat's claw. *Uncaria tomentosa* is the Latin name most frequently sold as cat's claw supplements, but these products vary greatly. Some contain the bark, some the stems, and others contain compounds from the leaves. All of these claim to aid the immune system.[23]

It is the root that actually contains the true health benefits. Scientists studying every part of the plant discovered that only extracts made from cat's claw root possess the healing power to treat and prevent disease. However, not all cat's claw roots actually contain healing properties.[24]

To find which roots DO contain healing properties we need to travel to the Peruvian rainforest where the *Uncaria tomentosa* thrives. It's a woody vine that's found at the base of tall trees in the rainforests. As it grows it winds up and around the tree, attaching itself to the trunk with curved, cat-like claws at the junction of the leaves. The Ashaninka Indians who make these rainforests their home have used the roots of the plant for thousands of years to cure illness and maintain health in the tribe. [23, 24]

Healers in the tribe attribute the healing properties in the plant to the "good spirits" that reside in the roots. Hence, to obtain these healing properties the correct root must be harvested. The healers know which root to use because they can actually see the good spirits hidden inside the root of the plant before they harvest it. If the plant with a good spirit is mixed with roots that do not contain good spirits, the healing power of the root is lost. While there are no visible differences in the plants or roots, only the tribal healers seem to be able to see the good spirit roots. [24]

Fortunately, the scientists who were studying the cat's claw root were given some good spirit roots by the Ashaninka Indians to study in the laboratory. They soon learned that they, too, could "see" the good spirit with the aid of a high performance liquid chromatography (HPLC) that identifies various organic chemical compounds. The good spirits were found to be important medicinal compounds called pentacyclic oxindole alkaloids, or POA's. [24] I think you can see why the pharmacy scientists thought they could make the POA's synthetically, but they failed because it is impossible to duplicate the spiritual essence of the plant.

By the same process they were able to identify the non-healing compounds in this plant as well. Again using HPLC they discovered the non-healing chemicals, tetracyclic oxindole alkaloids (TOA's). What an improvement in determining chemical analysis of organic compounds from the days of my college chemistry labs! It was a number of years after college when the company I worked for purchased their own equipment, which as I recall was very expensive. It was like doing math with long hand arithmetic before the invention of the computer. While the POA's have very powerful effects on the immune system, the TOA's have different effects in the body, none of which help the immune system cells at all. [25 – 28]

If the TOA's and POA's are mixed together (as so often happens in the vast majority of cat's claw supplements), the resulting product

234

is useless for healing and health. The TOA's cancel out the action of the POA's, making the cat's claw root extract ineffective. Even as little as 1% TOA content can cause the POA's to lose their ability to beneficially modulate the immune system. [24, 29]

This means that only cat's claw supplements that are 100% TOA-free from the root of the plant will provide the desired powerful effects in the immune system. [23,24,29] You can see the importance of knowing your source information when purchasing supplements, particularly biologicals. If the supplement is useless, no matter how cheap it is, it is a waste of money and effort. Unfortunately, there are many backroom formulators making a quick buck in the nutritional health industry. If the manufacturer will not reveal the exact active ingredients and the source of those ingredients, I would stay as far away from them as possible. This is why discount supplements are a waste of money and why some people's experience with supplements has turned them away from any supplement program at all, because the ones they tried didn't work. If the distributors can't supply the science behind their products and show good manufacturing practices, I would strike them off my list. Many healthcare providers use private label third party manufacturers for their products so be sure you can trust the distributor as well as the manufacturer.

Cat's claw isn't the only herbal supplement in which this scenario is repeated. Any supplement should be suspect unless proven otherwise. Make it a rule to have a consultation with your healthcare provider about these issues before starting a new supplement program. That is one of the reasons Cosmos Institute of Life's Transitions was founded. We don't want the Federal Government to be responsible for the validity of the supplement quality in the U.S. or we will be just as vulnerable as Europe is today about the quality of their supplements. Maybe this is why I call the FDA the Federal Death Agency.

LESSON: The Meatless Advantage.
" They (the Hunzas, who live in the Himalayas of Northern Pakistan; meat and dairy products combined account for 1 ½% of their calories.) work and play at 80 and beyond; most of those who reach their 100th

birthday continue to be active, and retirement is unheard of. The absence of excess protein in their diets engenders slower growth and slim, compact body frames. With age, wisdom accumulates, but physical degeneration is limited so the senior citizens of these remote societies have something unique to contribute to the lives of others. They are revered. "[32]
Robin Hur

Vegetarianism is not new but was practiced by the ancient Greeks. Many believed that both humans and animals have souls and all souls are equal in value. Plato has said that a vegetarian diet should be consumed by an ideal society, because plant foods promote health and also require less land to produce than do animal foods.

During Europe's Dark ages vegetarianism fell into disfavor for more than 1500 years. A lone exception was Leonardo da Vinci, who was a devout vegetarian. He said, "The time will come when men will look upon the murder of animals as they look upon the murder of men."

Darwin reviewed vegetarianism during the late 18th century Enlightenment when he challenged the justification for eating animals. He believed that humans and other animals were a part of the continuum of life, differing only in species, not in kind.

Food and diet are interwoven in the religion and culture of which they are a part. Beyond religion and culture people choose a vegetarian diet due to issues of animal welfare, environmental ecology, finances and personal health. Today we classify vegetarians by the food groups they predominantly consume as follows: [34]

- Semi-vegetarian: eats poultry, fish, eggs and dairy foods, but not all mammals.
- Pesco-vegetarian: eats fish, eggs and dairy foods, but not poultry or red meats.
- Lacto-ovo-vegetarian: eats eggs and dairy foods but no food that involves killing an animal.

- Ovo-vegetarian: eats eggs but no other animal food product.
- Lacto-vegetarian: eats dairy products but no other animal-derived foods
- Vegan: excludes all animal derived foods, including honey.

Becoming a vegetarian has long-term benefits on body/mind/spirit and healthy longevity. As your diet changes, you will find your point of view of life changes as well. Nutrition awareness and knowledge about foods also improves. Many report adopting a "green" lifestyle as their consciousness for animal welfare and environmental issues expands.

The healthy vegetarian diet is low in fats so it is now well documented that vegetarians have a lower risk for high blood pressure, heartburn, obesity, diabetes, osteoporosis, and cancer. Of course, potato chips and soft drinks are vegetarian, so it behooves us to make healthy choices outside the realm of animal products as well.

It takes only a fraction of the land, water, and money to grow fruits, vegetables and grains than to produce animal crops. In Dr. Page's book she has 2 ½ pages of statistics about the realities of production of meats versus fruits and vegetables, as well as the cost and effect upon animal life on the planet in the new millennium. I hope the world leaders and population will begin to do something positive about changing these depressing conditions before it is too late to reverse the damage. [34]

Dr. Haas talks about what he calls "the warrior diet." His concept of the warrior is that food is our fuel. We fuel the body by giving it what it needs for a continuous combustion of energy. He is talking about embracing life with feeling and passion. Food nourishment should support this and not devitalize us or generate excess aggressiveness or moodiness. His diet consists of small meals or snacks eaten every two to three hours throughout the day. he advocates simple meals and often only simple foods such as a handful of almonds or sunflower seeds, an apple or two, carrot or celery sticks, crackers with avocado, or a bowl of rice with sprouts or cooked beans. Big meals of lots of different foods can act as mental and physical sedatives. The warrior eats large meals only in celebration or ritual or at the end of the workday to relax. At this time we can let go of our physical concerns and tensions, be more aware of inner levels and digest our meal along with the day's experiences.[4]

The meat-eater's major objection to vegetarianism is that you can't get the required needs of protein from a no meat diet. The nutrition industry has been in disagreement on this issue so it is sometimes hard to know what to believe. In the final analysis, unless you are a growing child or professional athlete you should be able to obtain your protein requirements from vegetable protein rather than animal protein. Combining types of vegetable protein will make this happen, and there are many sources of information in how to accomplish this. If you want to insure you obtain the needed protein and essential amino acids you could add a little milk and eggs. And if the vegetarian diet you are using contains legumes, grains and nuts you will more than double the amount of protein you need to remain healthy.[4,33,34,35]

Another significant source of toxins in the diet is the feed given to the animals in their production. Animals are injected with hormones and antibiotics, and herbicides are sprayed on their food sources to increase production. All of these toxins become concentrated in the meat because it takes 12 pounds of animal feed to produce one pound of meat. When you consume this meat you increase your toxin load and possibly shorten your life. This is particularly true if you consume organ meats such as liver. The liver performs the same function in animals as it does in humans, to filter out these environment toxins. Hence, you receive an overdose of toxins when you consume it. I never liked the taste of liver and when I discovered this fact, I was thankful I didn't contaminate my own liver with the poisons of someone else's liver.

In summary, it is wise to consult a Holistic Nutritionist when you want to improve your diet and health. This is probably why the subject of nutrition was such a large part of my master's and PhD course work in natural health.

BODY:
"The United States has the most sophisticated medical technology in the world, and one of the most temperate of climates. One of the highest consumers of meat and animal products in the world, it also has one of the lowest life expectancies of industrialized nations.[33]
John Robbins

If you have been a long-term meat eater and are convinced of the benefits of vegetarianism for you, there are some cautions you should keep in mind. Make the transition to vegetarianism easier by going slowly. Don't create a big trauma to your system by trying to convert to a vegan diet all at once. Start by cutting back on meats on a decreasing schedule, maybe dropping back to meat three times a week and after a month down to two and then one and then none. All the time you can begin learning how to combine fruits and vegetables to insure a completely healthy diet. Vegetarian cuisine is very diverse and interesting and will be very nutritious if the right vegetables are combined at each of the meals. Buy a vegetarian cookbook in order to learn new ways to tempt your taste buds.

How long you have been a meat eater will determine how long it will take you to make the transition to being a vegetarian. Don't try to rush it because it could take months to years to eliminate meat from your diet. You might try saving a meat meal as a reward for maintaining your diet for a specific time frame. It is easier to change your mind or give up on your program than to change your taste buds. Depending on your motivation, it may be easier to get a new spouse than make a healthy change in your diet. Whether it is worth it is up to you.

Until you are knowledgeable about vitamins, minerals and other nutrients and how to combine ingredients of each meal to insure you receive the proper nutrition, it is recommended that you also take a quality multi-vitamin with the meal.

MIND:

"And with such a (vegetarian) diet they may be expected to live in peace and health to a good old age, and bequeath a similar life to their children after them."
Socrates

One of the most common uses of hypnotherapy uses is to change bad habits and abusive activity. Hence, it lends itself nicely if you are trying to make lasting changes in your diet. A poor diet, lacking in nutrition, is really an abusive activity so professional hypnotherapy will help to make the transition easier and conquer the discouragement and frustration that often goes along with radical changes.

As mentioned above, make the change in small steps. This is most important if you want to avoid discouragement and ultimately, failure. You can practice visualization by seeing a slimmer, healthy you whenever temptation rears it ugly head. Maintain a image of the ideal you make for your goal. I know you can do it. Give it a try but remember to give it plenty of time – God has no timetables.

Many vegetarians report that when they eliminated meat from their diets, the tendency to get headaches disappeared and they experienced an increase in mental clarity.[35] This in itself may be worth the effort to eliminate meat from your diet. Just think of all the "good" days that may be in your future.

SPIRIT:

"Live simply so others might simply live."
Gandhi

As we look back to humans' early history and compare the skills and attitudes that prevailed in the two main groups of humans, the agrarian lifestyle and the nomadic pastoralists, there is a striking difference. The early agrarians lived in egalitarian, peace-loving communities, while the nomadic pastoralists were a more aggressive and warlike community. The pastoralists were able to easily dominate the peaceful agrarian communities and hence their

240

numbers eventually predominated in the areas inhabited by early man.[35]

When studying early cultures it appears that our ancestors who developed in warmer climates where they subsisted largely on fruits, nuts and leafy and root vegetables that could be easily gathered and grew year round, survived readily without the need to search for other food sources. When changing climatic conditions or migrations compelled them to take up hunting as the sole means for survival we can assume they had to adapt with some difficulty in order to survive. Thus an essentially peaceful food-gatherer had to develop the cunning and aggression necessary for stalking and killing his food. These peoples, whose biochemistry was previously adapted to vegetables and fruits, had to now adapt their biochemistry systems toward aggressiveness and hunting. As they adapted they became a permanent part of their heredity and would demonstrate this aggression when they consumed animal flesh or meat the by-products of digestion would then stimulate the hunting instincts and aggressiveness necessary to continue to survive.

The hunter's aggressive capabilities would easily been turned toward the conquest of more peaceful communities (the bully concept) and they increased and dominated in areas of early man. A civilization dominated by hunters might be more likely to turn toward senseless warfare with their neighbors, violence on their streets, or might experience incessant feelings of anger and hostility. One anthropologist has suggested that prehistoric Europe adapted toward warfare only after livestock breeding became common in rural communities. What had been a dual capacity for gathering or hunting with great adaptability potential could have become a major danger to survival. [35]

While this theory would be difficult to prove, it is interesting to note that for a millennium in India meat was prescribed for consumption by the warrior and ruling castes. In contrast, the castes that dedicated themselves to study and spiritual advancement were not supposed to engage in combat and were forbidden to use meat. This hypothesis that man has a dual biological potential and he can be geared to more aggressive behavior by eating meat became more controversial. There are reports of aggressive behavior by vegetarians as well. The science behind each side of the question is questionable and may very well be faulty as both sides seems to personal observations as the bases of their beliefs. Since human behavior is an area that often varies with the belief system of the observer this theory may be one of those that will never meet the stringent rules of the scientific method. For me, it only seems logical that if someone takes pleasure and enjoyment out of killing other animals then what makes them think twice about wanting control over humans as well. That has been my experience.

"In carnivores, the constituents of the meat which are not useful remain as wastes which must be eliminated. Such elimination requires a period during which the carnivore is rather sluggish and dull. This state of lethargy is contrasted with the active aggressive state involved in hunting. The classical Indian culture, which is predominantly vegetarian puts a high value on the maintenance of a state of calm equilibrium which avoids either of these extremes. The lion is viewed as a typical example of the vacillation from one extreme to another. Ferocious and aggressive during hunting, after the kill and after feeding, the lion lapses into a long period of dormancy during which the meat is digested. It was perhaps the understanding of the effects of flesh-eating on consciousness that led so many of the ancient teachers to advise against it. Pythagoras, who was a spiritual teacher and a mathematician in ancient Greece, wrote persuasively about the advantages of vegetarianism, as did Buddha and others."[35]

The effects that meat-eating might have on consciousness are also tied to the psychological and moral aspect of meat. Vegetarians object to meat-eating on the basis that it is not humane. Another moral objection is that it is wasteful and not economically sound. Ten to fifteen times more protein can be provided from a plot of land harvesting plant crops than raising beef cattle. If we wish to feed the world population with nutritious food, the economics of land use becomes very important. That is why it is a false economy to destroy tropical rainforest to raise beef cattle. We are destroying the tropical rainforest today at an alarming rate and soon the

242

tropics will begin to look like the north African desert or the desert of the American Southwest.

Many years ago my wife and I used to enjoy a veal steak very now and then until we saw on TV how veal was produced and the inhumane living conditions in which the calves were raised. That horror story was enough for us to swear off veal and tell everyone we could why we would no longer contribute to such a horrific treatment of animals just for the sake of our own pleasure.

And so are the Spirits of ourselves and the Spirits of the planet and all humanity linked. Our soul dies a little each time we contribute to the murder of another animal. Since all animals are connected spiritually, it is a true case of murder to take the life of any defenseless animal, human or not.

CHAPTER X
TRANSITIONS – Your World is What You Make of It.

The format of this the last chapter will be a little different than what has transpired before. This concluding chapter we will be discussing life's transitions, a vital area of concern for anyone wishing a long, healthy, happy, life well into the omega of their lifespan.

Transition implies change that is usually necessitated by growth in body, mind, and spirit. We anticipate that this growth is always positive, resulting from new learning as a consequence of accomplishing life goals. Of course, it could also be negative during a state of depression or failures. If we are paying attention as we age, we will notice that through the decades there are definite transitions in our body and mental facilities. As we age, our bodies change just as mechanical machinery systems begin to change and break down over time as a part of Nature's laws. The most obvious transition for all male and females is the passing through the menopausal stage of life when reproductive activity is no longer required. I used to think there was no such thing as male menopause until I experienced it. So for you younger guys – don't laugh at the gals, your time will come. Some transitions are forced on us and some are planned. We should all plan on the transitions we know will happen in the future and react intelligently to the unplanned transitions. An unplanned, seemly negative transition that will affect all of us sooner or later is the apparent loss of fortune such as finances and careers. When these dark clouds descend to test your resolve, remember the word "Apocatastasis" (see glossary) to regain your perspective.

This final chapter is also a summary and plan of action based on the first nine chapters of this work. You might want to review chapter II before starting the journey. To start, we suggest you begin with an understanding of <u>who you are</u> and a written "life review" to better understand where, what, and which lessons you have learned so far in your life's story.

If you are in the sixth decade of life and have not written your life story for the benefit of your caregivers and younger family members, it is past time to get cracking on this most vital project. You may also need to do a life story with your parents before it is too late to obtain it. You can do this if you act as an interviewer and record your parents' life story. I treasure the recordings we did with my parents and regret not doing one with my wife's parents. We had intended to do so but never got around to it until it was too late, leaving a big hole in her family's story. When they get older my grandchildren will enjoy and appreciate being able to see and hear the great-grandparents they never had the opportunity to know. Whether you are a current or future caregiver for a family member, or the future recipient of such care, I highly recommend the book *A Dignified Life: A Guide for Family Caregivers.*[23] In the meantime let me include here the outline the authors of *A Dignified Life* recommend for a comprehensive Life Story:

"We recommend the following ingredients to make a comprehensive Life Story. They are listed here in chronological order, but the events are not necessarily limited to those years. For example, someone may have been in military service throughout his or her working life." [23]

CHILDHOOD
  Birth date and birthplace (and /or adoption)
  Parents and grandparents
  Brothers and sisters
  Early education
  Pets

ADOLESCENCE
  Name of high school
  Favorite classes
  Friends and interests
  Hobbies and sports
  First job

YOUNG ADULTHOOD

College and work
Marriage(s)/relationship(s)
Family
Clubs and/or community involvement
First home
Military

MIDDLE AGE
Grandchildren
Hobbies
Work/family role
Clubs and organizations
Community involvement

LATER YEARS
Life achievements and accomplishments
Hobbies
Travel
Family

OTHER MAJOR INGREDIENTS
Ethnicity
Religious background
Awards
Special skills

Much of my Life's Story is described throughout my book, *An Odyssey into Past Lives: A Personal Exploration into Cellular Memories.*[24] Additional information was included on my website under Doc's Commentaries, *Cosmos Beliefs and Practices.* Since this was also the basis of my own Life Review and illustrates the ingredients of your personal review as the first step in understanding your life transitions, I've reprinted it below for your perusal and guidance.

In chapter II I encouraged you to first determine who you really are. From this awareness you can work to evolve into the being who you were meant to be. If it is good for you then it would be good for me to do as I preach. Hence, following are the fundamental principles that motivated me to start Cosmos Institute and were the basis of my Life's Review to understand the transitions that occurred for me.

What was the transition that caused me to start Cosmos Institute? When I closed the chemical business I had been involved with for 34 years I was faced with the question, "What am I going to do with the rest of my life?" Before I could answer that question I had to take a serious look at my life to understand how I got to where I was. Knowing that everything happens for a purpose and in its divine time frame, I was aware that there had to be a reason for the circumstances that caused me to close the business in which I had spent so much time and effort. So at age 52 I started along the path of that life review.

My years in the Jaycees and the corporate business world taught me that civic and corporate politics were not the right area of activity for Bill Warner. While there is nothing wrong with these worlds for many, for me I learned a lot but came to the realization that the political world was not the reason I was sent to earth in this incarnation. I gave thanks for the opportunities I had experienced in my life up to that point but determined to find another path to express the real me. I also understood from early in life, thanks to the teachings of my grandmother and parents, that I am personally responsible for what happens to me and I have the power to change anything I don't like.

As I looked over my past efforts there were a number of positive realizations I came to understand:
1. I was happiest when I was teaching and conducting seminars and workshops in subjects that I was interested in.
2. My interest in hypnosis goes back to my childhood. I understood that was the tool I subconsciously used to allow me to control my own mind and bring about all the good things that have happened in my life.
3. The early knowledge that I am a spiritual being and so is every other living organism. Therefore there is a spiritual guide within me that is involved in every decision I make. If

I consult that spiritual part of me, my decisions turn out well and if I don't, my decisions and situations turn out badly.

4. I determined that I should study hypnotherapy so I could better utilize this wonderful power more efficiently for the remainder of my life. During that time I took a certification workshop for Past Life Regression and Time Line Therapy.

5. In that earlier part of my life I was involved with chemicals used to make gunpowder and war material. Even then I was opposed to war as a way to solve mankind's problems and I left the chemical business at that time. Now I know the source of my beliefs about war and why I was born when I was; I was too young for Korea and too old for Vietnam. And I also know why I made a decision in 1959 while in the Navy Reserve to allow me to miss that unfortunate war. Again, everything happens for a reason. In my life I can thank the Lebanon crisis of 1959 for leading me to the decision to leave the military after fulfilling my obligation and not to pursue the path of a Naval Officer. While I supported our troops and grieved when I saw the American people's display of non-support for our military, I don't approve of the aggression of war, which has never solved any problems, only created more problems. When it was all over, the south Vietnamese people were not free to experience the blessings of a democratic state. During that time in my life, my experience in the chemical industry made me realized that celebrated advances in chemistry have resulted in major damage to our planet, world peace, and our own personal health. With that realization, I didn't want to be a part of it any more. In fact, I suspect my parents' activity in the chemical business may have had something to do with their later challenge with Alzheimer's. The probability of both husband and wife contacting Alzheimer's is unusually low.

6. I realized I was blessed with a healthy genetic start in life and it was my responsibility to keep my life in a healthy condition. I couldn't do that by poisoning the environment that I lived in or by an unhealthy lifestyle if I expected to stay healthy for a long and productive life.

7. I enjoyed the intellectual exposure of a continuing education and realized that educational pursuits would be a part of my activities for the rest of my life. Learning is a life-long experience. When I saw my parents suffering the dementia of old age I determined I wasn't going to let that happen to me. I needed to find a way to improve my situation in the last decades of life. I realized I enjoyed and functioned better in the stimulation of the academic world than the stress of the corporate world.

With these points in mind, Cosmos Institute began to take shape. Now that I knew the reasons I left the chemical business, I could let that part of my life go and transition into a new adventure. I have no regrets in life because I can always reframe problems I experience in a positive way and appreciate the lesson learned. Following my past life survey I was able to understand the events in my life and why specific challenges came my way. The past life survey is a vital step in conducting any life review attempt. Unless you can understand your life it is impossible to have an accurate perspective and hence, you are a ship without a rudder floundering in the winds of life.

At that time in my life I was searching for what to do. I knew to be thankful to my spiritual guide for the blessings of a healthy genetic inheritance. Both my parents were blessed with good health and my mother especially took excellent care of my brother and me while we were developing in the womb. While all the members of my family understood the power of the mind to accomplish good, there came a time when it was put to a severe test. I watched it happen. We didn't understand environmental toxins and their long-term effects but the breakdown started first with my younger brother. He experienced a significant stressful event that allowed a tendency toward alcoholism to blossom into full view, leading to adult-onset diabetes that rapidly developed into a liver disease. While Dick understood the principles of apocatastasis he couldn't apply the knowledge when it counted. Hence, when the major stressful event happened in his life all these negative experiences spiraled out of personal control, resulting in an unfortunate untimely passing. It gave me a wakeup call that started a number of significant changes in my life.

Then the major stressful event happened to both my previously healthy parents. I can't remember any contacts they had with the medical profession earlier in life other than a few insignificant trauma events. But neither one of them was able to accept my brother's passing. I watched their health begin to deteriorate shortly afterwards. Even with their strong spiritual faith, I believe they were personally blaming God for his passing. They, too had forgotten the principles of apocatastasis and its beautiful message. A decade before Dad's passing with Alzheimer's disease, I closed the family chemical business. I'm sure that didn't help his personal stress level. Mother made her transition almost two years before Dad. By this time they were both in the same nursing home but in separate wings. I know Dad was mentally aware even though he was in the severe end stage of Alzheimer's. He was staying around because he still believed he was running the chemical business and was needed to lead the family.

Dad passed while in the emergency room of the hospital when the nursing home took him there to investigate a bleeding stomach. Dick's widow was there and holding his hand when the nurse went to get the equipment they would require. She said to him, "Dad, it is OK now, everything is fine, you can go home to Mom if you wish." He looked up at her, smiled, and made his transition in peace before the nurse returned. I think he was holding onto life because he felt he was needed to run the family even though his innate desire was to reunite with his wife of almost sixty years. At Mom's passing I saved her ashes because I didn't think Dad would last long without her. They demonstrated the theory that couples that have been together for many years frequently make their transition within a couple of years of each other. Then we could have the family memorial service and Mom and Dad's ashes would be joined with those of my brother and maternal grandmother in the waters of Tampa Bay.

My maternal grandmother passed at age 79 and wished to make her transition in peace. She was a very healthy and wonderful mentor to my brother and me. The whole family learned many lessons from her and she was an inspiration to everyone she met. Her husband had passed on many decades earlier, before I was born. She never remarried because she knew she would be with him again in their heavenly home. I had never seen my grandmother ill so I was surprised when I was told she was in the hospital with cancer. In those days she was operated on and closed up and sent home to die. She made her transition two weeks later at home. During my last visit to see her in my parents' home, she told me, "I've lived a fulfilled life, I've seen seven of my great-grandchildren, I'm not needed by anyone any more, all my friends have already made their transition, and it is time for me to leave and be with Daddy Bill again." She made her transition the next day. My brother Dick flew the plane as Dad and I released her ashes into Tampa Bay.

All these experiences had a profound influence on my life. In the case of my grandmother, brother and father, and to some degree my mother who died from complications of pneumonia, modern medicine could have kept them alive for some undeterminable time in the future. But what would their future have been? It sure wouldn't have been what they wanted. By the time it was my parents' turn they had the legal tools to insist that no heroic efforts be made to keep them alive. My grandmother wanted to leave this earthly plane because she believed her divine plan was completed. In the case of my brother, he didn't want to leave because he still had a growing family to influence and was engaged in a work he enjoyed with the total support of the small community they lived in. In fact, at his passing the community flew flags at half-mast for a week. I sat at his bedside the whole day before his passing and held his hand. The only words he was able to utter were, "Why is my body doing this to me?" I kissed him because I couldn't answer him truthfully at that late date.

The common thread in all these experiences is that the genesis of our own mortality is of our own making. I believe we each have challenges along the path of life. How well we handle these stresses will determine whether we stray from our path and destiny and start down that slippery slope that leads to our own transition.

Hence, the ability to properly handle stress is a requirement for each of us if we wish to fulfill our divine plan during this incarnation. This is why Go With the Flow became the first program developed by Cosmos Institute.

The next lesson I became aware of was, if we wish to have a fulfilling life that means accomplishment of our goals and maintenance of good health throughout life, we must start early. That means, the sooner after you are thirty years of age you begin to understand your destiny and make the lifestyle changes that are necessary, the greater is your probability of success. While modern medicine can work miracles, they are engaged in a contest to keep the symptoms of our illnesses at bay. I felt that if we maintained the philosophy that we are responsible for our own health and allowed Mother Nature to rule, then prevention of illness is more cost effective and comforting than treating the results by turning our care over to someone else. Nature has a solution to every problem and if we turn to that solution and learn her lessons we will be healthier until the completion of our own divine plan.

I am a walking billboard of this philosophy so it only seems practical to teach others how to stay on the path. I realized there are four areas that have a significant impact on our healthy longevity, and if we can teach people to control these areas before it is too late and the medical community gives up on them, then we can make a significant contribution to the health of the planet. These four areas of concentration are stress management, elimination of substance abuse, a healthy diet, and daily communication with the Physician Within (the God of your understanding).

Having worked within the environment of the western medical community for many years as an Emergency Medical Technician, I came to realize that basically, western medicine doesn't treat the root of the problem, only the symptoms in order to alleviate the suffering. But usually, once you become involved with the medical community it is a cycle from which there is no escape. The path toward a healthy longevity is in preventing illness and disease rather than correcting the problem after it occurs. In order to

252

accomplish this we need to return to the source, Mother Nature, and learn from her the natural divine way to health. This entails the confluence of the natural waters from the rivers of Body/Mind/Spirit into one treatment modality.

Unfortunately, as our science has improved we have tended to specialize our efforts and with the damaging effects of ego thrown into the equation, we have improved our lives but at a cost. Each of the disciplines has jealously protected its turf and felt theirs was the only way toward perfect health. The medical doctors treat the Body, the psychologist treats the Mind, and the spiritual leaders treat the Spirit, and never shall they be reunited. While nobody can be an expert in everything, we need to recognize that no one has the full answer to solving our problems. How many physicians truly believe that if their patients will take a positive mental attitude and place their care in the hands of their God, then the physician's success rate of healing will be infinitely improved? Physicians are personally responsible for only one third of the healing.

Therefore Cosmos Institute was started to be an advocate for PREVENTION OF ILLNESS AND DISEASE rather than attempting to become a healing source once the illness has progressed to the point when expensive and aggressive intervention is required. Healthcare futurist and medical product inventor Nicholas J. Webb says in a book entitled *The Cost of Being Sick,* [30] "Lousy nutritional habits, a 'treatment vs. prevention' medical industry mindset and the high cost of paying for prescription drugs are all merging to create a health care 'perfect storm' that will, if left unattended, swallow the health care industry whole and take a lot of Americans down with it." Reading that small book will convince you of the need to change your mindset in order to avoid the crash that is sure to come.

We are all aware that the cost of living has risen significantly over time. When I think about how cheap things were years ago I have to remind myself that everything is relative. While it was cheaper to buy things and there were fewer things to buy that we thought we needed, the income to purchase those things was also less. I remember after graduation from Georgia Tech, my first job paid $600 per month, a sum college graduates would laugh at today. My college fees, books and other expenses were paid out of war bonds I had saved during WWII. The source of those bonds came from selling city maps to the soldiers stationed in St. Petersburg during the war ,plus my parents and grandmother who gave us bonds at gift-giving occasions. Just before my brother and I returned to college each quarter, Dad would take us to the bank to cash in our bonds in the safe deposit box to pay the fees, books and other expenses. in the amount of $400 per quarter. I don't know what the cost is today at Georgia Tech (I was an out-of-state resident) but I'm sure it is a long way from $400.

I remember most young children during WWII bought stamps by turning their "odd job" pay and their allowances in at school each Friday. When we filled a book with stamps we turned the books in for the war bonds. So I guess the children's support of the war consisted of our financial support (from odd jobs – in my case selling maps to soldiers and sailors), suffering from the rationing (and standing in long lines), and not having a father present in our early growing years. I was one of the lucky ones because my Dad came home in one piece after about 4 years. I'll never forget the day Dad returned – what a wonderful day that was. My brother and I were in the bathtub when suddenly Mom appeared at the door with her arms around a man that we didn't even recognize until Mom reintroduced us to our father who had returned. We knew he was overseas fighting for our freedom in Italy but he had changed when he returned. We couldn't get Dad to talk about his experiences, even many decades later when we recorded Mom and Dad talking about their early history and our family history on film. I treasure that film but his side of the story during the war years is sadly absent. I guess it was a part of his life experience he wanted to forget.

I can remember 25¢ per gallon gasoline, and when the price was nearing $1.00 per gallon I thought $1.00 was some sort of magical ceiling that would never be exceeded. Boy, was I wrong! I went to college in the hometown of Coca-Cola and I paid a nickel for a bottle of Coke in a glass container.

Consider a real problem facing everyone today. How am I going to be able to retire and still be able to afford to maintain my current lifestyle and standard of living when medical costs will consume a predominant proportion of my income and life expectancy means I'll be living to an older age than is average today? Your income will have to come out of savings and what social security *might* be able to support. Assume you want to maintain your lifestyle of $30,000 per year ($2500/month) and you start to save at age 30 years old, planning to retire at age 65. With a modest inflation rate of 4%, which is historically conservative, you will need $12,138 per month by the time you retire. Where is that going to come from?

How far are you from retirement? How can you pay for it if you are not able to make the savings now because of the personal health care costs due to being unable to afford health insurance? This issue is the plight of more than 50 million Americans. If you live long enough, financial security will without a doubt be your life's most troubling issue. Suicide is not an option. God doesn't need you to "cop out" of your divine destiny.

So how could Cosmos Institute of Life's Transitions use the holistic approach for prevention? Recognizing that holistic prevention must involve the integration of Body/Mind/Spirit, our programs for each of these parts of the whole person are designed to return us to the natural order of life. A paradigm shift is in process where the old techniques of healing are no longer working. In spite of the attempts, we as a culture are becoming sicker. Cosmos Institute is a part of the new paradigm where healing is a process of bringing the Body/Mind/Spirit into an integrated balance. According to the laws of nature, as one paradigm fades away another, more evolved system is taking its place. A phoenix is born from the ashes of complacency and ignorance.

BODY:
"It is the entire man that writes and thinks, and not merely the head. His leg has often as much to do with it as his head – the state of his calves, his vitals and his nerves.

255

Leigh Hunt (`1784- 1859)
English poet and essayist

Since we believe invasive techniques and the use of drugs (toxins) are contraindicated to the natural divine order of the universe, we advocate different techniques as preventive measures. We also take to heart the first dictum of the father of medicine, Hippocrates, "to do no harm." This would be impossible if we allowed toxins to invade our bodies. As an alternative, we advocate the philosophy of Traditional Chinese Medicine (TCM) where physicians were paid to keep their patients well and when they became ill they were treated without compensation. TCM is an energy modality where health is attained by maintaining balance within the bio-system.

The practice of Homeopathy and Herbalism are also advocated as natural methods to promote a healthy longevity and lifestyle. Whenever a prescription drug is recommended, a homeopathic or herbal alternative is usually available.

The act of living creates toxins in our bodies from both internal and external sources. The most efficient and cost-effective way to control these toxins is through a high quality supplement which supplies the proper quantities and forms of antioxidants to neutralize these poisons. Cosmos Institute has spent considerable time finding a supplement that meets the high quality and science standard I demanded for myself. If your supplement program isn't providing you assurances that your long term health is improving and your program is working, then no matter how economical the cost, the money is wasted. It would be a tragedy to reach old age only to find out the program you were using didn't work. I want assurances long before it is too late to do anything about it.

A restricted caloric intake is still the most proven program to attain a healthy longevity. It has been proven repeatedly as the best and healthiest diet. The established rule when at the dinner table is to eat only until you are 80% full.

Physical activity is important at any age. A good health program must include time for this important activity. Regardless of your current physical status, there is always need to improve and maintain it. Without sufficient activity, ill health and a loss of weight management will surely follow. Cosmos Institute can help you on the path to safe, efficient physical program choices.

MIND:
"The unleashed power of the atom has changed everything save our modes of thinking and we thus drift toward unparalleled catastrophe.
Telegram to prominent Americans, 24 May 1946
Albert Einstein

The mind is an awful thing to waste. The mind is like a machine – it needs constant use and maintenance. The word "retirement" isn't in my vocabulary as that signifies to stop learning. I keep my mind actively growing by learning new skills to keep all the pathways open and growing. A model for me is the 105-year-old mayor of Okinawa who still goes to work every day in his office.

In the Okinawa Program[31] it is noted that the relaxation response is a critical skill to attain a healthy longevity. The modality advocated by Cosmos Institute is the ability to go to your personal Serenity Place through the use of hypnosis. Staying in your Serenity Place will maintain a healthy program for you. Today migraines, stress-related illnesses and chronic pain are the most common problems treated by hypnosis. Developing a relationship with your favorite local hypnotherapist will pay many benefits during your life.

SPIRIT:
"God is the author of change."
"When spiritual evolution is taking place it signals a need for new answers
to old questions."
"Those who promoted change were peacemakers like King, Gandhi, Jesus."
"A need to change God, is giving us a wake up call."
Misc. quotes from unknown sources.

The authors of *The Okinawa Program* had this observation about spirituality: "Spirituality connects us to our deepest values, beliefs, and feelings. It also gives meaning and purpose to our lives, and affects the way we feel about aging, how we deal with illness and death, and what kind of lifestyle choices we make And in the larger sense, spirituality reflects humankind's eternal quest for something greater than our limited selves."

The tools we use to access our spirituality are prayer, meditation and participation in a religious social network with other like-minded people, both young and old. The authors also offer seven healing prescriptions for the psyche and spirit they derived from their studies. The healing prescriptions are:
1. Use prayer to enhance your innate healing power.
2. Create a healing space.
3. Embrace life, accept death.
4. Celebrate aging through rites of passage.
5. Make use of healing imagery and visualization.
6. Create healing affirmations.
7. Find a Guide.

The Okinawa Program is based on a 25-year study to find how the world's longest-lived people achieve everlasting health and how you, too can understand and apply these principles. The foreword is written by Andrew Weil, M.D. and is filled with research results and techniques you can put to practical use today. There is nothing different about the people of Okinawa that can't be applied to you – we are all members of the human race and come from the same source. I think the main quote from the book which tells the reality of life as a human and gives an explanation of the need for an understanding of life as experienced by all humans, is this:

"IN OUR EXPERIENCE WITH THE OLDEST OLD WE RARELY FIND THAT THEIR LIVES HAVE BEEN EASY OR WITHOUT HARDSHIP. ELDERS DO NOT REACH A HEALTHY OLD AGE BECAUSE OF HAVING AVOIDED STRESSFUL LIFE CIRCUMSTANCES. RATHER THEY HAVE RESPONDED TO CHALLENGES IN AN EFFECTIVE AND HEALTHY MANNER."

Unless you were born with a silver spoon in your mouth you may not be aware that your job skills, opportunities and education are directly related to your financial security. As such, your job and its compensation will probably be either a blessing or a traumatic transition during your life. Yet your ability to move smoothly through these transitions is vital to your financial health. Often these events are out of your control, such as during economic and political downturns. But you still need a goal with a financial plan for its accomplishment.

In the United States there are only four ways to earn a living. Which one do you aspire to?

Employee: 80% of the workforce works in this category. As an employee you are working for someone else for a wage. Today you can't be sure of the security this type of employment offers. You are subject to the whims of the boss and your ability to earn extra money is limited. You could lose that job at any time through no fault of your own. Hence, financial growth is difficult unless you are able to get a raise in your salary or a promotion. Today it is almost impossible to find someone who has worked for the same company throughout their career. Even pensions have gone the way of the dodo bird. Now they call them 401K retirement accounts and a lot of those today are worth less than the contribution made by the employees.

Self-Employed: This group is the first level to escape the controls of the employee's situation. They are distinguished from the business owners (listed below) because their income is controlled by their own efforts. They don't have any limit to their income other than their own time. They can increase their income by increasing their fees. However, if they don't personally do the work, there is no income being produced. These are usually professional persons (doctors or lawyers, counselors, advisors) or producers of services (plumbers, carpenters, beauticians, musicians). If they are not personally performing the job there is no income but there are still overhead expenses. These people have complete control over the potential income because they set the fees and can increase their income by raising fees or getting new clients.

Business Owner: The next type of employment up the hierarchy is the business owner. This individual has more freedom of his time because his income isn't tied directly to personal activity. His individual efforts will produce the income or he can have residual income that continues regardless of his personal time. The owner of a McDonald's franchise is an example. The business is so organized that it can run itself in the absence of the owner. In other words, the owner's income continues because the employees continue to produce income in his absence. The business owner can increase his income by hiring more producers or buying more franchises. The business owner is really in the people business, producing a product or service. He then manages the business plan by planning, organizing, staffing, directing, and controlling. He is the ultimate single boss of his organization. He has complete control over his destiny. The downside to this arrangement is a case in which the franchiser is an organization that has control over your ability to stay in business. The chemical business I was in for 35 years is an example of this difficulty. I closed the business due to the sale of my major supplier to a competitor corporation. Rather than take on competing lines and deal with the market changes that were taking place then, I decided to leave the chemical industry. I was the owner so I could decide my own destiny. Any mistakes I made in those cases were completely my responsibility but I still retained the control.

Investor: This is the ultimate business activity for the entrepreneur. This is where a successful business owner can diversify by investing in other business. If they want to increase income they can invest the earnings in other businesses. They are using money to produce more income rather than investing in more people to work their base business. This is the free enterprise system working at its best.

The main question you need to decide is, which type of income do you want for your life's work? All of the options contain advantages and disadvantages. Each one is best for different people depending on their skills and motivations. Any of the choices, however, will result in a number of financial transitions throughout your life so your success will depend on how you manage these transitions. The choice is up to you but so are the risks and rewards.

The choice is yours to make so what you are willing to invest time and skills in will determine which type of income you wish to pursue. Whatever you decide, be sure to first create a detailed description of what you are looking for and then seek and ask for guidance from that Physician Within. Then go for it, putting everything you have into the successful completion of your goals. Recognize that there are no simple solutions – no matter what you choose there are still going to be challenges and transitions on any path – that is the reality of life. So don't blame any difficulties on life; the one you need to talk with is always available.

As an example, let me show you what I mean with the description of the business I was considering. This final effort is a result of years of experience and many transitions in my life. I am currently 73 years old and anticipate at least two decades left before the sun sets on my current incarnation.

I am searching for the following in an organization to which I wish to dedicate the rest of my life, that will add stability to the omega of my life.

1. In an industry that is universally required by most of the people on earth with emphasis toward the maligned middle-income sector.
2. Will provide income both current and residual to last through the remainder of my life.
3. An activity I enjoy and will allow me to have complete destiny over my income.
4. Whose potential market is anywhere on the planet I decide to live.
5. A professional type activity that has the potential to produce significant income and allows me to grow in a continuing learning experience. I don't want to fall into the

trap of allowing my mind to retire. As Kettering said, " The only benches in life where one can stop and rest are directly in front of the undertaker's office."

6. An organization that allows me to associate with positive winners.

7. The organization must have a good track record of innovation and support for its associates, plus financial strength with market needs regardless of the environmental conditions of the marketplace.

8. With no or low start up cost. I'm not interested in paying high priced franchise fees. Nor do I wish to involve myself with some kind of inventory which requires investments and probable losses due to downturns in the market place.

Such are my dreams. I believe I've found the organization that fits this bill of potentials.

I've seen and experienced the success demonstrated by this organization and I'm enthusiastic for the future, as it can become an adjunct to the goals of Cosmos Institute.

If this sounds exciting to you and you would like to investigate what I've found out, send me an email with a phone contact number and I'll contact you with information for your perusal. Send your goals and interest to wellnessdoc@mac.com.

Let me close with a story about the transition that happens in every life and that is a happy occasion, or should be. By this I mean the time in every life when we transition from the spirit world into this world (birth) and when we transition once again from this life to the spirit world, both ourselves and other family members as well. I have discussed the idea of the final transition a number of times throughout this book already. I refer to this final transition as a celebration of life because that is what it really is – just a movement to a higher frequency of awareness and a return to your spiritual home. In the appendix you will find a true story entitled "Connecting the Heart – Transition." It came to me from Barbara Rother, one of the principles and founders of Lightworker. I hope you, too will find inspiration from it. [36]

GLOSSARY

Akashic Record:

Everyone accesses the Record unconsciously through intuitive feelings, sudden urges, vivid dreams, inspirations, spiritual insights or gut feelings. So what is this record that we all accessed so often and what does this record tell us? The Akashic Record has a number of other names: The Book of Life, Hall of Records, The Collective Consciousness, St. Peter's Holy Book, An Energy Field; my grandmother referred to the Akashic Record as the way we earned the bricks to build our house in heaven – when we were good we added to the total of bricks we would have and when we were bad a brick was taken away. So the size of our house in heaven is directly proportional to the number of good things we've done on earth that exceeds the bad things we do. It is the construction bill of materials for our heavenly home. It keeps track of our debts and credits in our karma ledger. It is the record we individually consult when we return to spiritual consciousness after this incarnation on earth to evaluate how we did toward the fulfillment of our Divine Plan. It is also used to plan our next incarnation on earth. Humanity has been aware of the Akashic Record for thousands of years; successful futurists and prophets have long accessed the records to form their predictions. The term Akashic originated from ancient cultures of northern India and Tibet, putting the earliest historical evidence around 7500 BCE. Edgar Cayce found how to access the Record, which is the source of much of the accuracy of his predictions. Your personal record holds your thoughts, idea, verbal utterances, accomplishments and failures. So why can't I see my own records if they are so important? You can. Unfortunately, modern western religions, each with their need to be the only way to spiritual realization, prefer that we not have this access. As we grew in consciousness we realized that the ideas we were taught about God by these big religious institutions were meant to be controls. Hence many religions have defined the Record as supernatural and we are cautioned against its use. Accessing the Record is a learned skill that anyone can develop with a little practice. But it does require a shifting of your belief system in order to accomplish it. Today there are a number of how-to books written on the subject if you wish to peruse them.[8] Each one of us is a cell within the Collective Mind which resides in the 4th and 5th dimension in nature, making it difficult for modern man to comprehend.

Apocatastasis:
The serendipitous secret that in every seed of seeming tragedy is hidden the fruit of glory and reward. Until tomorrow becomes today men will be blind to the good fortune hidden in unfortunate acts.

Bell's Theorem:
John Stewart Bell, an Irish physicist, proposed an experiment that was a variation of the EPR apparatus to test the classical physics assumption that nature works in a "local" or mechanistic way. The results were that nature at the subatomic level is nonlocal, showing that the classical assumptions were wrong. See nonlocality below. This means that at a deep and fundamental level, the separated parts of the universe are connected in an intimate and immediate way. Everything we know about Nature is in accord with the idea that the fundamental process of Nature lies outside space-time, but generates events that can be located in space-time. Thus physicists have been forced to consider the possibility that the superluminal transfer of information between space-like separated events may be an integral aspect of our physical reality.[12]

Big Bang Theory:
A point of infinite compression is known to physicists as a "point of singularity." It is believed by most physicists that once upon a time (thought to be approximately 15 billion years ago) there was a great big bang or explosion that began the Universe from that singularity. All the matter and energy in the Universe today was compressed into that point of singularity and was released and has been expanding ever since and continues to expand. Einstein's General Theory of Relativity predicated the Big Bang. There is a lot of science developed since then to prove the nature of the early ancient Universe, but it is too extensive to include here. Faced with the validity of the Big Bang Theory many religions believe the moment of singularity was the beginning of time when God

created the Universe by releasing all the forces of Nature to manifest his Creation. [11,12,13,14]

Conservation of Mass-Energy:
The Special Theory of Relativity combined mass and energy (Einstein's famous equation $E=MC^2$). The conservation of mass or energy says the total amount of energy in the universe always has been and always will be the same. We can convert energy and mass from one to the other but the total amount in the universe does not change. [12]

Entropy:
Temperature and internal energy are both state functions that can be used to describe the thermodynamic states of a system. Another state function related to the Second Law of Thermodynamics is the entropy function. When thermal energy is absorbed by the system, the change in entropy is positive, the entropy increases. When thermal energy is expelled by the system the change is negative and the entropy decreases. Note that the function does not define entropy but the change in entropy. Change in state always accompanies heat transfer so the meaningful quantity in describing a process is the change in entropy. Hence, isolated systems tend toward disorder and entropy is a measure of this disorder. The entropy of the Universe increases in all processes. An everyday example how entropy is important to us is how we use heat to stay alive. We use heat as a by-product of the biochemical reactions of our bodies to keep us at the temperature that our bodies need at 98° F.. If our bodies fight in cold weather to keep our inner organs at 98° F, will we be at ease in 98° F weather? Except for the inevitableness of entropy's increase, we might be. Our metabolic processes even when we are at rest produce so much extra heat, never to be recovered, that we have developed an entire system, that of perspiration, to remove this excess heat by evaporative cooling. [10]

Hatha Yoga:
Hatha represents opposing energies: hot and cold (fire and water, following similar concept as yin-yang), male and female, positive

and negative. Hatha yoga attempts to balance mind and body via physical postures or "asanas", purification practices, controlled breathing, and the calming of the mind through relaxation and meditation.

Hologram:

A principle of laser physics called a hologram is a three-dimensional picture or in our case, a memory whose segmented part represents the whole. If you look at the picture you have the picture of the whole. However, if you cut the picture, extract a small segment and project it on a screen you would find the small segment image still contains the picture of the original whole. It is now felt that each cell in our bodies is a hologram that contains the whole story of our life and all previous lives. A hologram is made by illuminating the subject with a beam of laser light that has been run through a beam splitter, resulting in two beams – exposing a sensitized glass plate to the light reflected from the subject. The plate contains no visible image, but when illuminated by a similar pair of coordinated beams of light it produces a three dimensional replica of the hologrammed subject that seems to hover in space. Break a hologram, put one of its fragments in the laser beam and what you see is not a piece of the original image but all of it.

Karma:

Reduced to its essentials Karma is the law of cause and effect. It is involved with adjustment rather than punishment. Karma may be damaging to your self-esteem but it does not lessen its equity. Justice is commonly difficult for the convicted to understand. Karma is about free will. It doesn't mean an inhibiting fatalism which prevents a man struggling against his lot. Everyone has complete liberty to think as he will, speak as he will and act as he will. Each thought, action and speech will result in reactions which sooner or later will result in his being given a situation to face. How he faces it will depend entirely upon himself and upon the experience he has gained in his past.[17]

Law of Diminishing Returns:

The law states that we will get less and less extra output when we add additional doses of an input while holding other inputs fixed.

266

Nonlocal correlation:
A phase relationship that persists even at a distance between two quantum objects, which have interacted for a period and then stopped interacting. The EPR correlation corresponds to a potential nonlocal influence between the objects.

Nonlocality:
An instantaneous influence or communication without any exchange of signals through space-time; an unbroken wholeness or non-separability that transcends space-time.

Physician Within:
The Physician Within is the spiritual aspect of the trilogy of the three-legged stool. You cannot sit comfortably on a three legged stool if one of the legs is missing. At Cosmos Institute we believe the Physician Within is the God of your understanding, just as we advocate the return to Spirit Medicine and Mind which means the recognition that the God of the universe is present in every thing, person, and event which includes everything in Nature. We must connect with the spiritual oneness of the cosmos to achieve our Divine destiny.

Placebo Effect:
The tendency of any medication or treatment, even an inert or ineffective one, to exhibit results simply because the recipient believes that it will work. In recent decades reports have confirmed the efficacy of various sham treatments in nearly all areas of medicine. Placebos have helped alleviate pain, depression, anxiety, Parkinson's disease, inflammatory disorders and even cancer. Placebo effects can arise not only from a conscious belief in a drug but also from subconscious associations between recovery and the experience of being treated — from the pinch of a shot to a doctor's white coat. Such subliminal conditioning can control bodily processes of which we are unaware, such as immune responses and the release of hormones. Researchers have decoded some of the biology of placebo responses, demonstrating that they stem from active processes in the brain.[9]

Quantum memory:
Memory based on the modification of the probability calculus of nonlinear quantum equations that govern the quantum dynamics of the brain, mind, and the spirit. As a result of this memory, the probability of recall of learned responses is enhanced.

Quantum:
A discrete bundle of energy; the lowest denomination of energy or other physical quantities that can be exchanged.

Second Law of Thermodynamics:
When two systems are placed in thermal contact, the direction of energy transfer in the form of heat is always from the system at the higher temperature to the system at the lower temperature.[15]

APPENDIX

1. The station
2. You have a choice
3. Connecting the Heart – Transition
4. The mysteries and challenges of life and death.
5. Research on meditation
6. Effectiveness of spiritual healing practices
7. Being fat and free radicals
8. Our bodies are toxic chemical repositories
9. Contamination of Food Supply by Dioxin
10. Why Did 9/11 happen?
11. Study provides hope for the healthy Non-Smoker
12. Most heart attacks caused by unhealthy lifestyle, not bad genes
13. Oldest survivor in the world
14. Self test spirituality & well-being
15. Study - youngsters who smoke cigarettes are more likely to use marijuana
16. Effective battle plan for flu season
17. Effect of vitamin/mineral supplementation on juvenile delinquency
18. Mandatory drugging of our children??
19. Does the FDA represent the people or private interest??
20. Formula for a successful prayer

THE STATION – By Robert J. Hastings

Tucked away in our subconscious is an idyllic vision. We see ourselves on a long trip that spans the continent. We are traveling by train. Out the windows we drink in the passing scene of cars on nearby highways, of children waving at a crossing, of cattle grazing on a distant hillside, of smoke pouring from a power plant, of rows and rows of corn and wheat, of flat lands and valleys, of mountains and rolling hillsides, of city skylines and village halls.

But uppermost in our minds is the final destination. On a certain day at a certain hour we will pull into the station. Bands will be playing and flags waving. Once we get there so many wonderful dreams will come true and the pieces of our lives will come together like a completed jigsaw puzzle. How restlessly we pace the aisles, damning the minutes for loitering – waiting, waiting, waiting for the station.

"When we reach the station, that will be it!" we cry. "When I'm 18." "When I buy a new 450 SL Mercedes Benz!" "When I put the last kid through college." "When I have paid off the mortgage!" "When I get a promotion." "When I reach the age of retirement, I shall live happily ever after!"

Sooner or later we must realize there is no station, no one place to arrive at once and for all. The true joy of life is the trip; the station is only a dream. It constantly outdistances us.

"Relish the moment" is a good motto, especially when coupled with Psalm 118:24: "This is the day which the lord hath made; we will rejoice and be glad in it." It isn't the burdens of today that drive men mad. It is the regrets over yesterday and the fear of tomorrow. Regret and fear are the twin thieves who rob us of today.

So, stop pacing the aisles and counting the miles. Instead, climb more mountains, eat more ice cream, go barefoot more often, swim more rivers, watch more sunsets, laugh more, cry less. Life must be lived as we go along. The station will come soon enough.

YOU HAVE A CHOICE
Author Unknown

Michael is the kind of guy you love to hate. He is always in a good mood and always has something positive to say (reminds me of my grandmother Cappy). When someone asked him how he was doing, he would reply, "If I were any better, I would be twins!"

He was a natural motivator. If an employee was having a bad day, Michael was there telling the employee how to look on the positive side of the situation.

Seeing this style really made me curious, so one day I went up to Michael and asked him, "I don't get it! You can't be a positive person all the time. How do you do it?" Michael replied, "Each morning I wake up and say to myself, you have two choices today. You can choose to be in a good mood or you can choose to be in a bad mood. I choose to be in a good mood. Each time something bad happens, I can choose to be a victim or …I can choose to learn from it. I choose to learn from it. Every time someone comes to me complaining, I can choose to accept their complaining or ….I can point out the positive side of life. I choose the positive side of life." "Yeah, right, it's not that easy," I protested. "Yes, it is " Michael said. "Life is all about choices. When you cut away all the junk, every situation is a choice. You choose how you react to situations. You choose how people affect your mood. You choose to be in a good mood or bad mood. The bottom line: It's your choice how you live our life."

I reflected on what Michael said. Soon thereafter, I left the tower industry to start my own business. We lost touch, but I often thought about him when I made a choice about life instead of reacting to it.

Several years later, I heard that Michael was involved in a serious accident, falling some 60 feet from a communications tower. After 18 hours of surgery and weeks of intensive care, Michael was released from the hospital with rods placed in his back.

I saw Michael about six months after the accident. When I asked him how he was he replied, "If I were any better, I'd be twins. Wanna see my scars?"

I declined to see his wounds, but I did ask him what had gone through his mind as the accident took place. "The first thing that went through my mind was the well-being of my soon to be born daughter," Michael replied. "Then as I lay on the ground, I remembered that I had two choices: I could choose to live or ....I could choose to die. I chose to live."

"Weren't you scared? Did you lose consciousness?" I asked. Michael continued, "The paramedics were great. They kept telling me I was going to be fine. But when they wheeled me into the ER and I saw the expressions on the faces of the doctors and nurses, I got really scared. In their eyes, I read "He's a dead man." I knew I need to take action."

"What did you do?" I asked. "Well, there was a big burly nurse shouting questions at me," said Michael. "She asked if I was allergic to anything." "Yes," I replied. "The doctors and nurses stopped working as they waited for my reply. I took a deep breath and yelled, "Gravity."

Over their laughter, I told them, "I am choosing to live. Operate on me as if I am alive, not dead."

Michael lived, thanks to the skill of his doctors and nurses, but also because of his amazing attitude. I learned from him that every day we have the choice to live fully. Attitude, after all, is everything.

Therefore do not worry about tomorrow, for tomorrow will worry about itself, Each day has enough trouble of its own. Matt 6:34.

After all, today is the tomorrow you worried about yesterday. You have two choices now:
1. Ignore this.
2. Share it with the people you care about.

You know the choice I made because I care about the readers of my book who are seriously searching. God bless you all.

CONNECTING THE HEART – TRANSITION
By Barbara Rother, Co-Founder, Light Workers

Steve and I had just returned from Belgium. As always, we had a wonderful time connecting to spiritual family there. We presented a one-day event and two three-day seminars, Transition Team and Inverse Wave Therapy. I enjoyed them all but the transition event was the one that meant the most to me this time because of what I had been experiencing before this trip.

A month ago I received a phone call telling me that a dear friend of mine had suddenly lost her eight-week-old baby. He died in his sleep. It is hard enough to have a child die but to have no warning makes it worse. For a few days I tried to process and understand this situation. The day of the memorial service I kept telling myself not to be so upset. This was about my friend, not about me, but her pain was my pain. I arrived to the viewing early so I could help. I wanted to do something but felt helpless because no matter what I did I could not take away the pain of the family who lost this angel. I arranged the baby pictures around the room and greeted people. I hugged my friend as she cried while looking at her precious son who looked like he was in a peaceful sleep. I could feel his soul had transitioned. I thought I was coping well with this sad situation until I was driving home. My grief overcame me, as my tears would not stop. For the next week I felt myself tumbling down a black hole of depression, followed by anger. How could God take away such a precious soul? I experienced fear that one of my loved ones or I could die at any moment. I reached out to friends and family to tell them I loved them. I now realize I was going through the stages of grieving.

As time went on I started to feel more at peace with what had happened. Life continued at a busy pace moving me forward. Then I received another phone call. This time it was about a sudden death of a friend's daughter-in-law. I am such a sensitive person, as I know many of you are. Even though this was not my personal tragedy I felt the sadness as it was. Steve was asked to give a talk at the memorial service. His words were so beautiful and comforting. I looked around at the family and friends who were mourning this young woman's transition. Her husband broke down in tears while I hugged him. The young daughter didn't seem to fully conceive the situation at the moment. I am sure it was all so overwhelming for her. I also lost my mother when I was young. It saddened me to know what she would be going through.

This all happened in the month of January, a time of new beginnings. I began the New Year with such optimism and hope, only to now be feeling deep sadness. I was confused with all that had happened as my emotions drained me. Time has a way of healing and helping us move on. One day soon after all this I woke up feeling I was back to being myself again. The sun was shining and I felt joy in my heart. It was like I awoke from a long, bad dream and was back in my wonderful reality. I still think about both of my friends' losses but I know they are moving on with life and so am I. What I began to feel is appreciation for my life and all those around me. Death is only sad for the ones left behind who miss their loved ones. The ones who have crossed over are back home and feel no pain.

I had to laugh as I realized that all this happened shortly before Steve and I were going to present the Transition Team training in Belgium. I felt Spirit telling me that all this came into my life at the perfect time. As I talked about this experience during the seminar I came to the realization that both of these people gave me a gift. The group says that grieving is not about getting over a loss, but rather about finding a part of that person to keep in your heart. It was not just a gift for me, but I was able to share it with all those at the seminar and now with all of you. Hopefully my experience and sharing will help some of you through this process.

Transition, whether it is when a soul goes home, or when it enters this world, is just a part of life. Today I celebrate how wonderful my world is. Each day I understand more and more what life is about.
Love and Light.

Barbara
www. Lightworker.com

MYSTERIES AND THE CHALLENGES OF LIFE AND DEATH

After September 11, 2001 and the earthquake in Taiwan which took more than 3,000 victims, the people of Taiwan felt it was time to educate their citizens and school children on the new frontiers of human knowledge, the mysteries and the challenges of life and death. They wanted to understand the meaning of living and dying well amidst sufferings and tragedies. The Taiwanese hosted a conference in December with the purpose to explore these questions and also to seek solutions to their increasing problem of youth suicides. The speakers from throughout Taiwan emphasized meaning, purpose, religious beliefs and family support as major preventive factors. The keynote speaker, Paul T.P. Wong, is a professor and research director of the graduate program in counseling psychology at Trinity Western University in Langley, British Columbia. He spoke to the positive role of meaning and spirituality in death acceptance and in the transformation of grief.

Prof. Wong says, "The best way to be prepared for death is to live life to the fullest; to contemplate one's death is to contemplate the life that leads to that death." Konosuke Matsushita, founding president of Matsushita Electronics, once said, "To be prepared for death is to be prepared for living; to die well is to live well."

Prof. Wong summed up the conference in these words: "When young people understand the meaning and purpose of being alive, they are more likely to live a productive and fulfilling life. When the sick and the dying understand the meaning of suffering and death, they are more likely to engage life in a positive way, no matter how limited."

How true it is! I'm tempted to ask why in the western world the subject of death has to have such negative connotations. Learning about death is a lesson in living and when we accept that then our lives will be so much fuller.

RESEARCH ON MEDITATION

A brief outline of the research done on meditation will be of interest to all who wish to understand this important spiritual technique. One of the earliest western scientists to study meditation was Robert Keith Wallace, who in 1967 began his Ph.D. research into the physiological changes that take place during Transcendental Meditation. He measured the subjects' blood pressure, brain waves, heart rate, and oxygen consumption to indicate the metabolic rate of cells. He found that meditators would reach the alpha wave state and a state of deep relaxation within only a few minutes. Normally when we go to sleep it can take from four to six hours to reach a very deep state of relaxation while meditators were able to reach this level of relaxation in only a few minutes.

What was most significant about these meditators was that they hadn't gone to sleep, were not in one of the three consciousness states but were still fully awake internally, nor had they gone into a trance. They experienced an increased sense of awareness. Wallace called this state "hypometabolic wakefulness."

After a decade of working with the measurements and phenomenal mind/body states he turned to the study of aging. He set out to find out if the normal stress we have in life from environmental toxins, negative emotions, diet, substance abuses and the fast-paced lifestyle of modern westerners were responsible for normal aging. If that was the case, could meditation slow the aging process even while we are exposed to the detrimental factors? He investigated a group of adult meditators for biological aging factors. Wallace discovered that meditators as a group were significantly younger biologically than their chronological age would indicate. And the difference in these ages was very large; in the female subjects they averaged at least twenty years younger. There was a correlation in the amount of this biological age difference and the number of years the subject had been meditating regularly. He concluded that for every year of regular meditation the biological age was reduced by one year. In a later confirmation study this was confirmed again. A typical 60-year-old who had meditated five years or more would have the physiology of a 48-year-old. Imagine that, look twelve years younger with no surgery.

So meditation is well worth the time and effort. By putting in the time now you will extend your effective chronological age.

EFFECTIVENESS OF SPIRITUAL HEALING PRACTICES

Emory University Hospital, one of the premier teaching hospitals in the southeast, has begun clinical trials to see whether alternative medical techniques can improve life for Parkinson's patients. "We want to examine the quality of life as it relates to Parkinson's correlated to issues of spirituality," said Dr. Jorge Juncos, Associate Professor of Neurology at Emory. There haven't been any rigorous, controlled trials conducted to determine the effectiveness of spiritual healing practices.

Rev. Kathleen Kiley says that through spiritual healing one receives a healing so their body actually reverts to the natural form it had before the disease. Once the energy body is realigned and back to its natural order, the physical body follows suit. Medical doctors find it very difficult to talk with their patients about a healing technique when there is no scientific basis for their recommendations. Emory Hospital is endeavoring to supply some of that scientific basis. This study is especially encouraging since Emory is owned and supported by the Methodist Church. Maybe it will encourage more religiously-supported hospitals to conduct spiritual healing experiments.

BEING FAT AND FREE RADICALS

We all know that being "fat" is not good for your heart and health. A report in the medical journal Arteriosclerosis, Thrombosis and Vascular Biology described a study of 2,828 people in the Framingham (Mass.) Heart Study which attempted to determine why. The results confirmed what we already knew. The culprit was "free radicals" which are found in higher levels in obese persons than in thin persons. in other words, with obesity there are more chemicals available in the body to do damage to cells. In addition to losing weight we need to pay attention to reducing the available free radicals. We already know how to do that, don't we? In trying to determine whether you are within a healthy weight range, the Body Mass Index is a good measuring scale. So be sure to use the scale to set your goals for weight gain or loss. Earlier in this book we discussed the BMI in more detail.

OUR BODIES ARE TOXIC CHEMICAL REPOSITORIES.

The April 2003 *Life Extension* magazine had a most interesting article dealing with the carcinogens we consume in our diets. Life Extension is a research facility whose primary area of interest is research into extending the lifespan through lifestyle modifications and proper diet. An increasing number of Americans are now making lifestyle changes in order to avoid exposure to toxic chemicals. But even though we have worked very hard at
keeping these toxins out, two newly released studies show that our bodies have become toxic chemical repositories. It seems that despite all these efforts, even health conscious people have become significant pollution sites. There is still hope! Dr. Bruce Ames, a foremost expert on gene mutation (which is what cancer is) has long been a proponent of using DNA-protecting nutrients like folic acid to neutralize the effects of natural and synthetic carcinogens. He believes, and the new studies bear out, that nutrient deficiency causes cancer. "Deficiency of vitamin B12, folic acid, B6, niacin, vitamin C, Vitamin E, iron, or zinc, appears to mimic radiation in damaging DNA by causing single- and double-strand breaks, oxidative lesions or both... half of the population may be deficient in at least one of these micronutrients."

There are a number of practical suggestions we can utilize to protect our genetic pool. Take a look at the Life Extension website at www.lef.org.

CONTAMINATION OF FOOD SUPPLY BY DIOXIN

In a special update from the American Holistic Health Association, their feature news item dealt with a new government report by the National Academics which highlighted another reason to watch the fats in our diets – as if we didn't have enough reason already. They were warning of the increasing contamination of our food supply with dioxin, a very powerful, toxic carcinogen. Dioxin is difficult for the body to rid itself of because it dissolves in fats and has an average half-life of seven years in the human body. The WHO (World Health Organization) says that the higher one goes up the food chain, the higher is the concentration of dioxin. Remember, humans are at the top of the food chain. WHO's report says: "Short-term exposure of humans to high levels of dioxins may result in skin lesions and altered liver function. Long-term exposure is linked to impairment of the immune system, the developing nervous system, the endocrine system and reproductive functions. Chronic exposure of animals to dioxins has resulted in several types of cancer." The primary sources for exposure of humans to dioxins are from fatty meats, fish and full-fat dairy products. To help reduce your exposure, the consumption of a balanced diet including adequate amounts of fruits, vegetables and cereals might help. For more information on dioxins and their effects on human health, visit the following WHO website: http://www.who.int/mediacentre/factsheets/fs225/en/index.html.

WHY DID 9/11 HAPPEN?

The School of Metaphysics (www.som.org.) made the following announcement shortly after the 9/11 attacks:. "The attacks on September 11, 2001 stimulated all of us to ask, "Why?" "Why did it happen?" "What are the lessons we need to learn from this?" The urge to make sense of an event that seems so horrible, painful, and evil is the urge within us to know the mind of God. If we can understand how all of this aligns with Universal Law and what our soul needs to learn, then we can take steps to build understanding. With understanding comes peace."

STUDY PROVIDES HOPE FOR THE HEALTHY NON-SMOKER

The Aug. 5, 2003 issue of *Nutrition and Cancer* reported on a small study that provides hope for the healthy non-smoker. The study was done on 67 non-smokers at the University of California, Berkeley and suggested that vitamin C may protect non-smokers from the effects of second hand smoke. The researchers found that participants who took 500 mg. of vitamin C daily had lower levels of a compound that was linked to the oxidative damage caused by tobacco smoke. The study was short term so it didn't have any conclusions on the probability of not developing cancer or heart disease as a result of the vitamin C. But if you are a non-smoker and can't avoid second hand smoke, taking vitamin C, which has many positive side benefits, surely couldn't hurt.

MOST HEART ATTACKS CAUSED BY UNHEALTHY LIFESTYLE, NOT BAD GENES

That headline appeared in USA TODAY 11/19/03. The newspaper was reporting on two studies that were just released which took away all the "cop outs" commonly used by those who don't want to take responsibility for their health. As I've maintained many times, genetics is only a propensity for a condition, not a death sentence. We need to get back to the basics, the traditional risk factors.

This was a large, diverse population study with 30-year follow up on lifestyle studies. Basically, the conclusions reaffirmed the fact that roughly 90% of the people with severe heart disease have one or more of the classic risk factors like smoking, high cholesterol, high blood pressure, obesity and diabetes. All are factors that can be controlled through diet, exercise, and consultation with the Physician Within. When are we going to wake up to the truth as Shakespeare told us eight centuries ago: "The fault, dear Brutus, lies not in our stars but in ourselves that we are underlings."

OLDEST SURVIVOR IN THE WORLD

On 9/16/03 the oldest survivor in the world turned 116 years young. And as you would suspect she is Japanese; her name is Kamato Hongo. She is currently the eldest human after an American woman died last March at the age of 115. The same island that Hongo is from also produced the oldest human record holder for longevity, a woman who died at the age of 120. Do I have to move to Japan in order to become a healthy centurion, you might ask? Of course not; all you need to do is adapt the healthy lifestyle of the Orientals and move away from the pollution of the large cities. Ms. Hongo says the secret to her long life is "not moping around."

Healthy longevity has been extensively studied and an excellent resource is a book entitled *The Okinawa Program.*[31] The answers are known to us and only require us to commit to a change in lifestyle. The things that most people find too difficult to accomplish are still the only things that work. God never said that life was supposed to be easy; it is a learning experience and sometimes lessons are hard. The choice is yours to make. I wish everyone would realize that the time to start thinking about their health after retirement is soon after they start their fourth decade of life. With each year afterwards the ability to make effective lifestyle changes becomes more difficult.

SELF TEST SPIRITUALITY & WELL-BEING

Spirituality & Health Magazine has a self test to help you determine and investigate your personal spiritual practices. It is a simple test that you can answer in 10 minutes or less and you will receive your score and comments immediately. This test has also been validated by the US military, reducing their suicide rate from 804 to zero. By identifying the weak areas, you will be able to put forth an effort to strengthen your weaknesses.

You can access the test by going to the interactive website and following this path: www.spiritualityhealth.com > Community > Self Tests > Spirituality and Well-Being.

There are also a number of other self tests you may wish to try on a multitude of subjects. Good luck and have fun.

STUDY - YOUNGSTERS WHO SMOKE CIGARETTES ARE MORE LIKELY TO USE MARIJUANA

In September 2003 a study issued by the National Center on Addiction and Substance Abuse at Columbia University and the American Legacy Foundation said youngsters who smoke cigarettes are more likely to use marijuana than those who don't smoke. We all know that tobacco use has NO healthy, beneficial purpose. We know tobacco is not good for us and we know we are the role model for our children, so it is a crime to start them on the path to use an illegal drug which is also detrimental to their young bodies. Where is the justification to stop smoking while you are pregnant and then take it up after the birth? The child is still just as unhealthy by breathing in the toxins into a body that is not yet prepared to fight off the poisons. Even the kids recognize the connection between tobacco and pot use. When asked whether they think that a kid who smokes cigarettes is more likely to use pot, 77 % responded yes. Tobacco use is not easy to stop but it is possible, as thousands of people every day can testify. But what kind of legacy do we leave our children if we can't keep them from starting that unhealthy lifestyle choice? Isn't the motivation, while difficult, worth the effort? We must make the changes at home.

EFFECTIVE BATTLE PLAN FOR FLU SEASON

As the leaves begin to change color in the fall every year the press never lets us forget we are starting the cold and flu season. They warn us of all the dire consequences if we catch "the bug." Such negative press can be a self-fulfilling prophecy. When the only conversation is only about all those who are sick or the flu is running through everyone in the family, it is almost guaranteed you will get sick also, unless you strengthen your immune system and maintain a positive mental attitude so you can build your own shield against the "bugs." They warn us we must get our flu shots, and then tell us the vaccine is contaminated and in short supply. I'll not address the vaccination question here except to say that I don't take flu shots because I know my own body, if maintained properly, is a better defense against a foreign invader (the bug) than any poison I could put into it. In my whole history I think I've had the common cold only twice and never the flu. In fact, while a medic at a juvenile facility I was the one standing while 80% of the kids and over 50% of the staff were sent to bed and about 6 kids were in the hospital during a flu epidemic. In some cases the media will follow up their stories with suggestions of how to keep from getting the flu. This is one area we all agree on – that preventing the flu and colds is our best defense against the fever, chills and coughs that such illnesses produce (with the exception of the vaccines). So let me jump into the fray with my prevention plan that has always worked for me.

1. Wash your hands frequently during the day with soap and hot water, particularly if you have associated with other sick persons. Our hands are most often the route of transmission for the germs to enter our bodies. This is the one technique common to all prevention instructions.
2. Get plenty of rest. When you are sleep deprived your immune system is also depressed and having to work overtime.
3. Take a daily supplement of Echinacea or Astragalus to support the immune system in its work. The addition of a high quality multi-vitamin and antioxidant formula is also a good idea. I usually increase my vitamin C intake to 3000 mg per day.
4. Increase your fluid intake in order to stay hydrated.
5. If you think you will catch the flu because it "is going around" then you will. Don't let that lie slip into your consciousness.
6. Do not use tobacco or excessive alcohol, and review your current medications – many of them can depress the immune system and provide you with symptoms that imitate the virus. Many lifestyle conditions exacerbate the conditions.

You don't catch the cold or flu; the "bugs" are always around you. Your immune system has just become overwhelmed because you allowed your defenses to falter.

EFFECT OF VITAMIN-MINERAL SUPPLEMENTATION ON JUVENILE DELINQUENCY

This particular study was a randomized, double blind placebo-controlled study to determine the effect of vitamin-mineral supplementation on juvenile delinquency among American schoolchildren. The full study is contained within many pages and can be found in the Feb. 2000 issue of *The Journal of Alternative and Complementary Medicine,* pages 7-17. Let me quote from the conclusion, which confirms what we in natural health knew all along. "Poor nutritional habits in children that lead to low concentrations of water-soluble vitamins in blood impair brain function and subsequently cause violence and other serious antisocial behavior. Correction of nutrient intake either through a well-balanced diet or low-dose vitamin-mineral supplementation corrects the low concentrations of vitamins in blood, improves brain function and subsequently lowers institutional violence and antisocial behavior by almost half. This paper adds to the literature by enabling previous research to be generalized from older incarcerated subjects with a history of antisocial behavior to a normal population of younger children in an educational setting." While this study dealt with schoolchildren, the effects would be just as important for adults to consider. Just as we are experiencing increased diseases related to poor diet, so are we experiencing increased incidence of adult violence within the US population. All our prisons are overcrowded and the taxpayers have an increased burden to build more facilities just to house the growth of criminal activity in our society. Poor nutrition is still a major factor in the adult population as well.

MANDATORY DRUGGING OF OUR CHILDREN??

I recently (2004) was made aware of a scary scenario proposed for our country that reminded me of Germany in the 1930's. There are plans to screen every schoolchild for ADHD, depression, social anxiety disorder and behavior problems. These efforts are already in effect in the states of Illinois, Texas and New Jersey. In April 2002, President Bush created the New Freedom Commission on Mental Health. Its stated objective was to enhance mental health services to those in need. A lofty goal, but the commission has typically expanded its role to include the need to search for mental disorders, especially in children. They plan to use mandatory mental health screening for everyone, starting with the preschoolers. The commission goes on the say, "...the extent, severity, and far-reaching consequences make it imperative that our Nation adopt a comprehensive, systemic approach to improving the mental health status of children." What is the medical community's method for "improving"? You guessed it – drugging them. It doesn't take a mental giant to determine where the ideas for this dangerous policy comes from – the masterminds are the pharmaceutical companies who want to keep their coffers filled. The treatment protocols are based on the Texas Medication Algorithm Project which is a set of very specific medication recommendations which, of course, include all the newest and most expensive psychotropic drugs. Psychotropic drugs prevent children from truly experiencing childhood. The drugged child does not grow into and out of the various life stages of childhood. These drugs will prevent normal development of the human mind. Can you imagine what you would be like today if you had missed a half dozen years of your childhood?

If you want to test yourself to see how ridiculous these assessment tests can be, how one-sided they are, go to the website www. Prozac.com and take their 20 question self assessment test for depression screening. I personally took the test. It asks you to respond to the questions with sometimes, not often, often, or all the time. What happened to the "never" option? If a healthy person was to respond honestly to these questions they would probably check the "sometime" box for each question. When I did this my score was over 50 and I was advised to take a copy of the test to my doctor and ask to be evaluated for depression. I think I would be given a prescription to be filled as soon as I could make it to the closest pharmacy.

What can be done about it now? I think this is still in a development stage – it hasn't been approved by congress yet. But we must be watchful – remember what has happened to a number of generations with the advent of compulsory vaccinations in the US. The program sounded good in theory but decades later science showed the dangers that resulted. There are however, three states mentioned above where this program is being instituted. Fortunately, in the US we still have some control. They have to obtain the parents' permission; the drugging of our children can be avoided. So mothers and fathers, get involved to safeguard your children's and grandchildren's health.

DOES THE FDA REPRESENT THE PEOPLE OR PRIVATE INTERESTS?

In order words, I question whether they are doing their mandated job. Recently the FDA and the large drug companies have been having their problems. TOO BAD! This all started with the HRT (hormone replacement therapy) crisis, which increased the cancer risk rather than reduced it. HRT was rushed to the market too early to complete the long-term safety trials. Soon there will be more drugs that were also rushed to market before adequate testing was completed, resulting in unnecessary suffering by millions of patients who trusted their physicians to "Do No Harm." Other drugs that will soon be hitting the headlines are:

New cholesterol drugs that may weaken the heart...

New prostate drugs suspected of encouraging cancer....

New painkillers linked to everything from back pain to sudden death....

And in many cases they don't even suppress the symptoms they're supposed to! The real tragedy is that there are always safe alternatives without the side effects found in most prescription drugs. In addition, the drug companies knew of these hazards all along. The motivation to get these drugs to market was based more on greed than on a humanitarian cause, exacerbated by the FDA's relaxing the time frame for complete testing.

Unfortunately, the serious side effects don't come to light until long after their introduction. Could the drug companies in their search for profits finally come face to face with the immutable law that you cannot improve on Mother Nature? The return to nature is the only real solution to the planet's ills. The problem is that drug companies make their profits from patented drugs, and in order to get the patents you have to improve on nature – that is impossible. How can you fix the body vehicle with imitation parts when nature's original equipment wears out? And when you try, then for the rest of your life you are condemned to breakdowns that again need band-aid fixing, that will again break down, a catch-22 cycle. You have placed your foot on the slippery slope toward ill health.

When the U.S. Government, with lots of fanfare, proudly announced its new drug program for seniors, a senior executive with a large international drug company admitted that fewer than half of the patients prescribed some of the most expensive drugs actually derived any benefit from them. Did anyone hear that side of the story? The reason is that this comment was made by Dr. Allen Roses, Worldwide Vice-President of Genetics at GlaxoSmithKline during a hearing when Great Britain was investigating the cause of their soaring drug costs. He admitted, "The vast majority of drugs – more than 90% - only work in 30 or 50 percent of the people." That's close to the success attained by the placebo effect – 30%. These facts have been known to the drug industry for years and Dr. Roses was the first honest drug executive to go public with this industry secret.

Dr. Allen Roses, an academic geneticist from Duke University in North Carolina, spoke at a recent scientific meeting in London where he cited the following percentages on how well different classes of drugs work in real patients: Alzheimer's (30), Analgesics (80), Asthma (60), Cardiac Arrhythmias (60), Depression (62), Diabetes (57), Hepatitis C (47), Incontinence (40), Migraine (acute) (52), Migraine (prophylaxis) (50), Oncology (25), Rheumatoid arthritis (50), Schizophrenia (60).

This is yet another reason to go back to nature and a lifestyle of preventive and proactive medicine rather than being reactive, after the fact, to illness and disease.

We can make a difference. On June 21, 2004 Sen. Richard Durbin (IL) withdrew Senate Amendment 3255 from a DOD funding bill that threatened to restrict access to certain dietary supplements on military bases and place strict and unnecessary reporting guidelines on manufacturers who sell to these bases. This would have started a move to undermine the Dietary Supplement Health and Education Act (DSHEA) of 1994. This is the act that guarantees access to dietary supplements and information. Ever since this act was passed there have been forces at work to repeal the provisions of the act, and I believe you know who those forces are. This attempt was defeated by a groundswell of letters to Congress (over 12,500) from natural heath consumers across the nation asking to defeat the amendment in order to protect their free choice of medical care. There is a watchdog organization that keeps an eye on such lobbying attempts and their website is www.citizens.org if you would care to get on their mailing list to stay abreast of future developments. This organization is know as Citizens for Health. There are already a couple of herbal compounds that have been outlawed and are no longer available in America. Let's not let this happen to any other perfectly good natural substances just to line the pockets of Big Pharma's executives.

Big Pharma is still at it. As I'm writing this today (April 2010) I received another notice from another watchdog organization, Health Solutions Foundation, www.GlobalHealthFreedom.org and www.HealthFreedomUSA.org. To describe what is happening, the notice took three small-type pages to detail, but here is a short version. Back in 2007 just before Sen. Kennedy passed away, the "FDA Enabling Act" was passed, but it took hundreds of thousands of emails to keep Section 1011 in the bill in order to exempt and thus protect dietary supplements. Even so, the FDA used its new Section 301(11) power to ban interstate commerce in any food substance that had ever been studied for medical use in order to ban Pyridoxamine, a non-toxic form of vitamin B6.

In January 2009 the FDA banned Pyridoxamine, a natural, non-patentable, safe and historically proven vitamin to the American public despite its being protected under the DSHEA. The FDA is about to ban other forms of vitamin B6 as well. The drug company involved actually publicly stated, "Pharmaceutical companies developing new drugs must be protected from companies that may seek to market the ingredients in those drugs as dietary supplements. The marketing of such products has the potential to undermine the incentive for the development of new drugs because many people may choose to purchase the supplements rather than the drugs." Such blatant assumption of power should be treated as criminal activity against the public good.

Last year Sen. John McCain attempted to restrict dietary supplements again when he introduced S 3002. The bill died a month and half later because the public sent in a million plus emails in opposition to the bill. So now they are introducing another bill with a different name and number but still containing the worst parts of S 3002. After many hundreds of thousands of emails it looks like the new bill, S 510, will be amended to protect

DSHEA products, but it doesn't go far enough. The natural health legislation needs to protect natural health remedies and holistic techniques and all natural, local, community, family and farm food production. A better idea would be to DEFEAT S 510.

Until the powerful lobbies of Big Pharma, Big Agri, and Big Corp are eliminated we will continue having to fight to keep our health freedom until the freedoms are finally all eroded away. This fight has been going on since before DSHEA and it looks like there is no end in sight. Consider the following.

The following was reported in a news email by saveyourheart.com on 12/04/03. "100,000 people a year in the US die from the administration of pharmaceutical drugs – Lucian L. Leape, "Error in Medicine." JAMA 1994, 272:23 page 1851. Also Leape, "Medical Error Figures Are Not Exaggerated," JAMA 2000, July 5:284(1):95-97. Doctors are the third leading cause of death in the US, creating 225,000 deaths a year ; Barbara Starfield, JAMA vol. 284, No. 4, July 26, 2000. 12,000 deaths from unnecessary surgery. 7000 from medication errors in hospitals, 20,000 from other errors in hospitals, 80,000 from infections spread inside hospitals, and 106,000 from medical drugs correctly prescribed."

In 1990 the US Government Accounting Office reported about 50% of the medical drugs certified as safe and effective by the FDA and approved for public use between 1976 and 1985 were taken off the market or relabeled because of serious side effects. USGAO, FDA Drug Review: Postapproval Risks, 1976-1985, GAOPemd – 90-15, April 1990. In September 2003 (vol.21. No. 5) of the American Journal of Emergency Medicine: THE NUMBER OF DEATHS REPORTED FROM VITAMINS: NONE.

So my question to the pharmaceutical industry is: *WHY SHOULD WE HEARKEN UNTO YOUR COUNSEL?* And so it is and so I say –Amen.

FORMULA FOR A SUCCESSFUL PRAYER

1. Access the Physician Within.
2. Simple short statement of the concern – then release the concern.
3. Then a simple positive affirmation to replace the released concern.
4. Thank the Physician Within that the affirmation is manifested in your life NOW.

NOTES & BIBLIOGRAPHY

1. Boyle, Wade & Kirchfeld, Friedhelw, (2000). Nature Doctors: Pioneers in Naturopathic Medicine. East Palestine, Ohio, Buckeye Naturopathic Press. Pg. 14.
2. Dr. Marcus Bach. The World of Serendipity. Prentice Hall, Inc., Englewood Cliffs, N. J. , pg. 97.
3. Two studies on childhood obesity were released in Feb. 2010 in the *Journal of Pediatrics*. Some of the conclusions of the studies are as follows:
   a. The odds of obesity in minority children (Blacks and Hispanics) are greater than non-minority whites starting even before birth. 20% of Black and Hispanic children ages 2 – 19 are obese vs. 15% of whites.
   b. The researchers found signs of inflammation in obese children as young as 3 years old. Inflammation in adults is a marker for developing heart disease but was thought not to exist in very young children. "It is thought that fat cells in the body cause the inflammation that causes vessel damage," said University of North Carolina researcher Asheley Cockrell Skinner, the lead author. It is feared the 3-year-olds might already have artery changes.
   c. First Lady Michelle Obama's campaign against childhood obesity was praised by Dr. Reginald Washington, a Denver pediatrician heart specialist who says, "You still have to get the public to say we believe this is a problem, everybody's going to have to play a role here."
   d. Specific risk factors examined included: Mother smoking during pregnancy; unusually rapid weight gain in young infants; starting solid food before 4 months; mothers routinely pressuring young kids to eat more; children sleeping less than 12 hours daily between 6 months and 2 years; and allowing very young kids to have sugary drinks, fast food and/or TV's in their rooms.
   e. Many circumstances in these studies are more common in low-income, less educated families, including whites. The good news is that each of the risk factors can be changed.

4. Haas, Elso M.D. *Staying Healthy with Nutrition: The complete guide to diet & nutritional medicine.* Celestial Arts, Berkeley, CA.

5. "As a man thinketh ..." This aphorism has been part of my basic philosophy since my maternal grandmother led my brother and me in the power of positive thinking. All these years I thought the quote came from the Bible but never verified it personally. While writing this book, my editor (Laura Perry) asked me to include the source for the quote. That request started an interesting adventure trying to track down the source. I couldn't find the source in any of the three translations of the Bible in my library but there was a book entitled *As a Man Thinketh* that included James Allen's Greatest Inspirational Essays. In 1902 James Allen published his second book entitled *As A Man Thinketh in his heart so is he.* Allen combined Buddha's teaching, "All that we are is the result of what we have thought" and the Old Testament verse Proverbs 23:7 (KJV). The content in Allen's work and the Bible inscription are different. In the Bible the passage is referring to another person, and in Allen's work the passage is adopted to primarily refer to the reader himself. The quote is now in the public domain in the United States and most other countries.

6. *"The world's spiritual and transformative practices point to a place of refuge within."*   By Dr. Cassandra Vietten, a research psychologist & addictions expert. The Physician Within is the spiritual aspect of the trilogy of the three-legged stool. You cannot sit comfortably on a three legged stool if one of the legs is missing. At Cosmos Institute we believe the Physician Within is the God of your understanding, just as we advocate the return to Spirit Medicine and Mind which means the recognition that the God of the universe is present in every thing, person, and event which includes everything in Nature. We must connect with the spiritual oneness of the cosmos to achieve our Divine destiny.

7. According to published statistics from the AMA & CDC.

8. Bonnell, Gary. 1996 Third printing. *Your Book of Life: Accessing the Akashic Records.* Richman Rose Publishing , Atlanta, Georgia.

9. ScientificAmerican.com/mind.

10. Schroeder, Gerald L. PhD, 1992. *Genesis and the Big Bang.* Bantam Books, New York.

11. Davies, Paul (1992. *The Mind of God: The Scientific basis for a Rational World.* A Touchstone Book, New York.

12. Zukav, Gary PhD. 1979. *The Dancing WuLi Masters: An Overview of the New Physics.* William Morrow and Company, Inc., New York.

13. Pasachoff, Jay M., Professor of Astronomy, Williams College, 1991. *Astronomy: From the Earth to the Universe, 4th ed.* Saunders College Publishing, Philadelphia, PA.

14. Serway, Raymond A., James Madison University. 1996. *Physics for Scientists & Engineers with Modern Physics, 4th* ed. Saunders College Publishing. Philadelphia, PA.

15. Bothamley, Jennifer. 2002. *Dictionary of Theories.* Visible Ink Press. Detroit, MI

16. Bach, Marcus, PhD. 1970. *The World of Serendipity.* Prentice-Hall., Inc. Englewood Cliffs, N.J.

17. Rutter, Owen. 2000. *The Scales of Karma.* Aeon Publishing Co. Mamaroneck, New York.

18. Bradfor, Nikki, consultant editor. 2000. *The One Spirit Encyclopedia of Complementary Health.* Hamlyn, an imprint of Octopus Publishing Group Ltd. London. Pg.82.

19. www.orthmolecular.org/resources.

20. It was just announced by Natural News today 3/31/10 that GM crops (GMO's) cause liver and kidney damage. The following is summarized from that report. "A report published in the international Journal of Microbiology has verified once again that Monsanto's genetically modified (GM) crops are causing severe health problems... Adding to the mounting evidence that GM crops are dangerous all around, this information provides a damning indictment against Monsanto which continually insists that the GM products are safe. Not only are GM crops proving disastrous for the environment, but study after study, including those conducted by Monsanto itself, is showing that GM foods are detrimental to health.... The specific effects observed in tests indicated a buildup of hormones in the blood, that the liver and kidneys were not functioning properly. ... Dr. Seralini concluded that, because

GM crops are foreign substances that have never been a part of a normal diet, there is no telling what the long-term effects of consumption will be on people... significant disruption has been observed even in the short term.... Genetically manipulated food crops are not fit for human consumption....No legitimate study has ever proven them to be safe or nutritious... Today all data has revealed them to be unsafe. Claims that GM foods will end world hunger are baseless, propagated only by those that have a financial interest in converting the world's food supply to their own patented varieties in order to control it."

21. Reuters reported on 3/25/10 Bulgaria parliament bans GMO crops to soothe fears. "Bulgaria's parliament voted to tighten a law that effectively banned cultivation of GM crops for scientific and commercial reasons in response to public fears... There will be no field on the country's territory where GMO's can be cultivated said parliament... Authorizing GMO's for consumption, processing or cultivation in Europe is a politically charged subject with many openly hostile to what they call 'Frankenstein foods.'.... A March survey showed 97% of Bulgarians wanted their country to be GMO free. .. The new law bans GMO cultivation in nature protected areas and large buffer zones around those areas and fields with organic crops which effectively means scientific experiments and commercial cultivation will be impossible in the Balkan country... The amendments also forbid growing crops approved by the European Commission such as the GM potato, developed by the German maker BASF, and three modified maize types by US firm Monsanto...Fines for perpetrators were raised to one million levs ($698,300 US). The protesters said they were happy with the new law.....The parliament also tightened regulations for labeling products with GMO contents after checks by the health ministry showed that hundreds of food products had such ingredients above the allowed quantity."

22. Brody, Howard. M.D., PhD. 2000. *The Placebo Response: How You Can Release the Body's Inner Pharmacy for Better Health.* Harper Collins Publishers, Inc. New York City, NY.

23. Bell, Virginia, M.S.W. & Troxel, David, M.P.H. 2002. *A Dignified Life: The Best Friends Approach to Alzheimer's Care* . Health Professions Press, Inc. , Deerfield Beach, Fla.

24. Warner, Bill (The Wellness Doc), B.S., M.S. 2007. *An Odyssey into Past Lives: A Personal Exploration into Cellular Memories.* Booksurge, a division of Amazon, Inc. Charleston, SC.

25. Jim, RM, Chen CX, Li YK, Xu PK. *Effect of rhynchophylline on platelet aggregation and experimental thrombosis. Yao Hsueh Pao. 1991;7:246-249.*

26. Zhang W, Liu GX. *Effects of rhynchophylline on myocardial contractility in anaesthetized dogs and cats. Chung Kuo Yao Li Hsueh Pao. 1986;7:426-428.*

27. Zhang W, Liu GX. Huang XN. *Effect of rhynchophylline on the contraction of rabbit aorta. Chung Kuo Li Hsueh Pao. 1987;8:425-429.*

28. Kanatani H. Yamaasaki K. et.al. *The active principles of the branchlet and hook of Uncaria sinensis Oliv. Examined with a 5-hydroxytryptamine receptor-binding assay.* J. Pharm Pharmacol. 1985;37:401-404.

29. Wurm M. Kacani L. I., Laus G. Keplinger K. Dierich MP *Pentacyclic oxindole alkaloids from Uncaria tomentosa induce human endothelial cells to release a lymphocyte-proliferation-regulating factor.* Planta Medica.1998;65:701-704.

30. Webb, Nicholas J. 2003. *The Cost of Being Sick: A Prevention Initiative.* Sound Concepts, Orem, Utah.

31. Willcox, Bradley J. M.D., Willcox D. Craig, Ph.D., Suzuki, Makoto, M.D. 2001. *The Okinawa Program: How the World's Longest-Lived People Achieve Everlasting Health.* Clarkson Potter/ Publishers, NYC, NY.

32. Hur, Robin. 1975. *Food Reform: Our Desperate Need.* Heidelberg Publishers pg.95.

33. Robbins. John. 1987. *Diet for a New America.* Stillpoint Publishing, Walpole, NH. Pg, 154

34. Page, Linda, N.D., Ph.D.. 2002. *Cooking for Healthy Healing: Book One – The Healing Diets.* Traditional Wisdom, Inc., USA.

35. Ballentine, Rudolph, M.D. 1978. *Diet & Nutrition: A Holistic Approach.* The   Himalayan International Institute,. Honesdale, Pa.

36. www.lightworker.com.

ABOUT THE AUTHOR

Bill Warner, MS, PhD(c)
The Wellness Doc

Bill is the director and founder of Cosmos Institute of Life's Transitions. A healthy longevity in the Omega of life is the purpose of the Institute. Emphasis is placed on the integration of Body/Mind/Spirit and a return to a Nature philosophy. We accomplish a healthy longevity through Homeopathy, Herbal Therapy, Nutritional Therapy, Hypnotherapy, and access to the Physician Within. Bill has a BS in Industrial Management from Georgia Institute of Technology and an MS from Clayton College of Natural Health. After graduation from Georgia Tech Bill spent 34 years in the chemical business before resolving to commit to the principles of natural health in his personal and professional life.

Bill's professional and volunteer experience of 32 years with the National Ski Patrol taught him many lessons as he interfaced with the medical community as an Emergency Medical Technician. In 2000 Bill became certified in Hypnotherapy by the American Board of Hypnotherapy, and since then has specialized in Past Life research and therapy.

Bill's religious up-bringing was led by a Grandmother who lived with the family during most of his younger life, and hence had a great influence on his philosophy, along with being fortunate to have a stable, loving, religious set of parents. He was further blessed by being raised in the Unity Church were he was active in the Sunday school and youth programs. This training was instrumental in his awareness that spirituality is a vital part in the Mind/Body/Spirit triad. Bill served a term as President of the St. Petersburg, Florida Jaycees where they won 12 of the 13 activity awards in the state competition, including a first place in the religious programming. After moving to Georgia he continued his Jaycee activities by campaigned for the position of State Chaplain. During his tenure of office he made a number of significant changes; being the first non-professional cleric, he introduced a non-sectarian and non-denominational input into the diverse

Jaycee membership, changed the by-laws to allow the Chaplain position to be elected rather than a political appointment, and introduced the first Prayer Breakfast at the state convention, bringing the nationally recognized speaker Dr. Marcus Bach for the keynote address. His program won first place in the national competition for religious programming.

He has continued to advocate a return to nature at Cosmos Institute of Life's Transitions by founding the Nature e-Chapel as an advocate for a return to nature while accessing the Physician Within as a spiritual guide along the pathway of life.

CPSIA information can be obtained
at www.ICGtesting.com
Printed in the USA
LVOW10s1550161117

556553LV00026B/620/P